KICK BUTT

KICK BUTT

A Novel
by
DONALD HUBER

Sewanee Mountain

Published by Sewanee Mountain, a division of Proctor's Hall
Editor and Publisher: David Bowman

Printed in the United States of America
Designed by Latham Davis

ISBN 978-0-9706214-9-8

Library of Congress Control Number
2005937336

CHARACTERS
IN ORDER OF APPEARANCE
(Main characters are in bold type)

Tom Hanagan:	Athletics Director of Morgan University
Erin, Ashley, Katey:	Tom's young daughters
Jan Hanagan:	Tom's wife
Clifton Calhoun:	Jan's uncle, former Board of Trust member, super booster
Savannah McLane:	Tom's ex-twirler secretary
Bill Conner:	Tom's Assistant Athletics Director
Milt Lee:	Morgan booster, Metro entrepreneur
Noweeta Hayes:	Athletics Department Director of Academic Affairs
Buster Hooper:	President of the Houston Camelot Booster Club, real estate developer
Asswad King:	Morgan player
Arlo Plummer:	Morgan player
Brad Ballings:	Morgan strength coach, former professional body builder
Roscoe Barrett III:	Son of wealthy Athletics Department donor
Porky Wilson:	Morgan graduate assistant coach
Coach Tony Star:	Head Coach of Morgan Knights, Tom's lifelong buddy
Coach Ed Tarmeenian:	Star's defensive coordinator and former Pittsburgh Steelers teammate
Fernando DeGama:	Brazilian ex-soccer pro, now Morgan field goal kicker
Bo Hanks:	WSOT sports announcer
Bobby Brooks:	Female sporting goods sales rep
William R. Brewster:	Chancellor of Morgan University, ex-software salesman, and football fanatic
Lamont:	Brewster's driver
Anita Rogers:	Brewster's administrative assistant
Blake Stevens:	Ex-Morgan football player, head of National Camelot Boosters Club

Red Carlisle:	Sports editor for the Metro *Tribune*
Peaches Perdue:	Coach Star's secretary
Coach Jet Jackson:	Coach Star's offensive coordinator
Reggie Muggins:	Morgan starting quarterback
Jimmy Joe Wallace:	Morgan back-up quarterback
Coach Pete Cossacky:	Morgan offensive line coach
Roy Nash:	Morgan booster and athletics director of Living Waters Prep School
Stefan Bazitski:	Work-out instructor at Jan Hanagan's spa
Tootie Ruggles:	Quarterback Reggie Muggins' roommate and "main man"
Teeny McAdoo:	Reggie's sometime girlfriend
Symeon Smith:	Morgan player
Abe Koppel:	Milt Lee's old friend, owner of an Atlanta-based stadium concession accessory supplier
Boomer Cox:	Metro land developer, Chancellor Brewster's boyhood friend, Morgan booster, and Board of Trust member
Dewey Dobbins:	Morgan player
DeVon White:	Morgan player
Professor Paul Fisher:	Dean of School of Education
Dudley Dunning:	Peevish Mid-South business mogul, president of Morgan Board of Trust
Harlan Gooch:	Metro businessman, booster, wooed by Athletics Dept. for big gift
Felton Potts:	Metro businessman, booster
Senator "Lil Ed" Horton:	Former Morgan Law School student
Bobo Thomas:	Morgan player
Winnie Brewster:	Brewster's wife
Betty Cox:	Boomer's wife
Lamar Tubbs:	Attorney, friend of Boomer and Brewster, Board of Trust member
Craig Bumhoffer	Morgan player
Inez Calhoun:	Sports-crazy wife of Clifton Calhoun
Willard Sanders:	Morgan booster
Stitches Stevens:	Morgan head trainer
Sam Edwards:	Morgan provost, sports fan

Dr. Lucius Thompson:	Morgan's Sports Medicine program director
Mel Beerbauer:	Assistant offensive coordinator, Kansas City Chiefs, possible Morgan head coach
Doc Willis:	Morgan game doctor
Rose Star:	Coach Star's wife
Eddie Saxon:	Morgan player seriously injured
Pancho Arnez:	Morgan player
Dr. Barbara Sazlow:	Head of Morgan Student Athlete Tutoring program
Laverne "Mongol" Harris:	Morgan player
Pat Pitouchi:	Morgan assistant trainer
Coach Al Crimen:	Head coach of the UA Blue Wave
Bum Turner:	Al Crimen's offensive coordinator
Butch Sanders:	Game announcer, voice of the Morgan Purple Knights
Jacky Joe Wallace:	Father of quarterback Jimmy Joe Wallace
Billie Ann Wallace:	Jimmy Joe's mother
Tyson Culpepper:	Morgan booster, treasurer of the Morgan Board of Trust
Rob Williams:	Brad Ballings' roommate
Henry Robinson:	Morgan Assistant Dean of Students, disciplinary officer
Coach Wesley Woods:	Morgan defensive back coach, former lover of Nowceta
Rudy Marrow:	Butch Sanders' color commentator, former Morgan star
Coach Bobby Cheatem:	Head coach of Cotton Mouth Moccasins
Dr. Maurice Redman:	Tom and Jan Hanagans' marriage counselor
Bow Wow Turner:	Reggie Muggins' cocaine dealer
Coach Dim Haley:	Head coach of Raccoons
Dr. Tilford D. Stinson:	President of Cosmopolis University
Howdy Morrison:	Athletics Director, Cosmopolis University
Hamilton Pigg:	Cosmopolis booster, billionaire determined to hire away Coach Star
Tutomo Tongo:	Morgan player, Barbara Sazlow's star pupil
Dr. Louis Sazlow:	Barbara's husband

Grady Peckers:	Assistant Under-Secretary of Education
Mike Tubo:	Sports attorney, negotiating Star's contract with Pigg
Sweetie Pie Brewster:	Chancellor's daughter, Radcliffe undergraduate
Miguel Hidalgo:	Sweetie Pie's Venezuelan boyfriend
General Miles Ridley:	Man in charge of proposed Army bio-terrorism research program at Morgan
Bert Alpert & Hank Rowdy:	NBC game of week telecasters
Coach Bobby Bacon:	Cottonpicker head coach
BoDee Grimes:	Ultra-conservative, billionaire, Board of Trust member
DeeDee Grimes:	BoDee's daughter, presently a Morgan coed
Rodney Hampton:	Juvenile delinquent out on early release from Metro Detention Center
Anthony Gentry:	Third string Morgan quarterback, DeeDee's boyfriend
Clarence Drumbacher:	Publisher of the Metro *Tribune* and *Chronicle*
Coach Ron Carver:	Morgan linebacker coach
Nathan Cosby:	Sociology professor, head of Booker T. Washington Cultural Center
Manly Dunning:	Dudley Dunning's father, the real power behind the Dunning Empire
Jim Mack Brewer:	Retiring Athletics Director at A.S.U.
Dr. Faulkner T. Fentress:	President of A.S.U.
Coach Hoss Humphreys:	Coonhounds head coach
Obie Gamble:	Humphrey's offensive coordinator

FIRST QUARTER

FUNDAMENTALS

In life, there are three kinds of people: people who make things happen, people who watch things happen, and people who don't know what's happening.

JOHN MADDEN
The First Book of Football

CHAPTER 1

Thursday, August 18

'D addy, can I come in? . . . *Knock knock knock . . .* DADDY! I got to tinkle. Let me in."

"Sure, baby." Tom Hanagan opened the bathroom door, a white terry cloth robe wrapped around his once hard athletic body, his handsome, clean-cut face covered with shaving cream.

"Why don't you use your own bathroom, honey?"

"Erin locked the door." Ashley, the youngest of his three young daughters, pulled down her pajama bottoms and climbed onto the toilet.

"How 'bout the downstairs bathroom?"

"It's broken."

"I thought Momma was going to call the plumber."

"I don't know, Daddy," said Ashley, bumping into her father on the way out the door, causing him to take a slice out of his neck.

"Damn it!" Tom reached for toilet paper to stop the bleeding and found none. "DAMN IT, JAN! Why haven't you called the plumber?!"

No response.

"Can't you hear me?!" he roared.

"Did you say something, Tom?" asked his stylishly trim, thirty-four year old wife, turning off the blow dryer.

"I said why the hell haven't you taken care of that bathroom downstairs!"

"Don't scream at me, Tom!" she fired back, sitting down in front of the vanity mirror and beginning to apply her make-up.

"Look, Jan," he said, pulling a starched white, button down shirt from the dresser. "Football season starts in two weeks. I'm super busy right now. All you have to do is call."

"You're not the only one around here who's busy. In case you've forgotten, I've got a big formal wear show at the store next week."

"That's exactly what I mean," said the Athletics Director, his voice muffled by the clothing inside the walk-in closet. "You haven't seen my seersucker suit, have you?"

"Uhhh, I think it's still at the cleaners."

"STILL AT THE CLEANERS! It's been there for three weeks. And it's supposed to be a hundred degrees today."

"I guess I just forgot," she apologized, penciling a thin violet line beneath her eyes.

"You forgot?! Jan, why don't you quit that job of yours and—"

"Be a full-time house frau? Did it ever occur to you that women are just as entitled as men to have a career?"

"Jan, honey, with what I make, there's no need for you to run yourself ragged like you're doing. Besides, the kids could use—"

"To see their father sober at night for a change." Jan slipped into her dress and stormed out of the room.

As he stretched his paisley braces over his shoulders and looked at himself in the closet door mirror, Tom wondered if everyone's life was as screwed up as his. *It doesn't make sense, he thought. Here I am, Athletics Director at one of the most prestigious universities in the South, making over 300,000 a year, living in a million dollar house, with a beautiful wife, three wonderful kids....*

We should be happy, he muttered to himself twenty minutes later as he rolled down Steeplechase Boulevard past a dozen other red brick Georgian reproductions which, like his, sat on the treeless one and a half acre lots. *Maybe it's just this business I'm in ...* Tom nosed his Mercedes through the fieldstone gate of Fox Chapel Estates. *Nah, it's not just me, the whole world's going to hell. There's no such thing as a normal family anywhere anymore.* Then he stepped on the gas and reached for the cell to check his voice mail.

Bleep ... "Tom, this is Tony, callin' at 7:15 Thursday morning. We had a little trouble last night. Craig Bumhoffer got hauled in for a

DUI. Buddy Phillips had to bail him out. Give me a call when you get my message."

Tom rang up his head football coach. "What's up, Tony? What?... He ran two red lights? How much did he have to drink?... Registered point seven? Jesus!... Malenkovic and Bowers were with him and a girl with no clothes on.... Resisting arrest? ... You're sure Buddy can keep it out of the paper? ... Thank God. ... What?... " Tom grinned. "Yeah it does kinda remind me of that time we nearly wrecked my old man's car after the state championship game.... All right, I better call Buddy right now."

Ring Ring ... "Good morning, Gladys. Is Buddy in? ... Not till 10:30? I tell ya', you lawyers got the life."

After calling his golf pro and the plumber, Tom tuned in the radio to catch the Business Report and the scores from last night's games. Hearing that the market was up for the fourth day in a row and that the Braves were only a half game out made him forget his spat with Jan. And by the time he reached the light at Jackson Pike and Beauregard, where he got an admiring glance from a blond in a Lexus, he was feeling, except for a slight dull ache behind his eyeballs, like himself.

Maybe I did over-react a bit this morning, he thought as he pulled out in front of a harried looking commuter in a beat-up Volvo Station Wagon. *But I'm tired of living this way. The kids need a Mother around the house. Jan thinks all I do is go to football games and get drunk with a bunch of boring people. She's got some nerve criticizing me, with that pack of weirdos she works with—*

Bleep Bleep

Tom reached for the phone as he turned into the parking lot of Frank and Flo's Country Diner. "Hey, Bill, what's up? . . . You betcha! We'll go over those estimates as soon as I get in. . . . That's right, we've got to be absolutely certain about the price of those new sky boxes if I'm gonna run them by Brewster. . . . Okay, I'll see you in an hour."

Before Tom had slid all the way into the shiny red vinyl booth, Flo was pouring him the first of his daily dozen cups of coffee.

"You doin' all right, Mister Hanagan?" asked the gaunt waitress.

"Pretty good, hon. Got a little headache, but nothing serious."

"This here hot black stuff'll fix you up," said Flo with motherly affection. "Gonna be the us'al?"

"Yeah, but you can skip the biscuits today." Tom patted his stomach. "I'm tryin' to cut back a little."

"Anything you say, Mister Hanagan." Flo buzzed off to get his eggs, sausage patties, hash browns, and toast.

As Tom sipped his coffee, he started to think about the meeting he had scheduled with the Chancellor of the University later that afternoon. But finding the subject too unpleasant before he'd had his breakfast, he turned his attention to a gang of workers across the highway who were pouring a sidewalk in front of the monstrous new Piggly Wiggly. On what nine months before had been the rolling pastures of a pony farm now rose the nearly completed walls of the River Bend Mall. *It really is amazing how fast they can throw up a building these days,* he mused. But Tom's thoughts soon returned to the email that Chancellor Brewster had sent him from Hilton Head two days earlier.

Need to see you about the budget. Be back on the 18th. Call Anita. Brewster.

Though Tom was accustomed to being abruptly summoned before his imperious boss, the word "budget" chilled his heart. Budgets were something head administrators didn't talk about with athletics directors unless they were unhappy with their win/loss record. Like a learning disabled wide receiver who knows that his grades can be used as an excuse to terminate his scholarship anytime his first down percentages get too low, Tom knew the Athletics Department's perennial two million dollar deficit could be used as a pretext for relieving him of his duties whenever the Athletics Board wanted. Until now, Chancellor Brewster and the Morgan University Board of Trust had, like nearly all the NCAA's Division IA schools, been only too willing to keep siphoning money from the University's general operating budget to help offset the Athletics Department's shortfall. But after last year's 4 and 7 football season and the basketball team's first-round loss in the Mid-South Conference Tournament, Tom had felt the trustees' handshakes getting weaker, the alumni's backslaps fewer, and the boosters' howdeedos less vociferous.

Though officially a senior administrator, Tom was really little more secure than the coaches he hired. Unlike A.D.'s of old who received their directorships for life, usually as the reward for successful coaching, Tom was one of a new breed of cyber-savvy, athletics administration professionals whose ties with the university were only as strong as their won and lost percentages. When Chancellor Brewster and his Search Committee had contacted him about coming to Morgan, it wasn't just because he was married to the niece of the former President of the Board of Trust. No, Tom had been chosen to head up the school's foundering 18.4 million-dollar a year program because the members of the Board believed that he could make them winners. They took him at his word when he told them that he would transform their school into the next University of Miami—and do it without compromising Morgan's highly-esteemed academic reputation. Unfortunately for Tom, now in the sixth year of a seven-year contract, delivering on his promise was proving difficult.

When Tom walked into the lobby of Calhoun Athletics Complex forty minutes later he was met with a cold stare from his Uncle Clifton. A bronze bust of his wife's uncle had been installed in the vestibule in 2001 by the Metro Booster Club, in appreciation of Clifton's tireless effort in soliciting contributions. And the honor, as one could see, was not undeserved. Decorated with a golf-ball textured glass dome, basketball-shaped brass coffee tables, plastic armchairs molded in the form of upside down football helmets, and life-size glossy matted photos of Morgan players running, tackling and even graduating, the lobby looked like the front office of a professional sports franchise.

"Good mornin', Mr. Hanagan," said his secretary, Savannah McLane, jumping up to get him coffee as he pushed through the glass doors of his office.

"Good morning, Savannah." Tom slipped off his sunglasses and smiled at his attractive young assistant.

"You want cream today?"

"Thanks. Did Anita call yet?" Tom picked up a pile of will-calls from Savannah's desk and began thumbing through them.

"'Bout ten minutes ago." Savannah was a former Tar Heel twirler whom Tom had hired three months earlier as a favor to his old Carolina teammate Johnny McLane. "Anita said that Chancellor Brewster was gonna have to reschedule your meetin' for t'morrow."

"What?! After I rushed around all day yesterday?"

"That's what she said. Oh, and before I forget, Mr. Hooper called to say you're definitely on for lunch."

"I was afraid of that." Tom groaned and stepped into his purple-carpeted, mahogany-paneled office and noticed a copy of *The Dividend: Metro's Monthly Magazine of Business Opportunities* on his desk. "Hey thanks, Savannah."

"They brought it by this mornin'."

Tom lowered himself into his well-padded chair and picked up the magazine. On the cover was a photo of Head Coach Tony Star, wearing a gold blazer, purple-and-gold-striped tie, and uncharacteristically friendly smile. *Nice job,* thought Tom, thumbing to page thirty-six where he saw another photo of Star in sweatsuit and whistle, barking orders from the sideline. Opposite was a feature article by Nat Gold, the wife of *The Dividend*'s owner:

COACH STAR AND KNIGHTS
POISED FOR THE ATTACK

As the burgeoning business community of Metro moves forward with renewed optimism into the fourth quarter, Coach Star and his Fighting Knights are preparing for another season of Mid-Southern football. Ex-All American, former Pittsburgh Steeler and 2000 Mid-South Conference Coach of the Year, Tony Star has, with his no-nonsense, hard-nosed brand of blue collar football, been bringing J. P. Morgan University back to the pigskin prominence she enjoyed in the 40s and 50s under Doc Fulsom. Since taking over the helm of the purple and gold in 2000 when the team went 7 and 4, he has compiled an impressive 23 and 22 record. With 18 of his 22 starting gridiron warriors returning, we are all expecting big things this season at Fulsom Field. *The Dividend* was lucky enough to be able to get Coach Star alone for a few minutes last week for this exclusive interview.

"So Coach, how do you think it looks for Morgan this season?!"

"Fantastic, Nat. As you know, we lost only four starters from last year's squad. We had a great Spring practice. Everybody is in good shape physically and mentally. If we keep our attitude right, there's no telling what might happen."

"I guess going 4 and 7 last year must have been a bit disappointing for you and the team. It wasn't until November you really seemed to hit your stride."

"Yeah, we had some bad-luck injuries at the start of the year, but by the end of the season this team was looking like the championship outfit I know they are."

"There's been some talk about quarterback Reggie Muggins as a possible All Conference contender. What do you think?"

"Reggie came on strong at the close of the season, over seven hundred yards in five games. If he can start this year like he finished up last year, I wouldn't be at all surprised to see him on the top of a lot of people's award list."

"Coach, you and your A.D., Tom Hanagan, go way back together. In fact, it was largely through Tom's efforts that Morgan was able to induce you to give up your assistant coaching position with the National Champion 'Wildcats' and come here. Do you think having someone you've known intimately so long has helped you put this program back on its feet?"

"Positively. Tom is one of my oldest and dearest friends. We played high school football together at St. Mary's in Pittsburgh. I think it was one of the happiest days of my life when he asked

me if I'd take over the program here at Morgan. Tom and his staff have been supportive every step of the way."

"Now this is something that you don't have to answer, Coach, but do you seriously think a topflight academic institution like Morgan with its high entrance standards and its reputation for classroom excellence can really compete successfully on a regular basis with the other schools in the Mid-South Conference?"

"Without a doubt. I think we can maintain the academic integrity of our scholar/athletes and still be at the top of our conference. Chancellor Brewster, Tom Hanagan, and my staff are all committed to bringing the best and brightest to our campus to receive the finest education possible."

BUZZ BUZZ

"Yes, Savannah."

"Mr. Conner's here."

"Send him right in."

"Hey, Billy Boy!" blurted Tom, holding up *The Dividend* for his young associate to see. "You see this yet?"

"It looks great, doesn't it?"

"I'll say." Tom smiled. "So, you got those figures for me?"

"Got 'em right here," said Bill, plopping down in front of Tom's desk. "It's just like I—we thought. Figuring the yearly contribution on those new sky boxes at a hundred fifty thousand each, we should be pulling in, provided we install at least fifteen new boxes, about 1.5 a year within six years."

"You're figuring the installation cost at about nine hundred thou?"

"Give or take fifty grand," said the wavy-haired, former Clemson field goal kicker.

"Looks like a good game plan to me." Tom eyed Bill's lavishly prepared proposal.

"You still meeting with Brewster today?" asked Bill.

"Uh…not today," hesitated Tom. "We had a little scheduling conflict, and I suggested we move it back."

"I see—well I'm sure you can sell him on the idea if anybody can."

"Jus' gotta know when to play your cards, Bill. That's the whole secret of this business. Did you get those quarterly budget figures wrapped up yet?"

"I'm just about done. And if my projections are correct, I think we'll actually be looking about a hundred grand better than last year."

"Really?"

"Yeah, I've trimmed the per annum deficit down to about 1.89 million."

Tom nodded approvingly.

"If only we didn't have to pay that interest on the past ten years, we'd be going in the red less than a million and a half this year, which isn't bad."

"You're right. All things considered, that isn't bad."

"By the way, Artie Sawyer told me you birdied the 8th hole at Magnolia last week."

"Damn near a hole-in-one." Tom lit up. "You know, Billy, we gotta get you out there with us sometime."

"Love to," said Bill, eager to show off his improved swing and spend an afternoon recreating with the man he planned to ask for a raise.

"I like that boy," said Tom to his secretary after Bill walked out the door.

"Me too," replied Savannah. "He's cute."

Before Tom had time to consider whether or not he liked Savannah's obvious admiration for his ambitious young assistant, Morgan Business School alum and booster extraordinaire Milt Lee walked through the office door for his 10:15 appointment.

"Hey big man! What's goin' on?"

"Hello Milt. C'mon in."

Milt Lee, formerly Milton Leopold of Brooklyn, New York, was a member of a new generation of "good ole boys" who with each passing fiscal year are becoming increasingly influential in the New

South. A former scholarship student at the Morgan University School of Business, after completing his MBA in '82, Milt decided to settle in the land of cotton, where in twenty years he had become one of the biggest barbecue-eatin', bass fishin', hound dog-lovin' entrepreneurs around.

"Two weeks left to go. Y'all ready?" Milt took a seat in the brass-studded, leather armchair in front of Tom's desk.

"Yeah we are, Milt, and I think it's gonna be a big year."

"Speakin' of big ones, who's the sweet thing you got out there mindin' the desk?"

"Miss McLane?"

"Hubba hubba hubba. I tell you, Tommy, any time you get tired of her you can send her over to *work* for ole Milt. I'll keep her busy. You can bet on that, pardner."

"I'm sure you would, Milt," said Tom dryly. "So what's up? Artie told me something about you wanting to put a bid on the program printing."

"Not exactly, Tom. What I told Artie was that I'd print the game programs for you cheaper than anybody else in town. Guaranteed!"

"That's a hard offer to refuse, but—"

"I'll undercut anybody you got. It's the least I can do for my school. And I'll tell ya what I'll do for you in the bargain—"

"Whoa, hold on, Milt." Tom raised up his hands. "I let the boys in Promotions take care of those decisions."

"I realize that, Tom, but according to my calculations..."

As Tom listened to Milt try to sell him on the Lee and Jackson Printing Company and a new line of souvenirs that a friend of his manufactured in Atlanta, he wasn't sure whether this super-booster, dressed in a Morgan monogrammed polo shirt and gold blazer, was just hustling him or actually wanted to cut him a deal. In financial matters involving big time college sports, the line between benevolence and profit is frequently fuzzy. But either way, Tom knew it didn't matter, since the owner of the printer the Athletics Department used was former Morgan basketball star Skip Sawyer, son-in-law of Board of Trust member Olin T. Henson.

"Looks interesting," said Tom, folding the brochure back up, glancing at his watch. "But I got another meeting here in a couple minutes. I'll send this brochure over to Artie and make sure he looks at it."

"All right, pal." Milt extended a hand adorned with a large amethyst and gold Morgan class ring. "I'll call you next week. And I'll see you for sure at the party."

"You bet," said Tom, remembering without enthusiasm the Booster Club "Kick-Off" dinner and dance the 27th of August.

"Hey, Tom, just one more thing."

"Yeah."

"You think Star's gonna start throwin' the ball this year?"

"I think we'll all be surprised at what Tony's got up his sleeve."

"I hope so. Now, if it was me—"

"Love to talk about it some other time, Milt, but I'm really swamped today."

"Yeah, okay buddy."

After calling home to make sure that his housekeeper Aretha had given Katey her ear drops and put their Irish Setter O'Hara in his pen, Tom buzzed Savannah to send in his next appointment, Ms. Noweeta Hayes, the Athletics Department Director of Academic Affairs.

"Hey Noweeta, what's hap'nin'?" said Tom, assuming an air of street-smart familiarity which the former Tennessee State track star always found somewhat annoying.

"I've been very busy. How 'bout you?"

"Up to here." Tom smiled. "Hey, I love that dress. Is it new?"

"Yes, thank you, it is," said the well-spoken and attractive thirty year old administrator, taking a seat and demurely crossing her long legs beneath her zebra-striped silk dress. "I picked it up when I was in Washington."

"You have a nice vacation?"

"It was wonderful, just not long enough."

"They never are, are they? And how are you coming on your house?"

"Ugh," grumbled Noweeta, thinking about the home she was having built in the new Cottonfield Manor development not far from Tom's.

"Building is no fun, is it? Anyway, I wanted you to come in so I could tell you what a fantastic job I think you and Professor Fisher have done putting together this new Contemporary Communications major."

"Well thank you. It's been a real pleasure working with him."

"Paul's a great guy, isn't he? Too bad more of the faculty aren't as receptive to new ideas."

"Or to students with learning disabilities."

"Yes." Tom nodded his head in a grave and thoughtful manner. "I've been trying to convince people ever since I arrived here that a student's reading and writing skills aren't necessarily a true indication of their intelligence or ability."

"It's true."

"I mean, let's face it, the main thing that standardized tests measure is someone's socio-economic background."

"Absolutely." Dr. Hayes had been hired by Tom on the Chancellor's recommendation after he'd heard—and seen—her deliver a lecture at an NCAA conference in Miami on the "Validity of the Traditional Grade Point Evaluation Process."

"But with the latest court rulings and programs like the one you two have developed, we'll be able to graduate students we would have never even admitted a few years ago."

"Amen."

"Honestly, you should be proud of yourselves...."

By the time Tom finished reviewing a half dozen resumes for the women's diving coach position, and composing a letter to the General Manager of WBUX, begging him not to drop BUX's radio broadcasts of Morgan football and basketball games, Orvil "Buster" Hooper arrived for lunch. Buster, Morgan A.B. '64, was a real estate developer and President of the Houston Chapter of the Camelot Club. Dressed in a purple, pink, and green madras sport coat, bolo tie, and white bucks, the burr-headed half-pint wore a platinum-plated Rolex on one arm and a platinum blond on the other.

"Like y'all to meet Lou-Ellen," said Buster, marching into Tom's office and slapping him on the back. "She's a real football o-fic-i-o-na-do, ain't that right, honey?—Us't'a'be a cheerleader for the Cow-boys. So how's my buddy Tom doin'?"

"Great, Buster."

"Gettin' ready for a big year, I hope."

"Sure are."

"With all the money we've been raisin' for you down in Houston, we could pretty near buy ourselves a pro-fessional franchise, haw haw haw. But hey, let's not stand here jawin', I got a car outside waitin' to take us to lunch. Where's it gonna be, Mr. Ath-e-le-tics Di-rec-tor."

"The Alumni Club?"

"Long as they're serving cold drinks and hot steaks, it's awright with me."

The Alumni Club to which they drove in Buster's rented limo was located in a converted Victorian mansion six blocks from the Cal-houn Athletics Complex. Once the domicile of the Chancellor of the University, the blue limestone edifice had been restored to its velvet and silk grandeur when it was converted into a bar and restaurant in the mid '80s.

"So what's everybody drinkin'?" asked Buster, as an African-American waiter in a tuxedo shirt, purple bow tie, and gold lamé vest helped them to their seats.

"It's a little early for me, Buster," said Tom.

"Ain't never too early when you're havin' fun." Buster gave Lou-Ellen a hug. "C'mon now, Tom, whadda ya' drinkin'?"

"I guess a vodka tonic."

"Sounds good to me too. That'll be three. What's your name, son?" said Buster to their waiter.

"Marcus, sir."

"Marcus, that'll be three vodka tonics."

"Yassir."

"This sure is a pretty place, idn't it?" said Buster, looking around.

"So tell me, Tom, is this gonna be our year or not? Those pre-season reports I've been readin' haven't been any too optimistic."

"Don't worry, Buster, this'll be our year."

"I hope so, 'cause the last coupl'a seasons we sure as heck haven't been lookin' like that University of Miami dynasty you were talkin' about a few years back. And I still can't figure why. We got the money, the new facilities, and we certainly ain't got no Harvard University admission policy, judgin' by the number of minority students you got on the team." Buster winked at Tom.

"It takes time, Buster."

"I guess so. But I'm not lyin' when I say we're gettin' antsy for a Bowl game down in Houston."

"We all are."

"Now Tom, I know this here Coach Star's an old buddy of yours, but just between you and me, you really think he's the right man for the job?"

"Yes I do. Tony Star is one of the finest coaches in the country. Without his know-how and recruiting skills the Wildcats would never have been national champs."

"I guess so. But Morgan ain't Arizona, Tom. I know how excited you and Brewster were about Star comin' down here, but I cain't help but think maybe a local boy mighta been a better choice."

"I think you'll be surprised this year," said Tom dispassionately.

"You think maybe Star's gonna open up and do some passin' this year?"

"No tellin' what Tony's got up his sleeve," said Tom, hoping that his coach really did have something up his sleeve.

"You know the way I figure. . . ."

As Buster began to expound his philosophy of coaching, Marcus returned to take their orders.

Buster looked briefly at the menu.

"You like steak, don'tcha, Tom?—Good. Petit fil-ets for ev'rybody. And we'll all have a salad with that, baked potato, and another round of drinks."

As they ate Tom was relieved to have the conversation move from football to Buster's latest triumphs in real estate and Lou-Ellen's failure to land a recording deal with the demo tapes Buster had paid for her to cut in Nashville.

"No, there's no such thing as easy in this world anymore," expatiated Buster, washing down his last piece of cheesecake with a mouthful of coffee. "And I don't reckon there ever was, or we'd'a been national champs by now, eh Tom?"

It was almost 2:30 before Tom got back to the office. After checking out the three dozen calls that had come in while he was gone, he popped open the top button of his shirt, loosened his tie, and reached for a half-empty bottle of Rolaids he kept in his desk. *Jan's right, I gotta stop eating these big lunches and start getting more exercise. Gonna start tomorrow.*

At 3:30, after talking with Edith Mumphrey about season ticket sales (*Still slow, huh?*), Promotions Director Mike Shea about giving away free bags of Uncle Charlie's Pork Rinds to the first 5,000 fans on opening night (*Try to sell them some scoreboard time too*) and Memphis Booster Club President Vereen Kendricks about quarterback Reggie Muggins' stepfather (*Any kind of job you can get Muggins' father will be appreciated*), Tom reemerged from his office and took the elevator downstairs to meet with strength coach Brad Ballings.

Tom stepped through the swinging doors of the new Willard T. Sanders Physiological Development Center and heard the clank of metal on metal that is music to an A.D.'s ears.

"Anybody seen Brad?" shouted Tom, looking around the mirror-lined, supermarket-sized weight room where the football team was doing its afternoon workout.

"He in the back room with Arlo, Mr. Hanagan."

"Thanks, Asswad."

When Tom finally found the weight trainer, he was standing over a bench spotting for 290-pound lineman Arlo Plummer.

"Just one more set, Tom. I'll be right with you."

"Yeah sure, Brad," said Tom, irritated at having to wait for what promised to be an unpleasant confrontation. Though Brad Ballings was the most important person in the Athletics Department next to Tom himself—since none of the Morgan athletes, male or female, would have been competitive in any sport without Brad's help—Tom had spent little time in the company of the high-strung body builder. Brad had made it clear when he was hired four years earlier at the insistence of Coach Star that he was "a professional and didn't expect to have people meddling in his affairs." And indeed Tom had gone out of his way to accommodate the former University of Miami strength coach until he had recently discovered that several players on the football team were injecting a new human growth hormone called Bulloxen. Though strictly speaking Bulloxen was not illegal—since its molecular structure had been specially "designed" to differ slightly from banned substances with similar properties—Tom had read enough in the athletics journals to know that growth hormones were potentially dangerous to young men's health—and athletics directors' careers.

"Good set, Arlo." Brad gave the handsome lineman a lingering pat on the rear, "I'll be back in a minute and we'll finish up."

"Sure thing, Brad."

"So, what's up, Tom?" said the former Mr. Florida pulling a tee shirt over his sculpted torso, closing the door to his office.

"What do you know about this Bulloxen stuff?"

"Whadda you mean what do I know about this Bulloxen stuff?"

"I hear some of the guys on the football team are using it."

"I dunno. Coach Star hasn't said anything to me."

"Huh. Well, let me ask you a question. You think this stuff could be dangerous?"

"Dangerous. Not really. There's nothing about it that's illegal."

"I know it's not illegal. I mean dangerous to your health. I've been reading a lot of—"

"Anything is dangerous when it's not used properly, even multiple vitamins."

"Maybe. But they don't make your bones grow like a gorilla, do they?"

"No, not usually," said Brad disagreeably.

"And how 'bout these other designer steroids everybody's talking about? You don't think any of the guys are using them, do you?"

"Honestly, Tom, you'd have to ask them. I keep my eye out for the illegal stuff. Believe me, I'd know if they were doing something detrimental to their program."

"Yeah, I suppose you would."

"Listen. You let me worry about the kids' health, okay?" said Brad. "That's what you hired me for, right?"

"Well, yes, but—I tell you what, Brad, do me a favor. If you hear of anybody doing anything suspicious, let me know, will ya?"

Irritated by Brad's evasiveness, Tom returned to his office, turned on the Braves game, and began to slog through the pile of paperwork on his desk. *The last fucking thing I need is a drug scandal.*

BUZZ . . . BUZZ BUZZ

"Yes, what is it? "

"Bobby Brooks from Nike."

Tom hesitated a moment. "Sure—I'll take it."

"Hey, Bobby!" Tom turned down the sound on the TV. "You're gonna be in town when? . . . Tonight . . . Well, I'd kinda planned . . . Really? . . . Hum. Okay. Where should I meet you? . . . Awright . . . No, it's just been a long day . . . Yes I talked with Coach Callahan. He said Reebok's offered him an extra ten grand to wear their new slam dunk shoes . . . I know, I told him not to do anything before I'd talked with you . . . Awright Bobby, lobby of the Hunt Room at seven, see ya later."

Better call home and tell Aretha to let Jan know I've gotten tied up. What were we supposed to do tonight . . . Take the kids to Uncle Clifton and Aunt Inez's for dinner. Sheez! Jan's gonna hit the roof. But what am I s'posed to do? Business is business.

BUZZ BUZZ

"Mr. Barrett is here for his fo' thirty."

"Thank you, Savannah," said Tom, getting up to greet his last appointment of the day, and forgetting to call home.

Roscoe T. Barrett, III, better known as Junior, was the oldest son of

Roscoe T. Barrett II, President of Sun Southern Bank, one of the Athletics Department's largest corporate sponsors. Junior, like his father, was a Morgan grad and a former Knights football player. Unlike his father, who had been an All-American for the great Doc Fulsom, Junior had preferred banging cheerleaders to tackling dummies.

"Glad to see ya, Junior," said Tom, leading the handsome ne'er-do-well in the direction of a brass-studded, red leather couch.

"Been awhile, eh buddy?"

"Since the Golf Tournament in May. Where ya been, Junior?"

"I guess you haven't heard about Nancy and me."

"Just some rumors."

"Divorce is hell, Tom."

"I know. I've been there myself."

"Really? I didn't know that."

"Oh yeah, about ten years ago."

"Did you have any kids?"

"One." Tom sighed. "A three year old son."

"I've got four."

"Ooo, and there's nothin' you can—"

"No, it was strike three. She caught me red-handed."

"Anybody I know?"

"Julie Powers."

"The name sounds familiar. . . . "

"Works for WBUX—little blond."

"Oh yeah, I know the one." Tom nodded.

"The wife put an investigator on my ass. For four months he trailed me around."

"Man, that's cold."

"Yeah, I blew it. Big time. She's got pictures. And worst of all, Francine Nichols is her attorney."

"The ball buster."

"None other, and to top it all off, my old man's on her side."

Tom shook his head in commiseration.

"But I didn't come here to burden you with my personal problems."

"That's okay, Junior. Hey, you want a little pop? It's about that time."

"Don't mind if I do."

"Vodka on the rocks, right?" asked Tom, standing in front of a combination liquor cabinet-trophy case.

"Yeah, thanks."

"So what exactly *does* bring you over here to see me on this hot afternoon, Junior?"

"Well, Tom," said Junior, swirling the Grey Goose around the ice cubes in his glass, "I don't know how to tell you this, but Daddy is seriously thinking about dropping his sponsorship of the half-time field goal kicking competition."

"Whaaa—" Tom whirled around, visibly shaken by the thought of losing Sun Southern's $400,000 per year subsidy.

"Daddy's decided to sponsor his contest at Southern Baptist instead."

"But Junior, they're only a Double A team. Their whole stadium doesn't hold more than 25,000."

"I know."

"Besides your old man went to Morgan! Where's his school spirit?"

"Since that stroke of his last year he's been gettin' religious. I swear those Baptist boosters musta sent him a thousand dollars worth of flowers when he was in the hospital."

"I can't believe he'd—"

"And there's another thing, Tom, and this is just between you and me. Daddy hasn't been particularly happy about the kind of boys that Star has been recruiting for the last coupl'a years. He thinks maybe the Coach is prejudiced against white players."

"That's ridiculous!" trumpeted Tom in righteous indignation— and fear that other corporate contributors and ticket-buying citizens of Metro might be feeling the same way.

"That's what Daddy's been saying. And, of course, he'd deny it if anybody asked."

"And is his decision final?"

After several minutes of desultory conversation, Junior put his glass down on the coffee table and looked at his watch. "Wow, didn't know it was this late. Tell you what, Tom, I gotta run, but I'll give you a call next week. We'll get together for lunch at the Club, see if we can't figure out some way to change the old man's mind."

Tom rose slowly from his seat. "Sure, Junior, sure."

"Are you feelin' okay, Mr. Hanagan?" asked Savannah when the Athletics Director issued from his office several minutes after Junior's departure.

"Yeah, I'm okay, Savannah. I think the weather must be getting to me."

"It has been hot, hadn't it?" she said, gathering up her blond hair in a ponytail, preparing to go home. "I guess if you don't need me for anything more I'll go. "

"What?" asked Tom, whose mind had been wandering through the world of unbalanced budgets.

"I said you oughta go home and get yourself some rest. You've been workin' too hard, Mr. Hanagan."

"Yeah, you're right," he said, picking up the day's final pile of messages.

"You're sure there's nothin' else I can do?"

"No, you run along, I'll see you tomorrow."

"Awright, Mr. Hanagan, bye bye."

Once Savannah was gone, Tom made a beeline for the liquor cabinet where he poured himself two more fingers of Grey Goose. *I hope Brewster hasn't heard about this,* he said as he reared back and tossed off the vodka. That's the last thing I need.

Unable to concentrate, Tom shut off his computer thirty minutes later and headed out to the practice fields to kill some time before meeting Bobby Brooks for dinner. But by the time he reached the coaches' observation tower he regretted his decision.

"God it's hot out here!" he said, thankful to receive a glass of Gatorade from graduate assistant coach Porky Watson.

"Yessir, Mr. Hanagan. Two of the guys passed out while they were warmin' up."

"They're okay, I hope?"

"Fine, just the us'al."

"Huh, so how are the guys lookin'?"

"They're kickin' butt."

"Fired up, eh?"

"Yes sir. We've been havin' to pull 'em apart all week long."

"Hey Tommy, what's up?" said Coach Star, walking up to his friend.

"Damn it's hot."

The Coach smiled.

"Porky says the guys are lookin' good, huh?"

"Kickin' butt," said Star, repeating the team's new rallying cry— the words of which had been plastered on every locker and athletics dormitory wall. "Kicking butt," repeated Tom, steadying himself against a blocking sled on the sideline.

"I got a call from Ballings this afternoon," said Star a minute later, his eyes fixed on the field where the players were running through plays.

"Yes, I met with him earlier this afternoon."

"That's what he said. And I don't know what the hell you said to him, but—WHAT ARE YOU DOIN', MUGGINS?! When I say wait till the last minute to break, I mean it! You telegraph your moves like that against the Bearcats, they'll be all over you!"

"All I said to him, Tony, was that I was worried about the kids using these designer drugs."

"Uh huh . . . Awright, Dewey! Nice move! . . . Good hands, Musta-fa!"

"And?"

"And I don't know what your problem is, Tommy." Coach Star looked his friend in the eyes. "I've already told you the guys aren't doin' anything illegal."

"I know," said Tom, jumping back as 295 pound tackle Dubose Forrest drove Reggie Muggins out of bounds for a ten yard loss. "But, Tony, I still don't like it."

"Wake up, Caroon!" yelled the Coach at his new 6-foot, 11-inch defensive team specialist. "You aren't playin' basketball! ... I dunno, Tommy, I think you should just let Ballings do his job—15, 16, 17... Hold up! Hold up! Now, listen! When I say I want that next play off in 15 seconds, I mean 15 seconds! I don't care how hot it is. Start moving your asses!"

"But you're missing my point." Tom followed Tony down to the other end of the field where defensive coordinator Ed Tarmeenian was putting the first string defensive players through the paces against quarterback Jimmy Joe Wallace and the third string offense.

"That's the third time Holmes has beat you this afternoon, Lincoln!" screamed Ed Tarmeenian in the sweaty face of his left cornerback. "Who do you motherfuckers think we're playin' in two weeks? Harvard?"

While the offense prepared to run another play out of the Mississippi Bearcat playbook, Tarmeenian rambled over to Tony and Tom.

"What's up, Eddie?"

"Shit," grunted Coach Star's old Pittsburgh Steeler teammate and right hand man. "Wallace has been picking my boys apart all afternoon."

"I saw," said the Coach.

"NO NO NO!" screamed Tarmeenian as halfback Tutomo Tongo darted in front of linebacker Craig Bumhoffer and grabbed a flare pass from Wallace. "What are you guys DOIN'?!"

"Ten more minutes, Eddie," said the Coach. "I wanna give 'em at least a half hour on kicking drills."

"Yeah, yeah." Tarmeenian stomped back out onto the field.

"That Wallace kid's lookin' good, isn't he, Tony?"

"Yeah, not bad." Star mopped the sweat off his face on the shoulder of his tee shirt and led Tom across the field to where twenty seven year old true freshman Fernando DeGama was practicing field goals. "How's that leg feel?" he shouted at the former Brazilian soccer pro.

"Leg feel okay, Coach."

"No problemo?"

"No problemo!"

"Anyways, Tony, I gotta get goin'," said Tom. "But I still think we need to talk about this drug stuff."

"Okay, Tommy, but—"

"But what?"

"Relax. You're worrying too much."

As Tom dizzily made his way to the Calhoun parking lot across the steaming playing field, he started to think again about Roscoe Barrett and what a bad day it had been. Then he turned on the ignition of his car, and it got worse.

"It's not fair to blame it all on Tom Hanagan," came the voice of Metro's very own Bo Hanks, host of the WSOT sports talk show, over the radio. "I'm sure he didn't want to raise the price of football tickets anymore than anyone else."

"Well, if Hanagan ain't responsible, Bo, who is? I mean, it's got to where us workin' folks cain't hardly afford to go to a football game on Saturday no more."

"But even State had to raise the price of their tickets last year."

"Yeah, but only three dollars, and it's a far sight more entertainin' to pay three bucks more to watch them win, than five bucks more to watch our boys lose."

"All right, Norman." Bo Hanks chuckled. "Gotta go now. I'd like to hear what the rest of you out there think about the new price of tickets at Morgan—You're on the air."

"This here's Ned Bullins."

"Where you callin' from, Ned?"

"Boomers Fork."

"Go ahead, buddy."

"Well now, Bo, I kinda feel like maybe that last fella you was talkin' to had a good point 'bout Hanagan bein' responsible for our problems."

"How's that, Ned?"

"Well, 'fore he got here we might not 'a had much of a football team, but we at least used to win some basketball games, and it didn't cost—"

"ENOUGH!" blurted Tom, savagely punching the button on his radio.

At 7:05 Tom walked into the lobby of the Royal Hunt Room Restaurant. Located on top of the new Regency Hotel which had gone up five years earlier to accommodate the athletics event crowds that had as yet failed to materialize, the Royal Hunt Room specialized in serving over-priced Franco-American cuisine to businessmen with big expense accounts. Besides its proximity to the University, two blocks from the east end of campus, Tom was particularly fond of the restaurant because Manuel made the best vodka martinis in town, and Edwardo, the maitre d', could always be relied upon to find Seignior Hanagan a discreetly-located table and, if necessary, a room on the top floor in which to entertain really important clients after dinner.

"Meester Hanagan, how are you tonight?" The tuxedo-clad Edwardo gave Tom a low bow reserved only for his most extravagant tippers.

"I've been better."

The maitre d' looked concerned. "Evryting's all right, I hope."

"Yeah, I'll be okay." Tom looked around the dimly lit lobby for Bobby. "Not here yet. I think I'll go over to the bar a minute."

"Fine, Meester Hanagan. Your table is ready whenever you are."

"Meester Tom!"

"What's happenin', Manuel?"

"You want the usual?" asked the swarthy Puerto Rican bartender whose slicked back hair gleamed in the candlelight.

"Yeah, but make it a double," said Tom.

"Long day, eh?"

"I'll say. I thought it would never end."

"Dees will help." Manuel placed Tom's drink on top of a paper napkin on the bar.

"Ohh yeah." Tom gurgled with relief as the ice-cold vodka burned its way down his throat. "Hey, you wouldn't happen to have a cigarette, would ya?"

"Sure, Meester Tom, I din't know you smoked."

"Gave it up a coupl'a years ago, but I still get the urge every now and then."

"Marlboro okay?"

"Yeah, thanks." Tom sucked in a long drag.

"Ahh, that tastes good. Might as well mix me another while you're at it, Manuel."

"Make that two."

"Bobby!"

"And how's my all-time favorite Athletics Director doin' tonight?" Bobby Brooks gave Tom a big hug.

"Suddenly better," answered Tom, looking into the velvety brown eyes of Nike's number one mid-South sales rep.

"Well good!" said Bobby sitting down on the stool beside him, her dark hair falling in curly wisps across her provocative cleavage.

Tom sat there taking her all in.

"Long day, huh," she said, affectionately rubbing the arm of the man in charge of her second largest account.

"A killer," said Tom. "You ready to eat?"

"Sure."

Tom got up unsteadily from his barstool. "Edwardo!"

"Yes, Meester Hanagan, come right theese way."

Exercising his usual discretion, Edwardo led Tom and Bobby to a table overlooking the Metro city lights, hidden from view behind a row of potted palms.

"If I'd known you were so busy—"

"That's all right, Bobby." Tom took a long drink and smiled.

"Is everything all right? You sounded kinda upset over the phone."

"Yeah, everything's okay," he lied, beginning to feel his spirits revive under the effects of the alcohol and Bobby's presence.

"I hope so."

"I've just been under a lot of pressure." Tom drained his glass.

"I guess those pre-season ratings have people kinda upset, huh?"

"That's part of it," he said, wondering why Jan wasn't ever interested in his work like Bobby.

"Frankly, I was surprised you were ranked so low."

"Tell me about it." *Yeah, it really is nice having somebody you can talk to,* he thought as Bobby related the details of her day to him. *Hell, Jan's been so uptight lately I can't even mention football to her without her flying off the handle. Women like Bobby know how to make a man feel appreciated. I mean what's wrong with having a couple of drinks and a few laughs every now and then. I can't even remember the last time that Jan and—*

"Would you like to order now, sir?"

"What?" said Tom, wrenched from his thoughts.

"Would you like to order now, sir?"

"Yeah, sure."

"And don't worry about Callahan goin' to Reebok," said Tom a half hour later after ordering another bottle of Bergsit Sauvignon Blanc as he and Bobby were served their cucumber bisque. "I'll takecarahim."

"I know you will," said the sneaker saleswoman. "You sho' we need more wine, honey?"

"Y'I'mawright," said Tom.

But by the time the waiter served their venison scaloppini and blackened Dover sole, she had begun to wonder.

"I don't know what thehellpeople 'spect from meanyway."

"I know, suga'," she said, patting his hand.

And by the time their chocolate parfait and Courvoisier arrived, she told Edwardo that Mr. Hanagan was going to need a cab.

"Hell, I'mthebesdamathleticdirector thisschools ever had."

"Of course you are, baby. The vera' vera' best," she assured him, clandestinely signaling to the waiter that it was time to bring their check.

An hour later, loafers in hand, Tom tip-toed as quietly as a drunken man could up the creaky spiral staircase of his house. Then turning left on the upstairs landing, he walked down the hall to the master bedroom and turned the doorknob. Locked. Tom would have liked to go in and curl up beside his wife, but he knew better than to risk it at this hour with alcohol on his breath. Instead, he felt his way downstairs and after painfully stubbing his toe on a dining room chair, entered the dimly lit kitchen where, to his surprise, he found his five year old Katey in her dinosaur print pajamas pouring herself a glass of Diet Pepsi.

"Katey, what are you doin' up at this hour?"

"I can't sleep," said his redheaded daughter, her blue eyes filled with accusation and tears. "Mommy says you don't love her anymore."

"What?"

"Mommy says you don't love her anymore."

"That's not true, baby."

"She told grandma that we were gonna move away from here and never come back."

"No, no, no," he said, reaching for his whimpering daughter, who wriggled away and ran out the kitchen door.

What a day! he muttered, suddenly feeling dizzy and grabbing for the butcher-block table as he stood back up. *What a lousy, rotten day!*

CHAPTER 2

Friday, August 19

Chancellor Brewster was in a foul mood as he rode to work. "Tell Hanagan to be at my office in forty minutes," he growled into his car phone.

Not yet 9:00 on his second day back from vacation, Morgan's head administrator had just been informed by the mayor of Metro that as of January 1 the University could no longer burn its toxic waste at the Hargrove County facility. That was just after his friend Boomer Cox, Vice President of the University Board of Trust, had called to tell him that the members of the Athletics Committee wanted to call a special meeting about the Knights' abysmal pre-season ratings.

"I don't know what I'm gonna do about this football team of mine," muttered Brewster.

"Did you say sumpin, sir?" asked his driver.

"I was just talking to myself, Lamont." Brewster opened his newspaper, skimmed over the headlines from the Near East and then turned to the sports section where he saw a photograph of State football coach Hoss Humphreys with a caption that read, "Humphreys and State set sights on another Mid-South championship." As he read through the upbeat article about Humphreys getting his Bowl-winning squad ready for the season in Sharpsville, Chancellor Brewster's blood pressure rose by almost as many points as State had beaten Morgan last December.

"But I'm gonna do something," he said, angrily recalling the way State University President Elmore Cudlip had high-hatted him at the governor's conference on minority education the month before.

If it's the last thing I do here at Morgan, I'm gonna get myself a winning football team.

To the man who has everything, or almost everything, not being able to get that one thing he wants more than anything can be profoundly disturbing. By all rights William R. Brewster should have been happy. He had health. At fifty-eight, tall, trim, gray-templed, and tan, he looked forty-five. He had wealth. At $825,000 per year, he was one of the highest paid university presidents in the United States. He had status and power. Under his directorship, J.P. Morgan had grown from a medium-sized southern university with a good liberal arts college into an internationally respected megaversity with top-ranked law, business, and medical schools. Listed in *Who's Who* as one of the movers and shakers in American education, Billy Bob Brewster, the son of a grocer and an elementary school teacher from Texarkana, Arkansas, had risen to the very top of American professional life. But he still didn't have a championship football team.

Despite his present agitation, by the time he pulled through the University's main gate, past the tarnished bronze statue of J.P. Morgan that stood in front of the Administration Building, the Chancellor had assumed that self-possessed and dignified mien with which men of his rank and stature are accustomed to greet the world.

"Good morning, sir," saluted Provost Dave Buntley as the Chancellor emerged from his car and climbed up the marble stairs that led to the arched Gothic doorway of Morgan Hall.

"Good morning, Dave."

"How are you today?" asked receptionist Peggy Anne Purdle.

"Just fine, Peggy, and you?" responded Brewster, marching through the wooden doors of his executive suite before he heard what she had to say.

"Good morning, Chancellor."

"Hello, Helen."

"Good morning, sir."

"Good morning, Henry."

Brewster halted before the arched doorway of his personal chambers and was greeted by his administrative assistant, Anita Rogers.

"And how are we this morning?" Anita smiled.

"Don't ask." Brewster put down his briefcase and began to look at the memos she handed him.

"Dudley Dunning wants you to call, the Reverend Dr. Bigsby in Memphis wanted to know if you would be staying for the night—I told him no—Mike O'Neill from the NCAA Executive Council will be in town Wednesday, your mother called five minutes ago, and—I love that new tie. Did you get it in Washington?"

"Why yes I did," said the Chancellor, breaking out in an ingratiating smile that vanished when he asked where Tom Hanagan was.

"He just stepped out to the men's room."

Fifteen minutes later, after talking to the Head of the University Hospital about the impending toxic waste crisis, and to his mother about her sick Chihuahua, Brewster buzzed Anita and told her to send in his Athletics Director.

Like Chancellor Brewster, Tom had also had a trying morning. At 6:15, Jan woke him up to tell him she wanted a divorce. At 9:15, Junior Barrett confirmed that his father was still intent on pulling out Sun Southern's subsidy. And just before coming over, Coach Star had reported that Brad Ballings was threatening to quit unless he left him alone. Nevertheless, dressed in his crisply pressed seersucker suit, Tom was all smiles as he entered the stone and oak-beamed interior of the Chancellor's office.

"Have a seat, Tom," said the Chancellor, nodding toward a chair in front of his desk.

"Ah, did you enjoy your vacation?" asked Tom, trying to get comfortable in the straight-back throne chair.

"Yes, I did, thank you," said Brewster, letting the silence surround them as he stared at Tom. "But I didn't ask you up here today to talk about my vacation." Tom shook his head, and Brewster rocked forward in his heavy leather chair and started to fiddle with a football-shaped paperweight on his desk. "Now, Tom, I'm sure you know how much I like you. And how much I believe in you. Otherwise, I never would have brought you here to Morgan." Tom nodded.

"And I'm also sure you're aware of what high hopes we had when you first took over in Calhoun. And for the first two years at least, it looked like we were headed in the right direction." Brewster paused again. "But unfortunately something appears to have gone wrong, dreadfully wrong. And I'm not sure why. I've pretty much let you have a free hand in running the department. I went along with you on hiring Star—over the objections of many of the Board members. And in spite of difficult financial times, we've spent millions modernizing our facilities—"

"May I—"

"And we're still on the bottom of the pre-season ratings."

Silence.

"Now as you can testify, Tom, I've never been a stickler about balancing the budget. I'm enough of a businessman to know that it takes money to make money. And I've been more than willing to invest in you in the hope that our institution would eventually reap a reward from our financial commitment. But I'm afraid that the members of the Athletics Committee have begun to have second thoughts about our investment."

Tom shifted uncomfortably in his chair.

"For the past five years, we've been running in the neighborhood of two million a year in the red."

"I know."

"Now if we had somethin' to show for our money, like a Bowl victory or a league championship, then maybe I could justify the outlay. 'Course, if we were winning like you promised, we wouldn't have to worry about any of this 'cause we'd be making some of those big dollars that NBC's giving away, now wouldn't we?"

"That's true," said Tom.

"YOU'RE GODDAM RIGHT IT IS!" roared Brewster. "And it's high time our football program stopped bein' the laughin' stock of the South. We're not paying you over a quarter of a million a year so we can sit in our sky boxes on Saturday and watch our team lose. Now, bein' a professional educator," resumed the Chancellor a moment later in a tone of voice more befitting the dignity of his office, "I understand that winning football games on Saturday afternoon should not be the end-all of our athletics program here at Morgan. But the members of the Board are tired of seeing the name of their Alma Mater on the bottom of everyone's list, and if you and your staff don't turn this program around damn quick, they're gonna start looking for someone who can. Have I made myself clear?"

"Yes," said Tom, feeling a sudden urge to jump across the desk and strangle Brewster.

"Well, good," said the Chancellor. "Then I don't s'pose there's much else we need to talk about right now, is there?"

"No, I guess not."

"And I suggest you tell your friend Star what I've told you. It might help to motivate him too."

The Chancellor fabricated a smile. "And now, if you'll excuse me, I have work to do."

By two o'clock that afternoon, Tom's head was splitting. He wanted to go home, take three Advil, and go to sleep. But The Tribune's feature sportswriter, Red Carlisle, was due in his office in five minutes. While he waited for Red to arrive, Tom was talking on the phone with Blake Stevens, the National Head of the Camelot Boosters Club.

"I tell you, Blake, I came this close to telling Brewster where to go this morning. . . . Maybe, but he's not gonna push me around. . . . Hold on a sec, would you? . . . Hey Blake, gotta go. Carlisle just walked in. I'll talk with you this weekend." BUZZ BUZZ. "Savannah, after you let in Mr. Carlisle, would you tell Coach Star to come up to the office."

"So how's Metro's number one sportswriter doin' today?" Tom clapped Red on the back and ushered him to a seat.

"Not bad, Tom, not bad at all," replied the journalist, somewhat surprised to find Tom so amiable after the hostile articles he'd been writing about Morgan. Red had never forgiven Tom for firing his fraternity brother Smiley Sims and replacing him with Coach Star.

"Good. I always like to see friends doing well. Have a seat, Red. Anything I can get you?"

"Well," said the forty-five year old, red-haired, red-faced, red-necked sportswriter, breaking into a grin, "maybe a date with that little secretary of yours."

"I don't know if your wife would like that, Red."

"What ole Joyce don't know never hurt her."

Tom grinned. "And how is Joyce?"

"Couldn't be better. She and the kids went down to see her sister in Mississippi last week. Since she left, ole Red's been catching up on his fishin', if you know what I mean."

Tom gave Red a wink. "So, anyway, before Star gets here, let me tell ya', I got him to agree to let you into practice."

"That's my buddy, Tom."

"But I'm afraid I could only get him to agree to once a week."

"Once a week?!"

"Six to six-thirty on Wednesdays. I thought Wednesdays would be—"

"Now hol' on jus' a second. Let me get this right. You're tellin' me that Star's only gonna allow me a half hour once a week?!"

"That's about the size of it, and believe me, it was tough just to get that out of him."

"I don't know who the hell that boy of yours thinks he is. I've worked Morgan football for twenty years and I've never been barred from anybody's practice."

"I realize how you feel, Red. Believe me, I'm on your side. But when I hired Tony I told him—"

"You told him what, that he could insult the press? This here's America, Tom, we got a right to know what's goin' on."

"I agree, but this year Tony and his staff decided, for the players' sake, it was best to limit the amount of press coverage."

"My readers ain't gonna stand for this."

"You know there's a lot a coaches these days who don't allow—"

"I don't give a goddam about those other coaches. This here is Metro and—"

Before Red had time to finish his sentence, Coach Star walked in. "Hey Tom."

"Have a seat, Tony," said Tom, jumping up from behind his desk. Red and I were just discussing your proposal."

"And," said Tony, slowly turning his head in the direction of the sportswriter who had turned his crimson face to the wall.

"And I'm gettin' tired of your bullshit, Star," shouted the columnist, whirling around in Tony's direction—and suddenly deciding to lower his voice.

"I'm sorry if you don't like the arrangements, Red, but that's how it is."

"My readers ain't gonna like this."

"That's up to you, Red," said Tony with a shrug he knew would infuriate the journalist—just as he and Coach Ed Tarmeenian had planned.

If we can really piss Carlisle off, we got it made, Ed had suggested to Tony the week earlier. *Surest way I know to get everybody's attention is to start feudin' with the press. You remember how Rudy Rose did it at West Virginia in '86. He stopped talkin' to the newspaper boys just before the season started and they couldn't stop talkin' about him.*

"My readers ain't gonna like this at all," repeated Red, bolting from his seat, shooting a threatening glance at Tom Hanagan, and heading for the door.

"See you next Wednesday, Red," said the Coach as the journalist stomped out the door.

"Jesus Christ, Tony! What are you trying to do?" Tom ran out of his office after Red.

Trying to save our jobs, pal, said the Coach to himself.

CHAPTER 3

As Tom Hanagan feared, Red Carlisle blasted the Morgan Athletics Department with both barrels in his column in the Sunday *Tribune*. "*If Tony Star spent more time working on his offensive game plans and less time worrying about the media bothering his players, he might be able to fill Fulsom Field on Saturdays. . . . No matter what Tom Hanagan or anyone in the Athletics Department thinks, it is our right as loyal fans to know what is going on behind the walls at Calhoun.*"

• • •

And on Tuesday evening, Coach Star, wearing a ballcap with *KICK BUTT* blazoned on the crest, did an interview with TV Channel 5 sports reporter Al South, in which he told the people of Metro that he'd decided to close practices for fear of leaks. "And if some people in town don't start practicing a little more responsible journalism"— he pointed to his cap— "they just might find out what these words mean."

• • •

By Wednesday afternoon, the Coach's feud with Red was front-page news: COACH *BUTTS* HEAD WITH LOCAL MEDIA.

• • •

And by Thursday morning, the first day of class at the University, ticket sales, precisely as Ed predicted, had risen forty percent.

"I gotta apologize, Tony," said Tom Hanagan over his cell as he turned down Stadium Drive. "You were right, that TV appearance of yours has the whole town talking. Ticket sales have jumped 40 percent. I'm sorry for reaming you the way I did after that meeting with Carlisle. . . . I know you wouldn't, buddy. . . . All right, Tony, I'll let you go."

Coach Star dreaded the return of the students for fall classes. Until school began he had his players to himself. Once classes resumed, he had to share them with the rest of the student body. No longer under twenty-four hour surveillance, his boys were on their own from the time they left the weight room in the morning until they returned to the weight room in the afternoon. That worried Star, for although J. P. Morgan had a reputation for being conservative, he knew that Morgan students were just as wild and crazy as college kids anywhere — even if they didn't make a political issue of their misbehavior like their more obstreperous brothers and sisters north of the Mason Dixon. Lurking on Morgan's magnolia-shaded walkways and in the creaky-floored classrooms of its ivy-covered Greek Revival buildings were just as many liberated, cocktail-swilling coeds, pot-smoking, coke-sniffing fraternity brothers, and anti-authoritarian professors as at any other top Top 20 American university. As he stood in the hallway outside the videotape room Friday morning, Tony Star was as nervous as a father whose daughter is out on her first date.

"Got that tape ready, Turk?"

"Few more minutes, Coach," said Turk Turley, the longhaired, ex-TV cameraman who headed up the Athletics Videotape Department.

"A FEW MORE MINUTES?!" snapped the Coach.

"Yeah, Porky screwed up the sequence." Turk moved the mouse across the screen. "You wanna look at the A-Team offense first, right?"

"With all this gear we got I don't know why we're havin' problems." Outfitted at three times the cost of the new language lab, the Calhoun video room was fitted with two Sony video editing boards, two duplicating machines, a library of tapes, and a battery of portable cameras and equipment with which Turk and his three full-time assistants filmed every minute of every practice and game.

"Just one more second, Coach and I'll have it. There you go, it's cued right up to where you want it."

"Thanks, Turk. I didn't mean to unload on you like that," apologized Tony, not wishing to antagonize a man whose technological expertise he needed to formulate strategy, scout opponents, and evaluate recruits.

"That's okay, I know how it is with the kids back in school."

When Tony walked into the football conference room five minutes later, defensive coordinator Ed Tarmeenian and offensive coordinator Jet Jackson were waiting for him.

"So whad'da you guys want for lunch?"

"I dunno, Tony, whatever you want."

"How 'bout pizza?" suggested the Coach, who was feeling even hungrier than usual from the nervous acid gurgling in his stomach.

"Sounds good to me. How 'bout you, Jet?"

"Yeah, sure."

Tony took his cell off his belt and rang his secretary Peaches Perdue. "Yeah, two monster size pies with the works. . . . What did you say, Jet? . . . That's one without onions. . . . All right, hon, thanks. And while we're waiting," said the Coach, "let's see what we got from yesterday. Lock those doors, would'ja, Ed? I don't want anybody interrupting us."

A little over a week to go until the season opener, the coaches had been allowing the players to hit each other with nearly game-like intensity. Tony and his coordinators were of the school who believed it was beneficial for the players to do some real head-banging before the first game. Like training soldiers with live ammunition, it was good for morale and unlikely to result in many injuries, except to the walk-ons on whom they blooded their starters. It also gave the coaches a chance to see if the line-up was working—and if it wasn't, to make adjustments.

The first few series of downs on the tape featured the A-Team offense vs. the B-Team defense.

"They looked okay on that play," said Jet Jackson, after they watched quarterback Reggie Muggins fake a dive to his fullback and dash between tackle and tight end for ten yards. "But watch what happens when he tries it goin' the other way. Give 'em hell, Pete!" Jet laughed as offensive line coach Pete Cossacky suddenly appeared on the screen and started screaming at Arlo Plummer. There was no sound, but it was easy to read Pete's lips.

"Maybe Pete's right about Plummer losing his balls," said Star.

"Could be," said Jet. "You wanna try White at guard?"

"Maybe we should. And I tell you what, have Cossacky send Plummer to see me."

As the Coach watched his A-Team offense working out of the T-Bone, a variation on the triple option that he and Head Coach Art Mink had used to lead the UA Wild Cats to the national championship five years before, he thought how ironic it was that he had earned his reputation as a coach by using an offense he didn't really believe in.

"And this time," said Jet, "Muggins is gonna try the weak side. Good snap, nice movement down the line—and he gets buried before he can get the ball off."

Though adept at coaching the option, Tony knew that big-time winning college football teams needed a pro-style combined air and ground assault. But athletes who were big and strong enough to play pro-style ball—even with the recent proliferation of bodybuilding drugs in high schools—were hard to recruit, especially at a place like Morgan.

"Hey Tony, check out this next play," said Ed Tarmeenian, watching with glee as walk-on Greg Forest collided with tailback Mongol Harris in mid air. *KABOOM!* . . . "Did you see that hit?!"

Yeah, life was definitely strange, thought the Coach as Ed ran the instant replay back so he could watch Greg Forest get two of his ribs broken one more time. *You do something you don't believe in and all of a sudden you're a big success.*

"Now, what I think we oughta do, Tony," said Jet after another set of downs, "is reverse the order of the plays in this series and send Mongol in motion on first down.

KNOCK KNOCK

"Pizza's here." Ed bolted from his seat and opened the door. "Thanks, Porky—here it is, boys, and still hot."

By the time the Coach had scarfed his fifth piece of pizza and second Dr. Pepper, he was starting to feel a bit more relaxed. And as he watched the C-Team offense—with freshman Jimmy Joe Wallace at quarterback—he felt that there might actually be hope for the season. *Maybe this Wallace kid can be my secret weapon*, he thought, as he watched him drop back and hit tight end Jeremiah Hardee for thirteen yards.

"Well guys, whad'da ya think?" asked Star, after they'd watched Wallace run through several more well-executed series of downs.

"I tell ya," said Jet, stroking the lobe of his left ear, "this wild scheme of yours just might work. Wallace is definitely lookin' sharp, and if we wait till the third game to use him, we might catch Bobby Cheathem and his boys off guard."

"Eddie?"

"If those pigs in front of Wallace can hold back the competition like they've been holdin' back our defense, Wallace could be dangerous."

The pigs to whom Ed was referring were the front five of the C-Team offense. Nicknamed the "guinea pigs" or "pigs" for short by Pete Cossacky, they had received their moniker not so much because of the humongous dimensions of their hams as for the enormous quantities of chemicals they'd been injecting.

"Yeah, it's amazing how those boys have bulked up," said the Coach. "Yeah, it is," chuckled Jet, "a miracle of modern medicine."

• • •

Tom Hanagan felt as if he were going to pass out as he bent over and fished his ball out of the cup on the 14th hole at the Magnolia Hills Country Club Friday afternoon.

"That's the third hole in a row you've won, Roy," wheezed Clifton Calhoun, leaning against his golf cart while filling in his scorecard.

"And let's see, Tom, you were—?"

"Three over." Tom wiped his sweaty face with a towel.

"And Bill?"

"A bogie, Mr. Calhoun," said the still fresh assistant athletics director.

"Well, I guess the honor's yours again, Roy."

"Awrighty, Clifton," said Roy Nash, the former golf pro and Bible salesman who was athletics director at Living Waters Christian Academy—a local private high school where talented athletes in whom Morgan was particularly interested matriculated through the generosity of anonymous boosters.

Nash, in a pink polo shirt, grass-green trousers and black and white golf shoes, pulled a number three Big Bertha out of his kangaroo skin bag. He stepped up to the tee, and Bill Conner made him a sporting wager: "I got an extra twenty says this is gonna be my hole."

"You're on, Billy," said Nash, to whom the foursome was already about two hundred dollars in debt.

WOOOOSH...SMACKKK.

"Looks like another beauty, Roy. Yup, just to the left of the green."

"You're next, Billy."

As Bill teed up his ball, Clifton Calhoun leaned over to Tom, who was helping himself to another beer from the cooler on the back of their cart. "You bettuh take it easy on that beer, Tom, it's pretty hot out here."

"Okay, Uncle Cliff"—*glug glug glug.*

"You sure you feel okay?" said Clifton, after Tom plopped down in the seat next to him. "Your game's way off today."

"Yeah, it has been for awhile."

"I know, and I've been meanin' to talk with you about it, Tom. As you know, I've never been one to poke my nose into other folks' business, but I've been noticin' that you just aren't on top of things lately."

"I've been under a lot of pressure, Cliff."

"Of course you have, Tom. I know what you're goin' through"—which wasn't exactly true, since Uncle Cliff had never worried about his job a day in his life after marrying a mining fortune just out of college. "It's a demandin' position you've got. But what really concerns me is what's hap'nin' with you and Jan—*Silence*—The other night Inez told me Jan said she was thinkin' of movin' back to Car'lina. Now Tommy—" Cliff laid his hand on the Director's knee with fatherly affection, "somethin's gotta be done about this situation. And mind ya', I'm not pointin' any fingers. I know how headstrong my niece can be. But on the other hand—"

"On the other hand what?!" asked Tom a little more forcefully than he meant to.

"On the other hand," said Clifton Calhoun, shocked at the way Tom had spoken to him, "I won't be havin' anybody make my little baby mis'rable. I've been like a daddy to that girl ever since my brother died," said the bronze-skinned, white-haired trustee, pulling the cart to an abrupt stop where Tom had hit his ball in the rough. "And there's nothin' in the world I wouldn't do to keep her happy."

"I know, Cliff," said Tom apologetically.

"The truth is," said Clifton, also softening his tone, "when things aren't right at home, it's bound to carry over everywhere else."

Tom gave Uncle Cliff a puzzled look. "Whad'da you mean, Cliff?"

"Well Tom, I'd be less than honest if I wasn't to tell you I've been hearin' things."

"What things? From who?"

"Just things, Tom, and it doesn't matter from whom. That's not the issue. The point I'm tryin' to make is that people are startin' to talk."

"Talk about what?" asked Tom defensively.

"Well, for one thing, about the way your hand starts shakin' every time you're not holdin' a drink."

Tom didn't know what to say.

Inez told me that you and Jan have started talkin' to some sort of marriage counselor."

"Yeah. We've been there once, but—"

"But nothin'. You keep goin' to see him. Maybe he can help you get a grip on yourself. Right now, though, you better go find your ball before they start wond'rin' what's happened to us."

As Tom blazed his way through the chiggers and poison ivy looking for his Pro Staff, woozy from the suffocating heat and warm beer, he was seething with anger—and apprehension. *Just once,* he said to himself, *I'd like to tell Cliff to take this job and—what am I saying? Uncle Cliff's not to blame. I should'a never left that job I had at Carolina. Hell, I never would have if it hadn't been for Jan— no, that's not true either. It was me who really wanted this fucking job. Besides, things went great for the first three years.* Tom finally saw his ball and motioned to Cliff that he'd found it. *How was I to know it would all go to shit.* The thought of himself branded as a loser working for a third as much in the athletics department of some podunk college or prep school literally made Tom shudder. *But I can still pull it out,* he told himself. *I've just got to get my life in control. Stop drinking so much—'course that's not gonna be easy with football season starting. But Cliff's right, it is starting to show. Tony's told me as much too. Yeah, they're both right. Of course, that's easy for them to say. Neither one of them has to report to Brewster or live with Jan.*

• • •

While Tom was stomping through the rough thinking about his wife, Jan was flexing her glutei maximi at Physiques thinking about him.

"Push! Push! Push that tush! Great! And wance again."

Maybe I have been too hard on Tom (HUFF HUFF), but the way he's been drinking lately, he's going to wind up like Mack. Mack was Jan's alcoholic ex-husband.

"Get those knees up, ladies! Wan, two, tree, stretch," said Stefan Bazitski, the handsome twenty-nine year old Russian émigré who worked as a part-time instructor at Physiques Spa to help pay for his tuition in the MBA program at Morgan.

I know his job hasn't been easy lately, having to deal with all those dreadful booster types every day (HUFF HUFF). Sometimes I wish we'd never left Carolina.

"Wan, two, stretch. And now other leg."

But horrible or not, he needs to grow up and stop telling me ridiculous things like I should quit my job (HUFF ugh). I only took my job in the first place because I was scared of getting stranded like I did with Mack. I can't let that happen again, not with three children.

"And now let's tighten up those tummies. Ready! Wan, two, tree."

And besides (PHEW PHEW), I like what I'm doing—and I'm good at it.

"And wance more! Okee dokee, ladies, you all look very good today. Especially you, Mrs. Ransom," said Stefan to the Mayor's once voluptuous, now dumpy forty-five year old wife. "And you, Mrs. Hanagan," said Bazitski, gracefully gliding toward her, the muscles of his torso rippling beneath his silver body suit, "you are lookink beauteeful as ever."

"Well, I don't know about that," said Jan as she toweled off her face.

"It's true, so athletic, so graceful."

"You sure that's me you're talking about?" Jan Hanagan smiled and removed the terry cloth band on her head and shook out her frosted blond hair.

"Have you ever been a dancer, Mrs. Hanagan?"

"A dancer? No—well, I did study ballet as a child. And I was in the modern dance troupe in college."

"I thought so," said the sandy-haired, blue-eyed Muscovite. "I too was dancer in St. Petersburg."

"Oh really?" said Mrs. Hanagan, throwing back her head and taking a drink of Evian water, her nipples standing out in relief through her pink leotard.

"Yes, for many years. Unfortunately I was injured in car accident and had to give up dancink."

"Oh, that's terrible."

"Yes, but then again, if I hadn't hurt myself I would never have come to Amerika—to Metro, where I meet wanderful person like you."

"Well, thank you, Stefan, that's nice of you to say that." Jan bent down to pick up her stair steps.

"Maybe we get together after class sometime and talk about dance."

"Uh—sure, that would be nice."

"Maybe next Wednesday?"

"Fine, Stefan. But I'm running kinda late. I'll talk to you next week."

"All right, Mrs. Hanagan. I see you next week."

CHAPTER 4

Saturday, August 27

Coach Star had reluctantly extended his players' curfew until one o'clock Saturday night. By eight o'clock that evening, all 102 members of the team who could still walk were out on the town, enjoying their first night of freedom since fall practice had begun.

"Did you see that mutherfucka's face when I showed him who you was, Reggie?"

"He almost had a heart attack, didn't he?"

"There you was, Reggie, right on the front page of the sports section, smilin' like you jus' won the lottery, and that jive nigga's tellin' us he knows Shaquille O'Neill."

Quarterback Reggie Muggins and homeboy Tootie Ruggles were cruising slowly down Stadium Boulevard on their way back from the JFK housing project, where they had just scored an eight-ball of coke at the apartment of Bow Wow Turner.

"I still can't believe he didn't know who you was, Reggie."

"That Bow Wow's got some dumb friends, don't he. But he's still got the bes' shit in town."

"You know dat's right," said Tootie, smiling at the man for whom he served as sidekick, procurer and confidante.

"Hey man, turn that up, will you?!"

Boom! Bam! Boom boom boom Bam!
Boom! Bam! Boom boom boom Bam!
Way you do me, baby, you know it's really sumthin'
Wid my hootchie in your cootchie pumpin and a humpin'

Drivin' through your tunnel, headed straight for heav'n
Shoot my load, girl, bam bam bam, like an AK47

"That's some bad sounds my boys be puttin' down."

"Yeah, Top-Z's the baddest," agreed Tootie, bobbing his head up and down to the deafening thump of the bass drum on the car's eighteen-inch woofers. "Hey man, you better slow down, der's the pigs."

"Where?" Muggins raised himself in his seat.

"Right over der, Reg."

"Shit, they just campus cops. They know better than to fuck with us."

Pulling on to Sumter Avenue—a junk food, video, music and hip clothing strip three blocks from the main university entrance—Reggie inched down the crowded street looking for a place to park near the Beta Alpha Delta frat house.

"Everybody gonna be here tonight?"

"I think so, Tootie," said Morgan's number one rusher, slamming on the brakes to avoid hitting two graduate students who had just stumbled out of the Gold Nugget bar.

"Those bitches from SAS gonna be here too?" SAS, Sigma Alpha Sigma, was the sister sorority of Beta Alpha Delta, the voluntarily segregated African-American fraternity on campus to which nearly all the black athletes belonged.

"Yeah they are," said Muggins, grinning at his friend.

"That Shanique St. Clair's bad lookin, ain't she, Reggie?"

"What?" said Reggie, suddenly swerving right to avoid colliding with a jeep full of screaming blond Tri-Delts.

"I said you get any pussy off Shanique St. Clair yet?"

"Wouldn't you like to know?"

"I knew it. You ain't fucked her yet."

"Who says? I come this close last spring."

"Yeah. An' how 'bout Tamika?"

"Tamika Gibbons?"

"Yeah."

"Ain't nobody hadn't had her, 'cept maybe you," laughed Reggie, poking Tootie in the ribs and pulling into a space that had just been vacated by an inebriated gang of Dekes in a Land Rover.

"I know the one you like, Reggie, it's that Teeny McAdoo, ain't it?"

"Don't you say nothin' bad about Teeny."

"I knew it," said Tootie testily, recognizing a rival for his friend's affection in the freckle-faced, pony-tailed cheerleader.

Before following the drum thuds up the stairs to the BAD fraternity house—a rundown two-story brick Victorian pile owned by the University—Reggie and Tootie checked themselves out in the florist shop window next to the frat house.

"How'm I lookin', Tootie?" asked the quarterback, who was wearing a pair of diamond stud earrings, a fishnet Morgan jersey (against regulations) with the midriff cut off, blue jeans, and three hundred-dollar sneakers.

"Fly, man. How 'bout me?"

Reggie and Tootie entered the frat house and were greeted by the BAD president, Alfy Winters, a light-skinned, capon-shaped, young black man in a goatee, rose-colored sunglasses, and a red, green and black imported dashiki.

"Wuz hap'nin, brothas?"

"You are, Alfy." Muggins gave his brother the fraternity's elaborate two-handed shake, then stepped in the un-air-conditioned house filled with music, laughter, and the scent of cigarettes, popcorn, and patchouli.

"Reggie!" squealed Shanique St. Clair, jumping up from a couch near the door. "You're here!"

"Yeah, I'm here." Reggie tried to act nonchalant as the buxom coed wiggled up to him in halter top and gold lamé toreador pants and threw her arms around his neck.

"Oooo honey, I'm so glad to see you."

"The feelin's mutual, baby," said the handsome football star, mugging for the crowd of laughing admirers congregating around their hero.

"Yo Reg, wuz goin' on," hooted Mongol Harris from across the room, giving the high sign to his teammate.

"What's hap'nin with your bad self," said Reggie to the muscle-bound halfback, whose initials MH stood out in hairy relief on the back of his shaved head.

"Yo, brother Reggie," said Zanzibar "Boo" Jackson, pushing his way through a crowd of hangers-on who had pressed the quarterback into a corner next to a poster of Nelson Mandela. "Here man, have som'a this."

"Thanks, Boo." Reggie took a plastic cup full of the fraternity's ritual "Knock-Out" punch. "You haven't seen Teeny tonight, have you, man?"

"Yeah, she went upstairs to try an' find Tamika."

"Oh yeah? You'll have to scuse me a second, brotha. C'mon, Tootie. Scuse me, people." Muggins began pushing his way slowly through the crowd, stopping every other step to exchange hugs, kisses, and high fives. When he finally reached the top of the stairs, he saw Teeny.

"Reggie, I've been looking for you all night," said the cheerleader, bouncing up to him in her cut-off jeans and SAS sweatshirt.

"Hi Teeny." Reggie smiled at her almost shyly and gave her a hug.

"Where you been?" she asked, stepping back to get a look in his eyes.

Before he could answer, the door in front of them burst open and Reggie, Teeny, and Tootie were dragged with a cheer into the fraternity house's inner sanctum. "Hey Brotha', you just in time," said Leroy Fosdick, the son of U.S. ambassador Luther Fosdick, handing Reggie a joint, trying to sound as home-boyish as someone could who had grown up in Paris and gone to Choate.

"Thanks, man." The quarterback took a hit and French curled the pot smoke through his nostrils.

"That's some bad shit, eh man?"

"Yeah, and so is this." Muggins pulled the coke he'd purchased earlier and threw it on the table in front of him.

"Awright, Reggie!" said honors student Maia Dobson, the granddaughter of the venerable Elmo T. Dobson, Federal Judge from Atlanta, also trying to sound as "bad" as possible as she opened up the baggie and began to pulverize the rock of coke on the table.

"I hope you haven't been doin' much of that stuff," said Teeny.

"You know me, baby, I'm cool."

"I hope so, Reggie, that's dangerous stuff you're playin' with."

At that moment the bedroom door burst open again, and in stepped the hulking forms of fullback Symeon Smith and linebacker Atilla Wilson.

"Yo, Symeon! Tilla!"

"Hey, everybody, what's goin' on?" blurted out Muggins' teammates.

"Just gettin' ready to do a little blow, man, want some?" Muggins ostentatiously rolled up a hundred-dollar bill.

"You doin' what?!"

"Man, you got hearin' trouble? (*laughter all around*) I said we gettin' ready to do a few lines, gimme that mirror, wouldja, baby? (*snifffff...sniff*) Here you go, Symeon."

"What'choo doin', man?! Don't you know that shit's bad for you?"

"I'm not smokin' it. Here, Tilla, try some."

"Not me, Reggie. They do a test on you, you're gonna get caught."

"Man. I got somethin' to take care 'a that."

"Besides, that shit'll mess you up."

"It didn't seem to mess up Lawrence Taylor too much. Maybe you oughta try some."

"Fuck you, man," said the insulted linebacker. "Coach is right, that stuff'll kill you."

"Man (*sniffff*),Coach don't know shit."

"He knows a lot more than you do, Reggie," said Symeon Smith, "if you're doin' that stuff."

"You're just sayin' that, brotha, cause you think the Coach is gonna help you get a big pro contract."

"That ain't true."

"You're just like all the rest of us poor niggers on the team, slavin' away for Massa Coach, hopin' someday the Big Boss Man is gonna take you to work on his professional football plantation."

"You talkin' crazy, Reggie."

"Yeah? You're jus' afraid to face the truth. Coach don't give a damn about you or anybody else he's got playin' on his team. Minute you get hurt, you're outta here. You remember what happen to Tremayne Stuart? And Rasheed Brown?"

"That was different."

"Oh yea? You get hurt and you see how long your friend Coach Star keeps you around J.P. Morgan University."

"You talkin' crazy, man. I'm gettin' outta here. Come on, Tilla."
Silence.

"Dumb mutha—Hey, somebody roll up another doobie. What are you lookin' at, Teeny?"

"I don't know, Reggie."

"Sometimes I don't know what's wrong with you, girl. You think I'm gonna get hooked (*snifffff*) on this stuff?"

"I don't know."

"Listen, baby, I'm too smart for that, ain't I, Tootie?"

"You know dat's right," agreed the athlete's companion (*snorrrrt*). You too smart for that, Reggie."

• • •

"I love it!" said Milt Lee into the speaker phone while he examined one of the tee-shirts from the shipment of KICK BUTT apparel that had arrived at the Lee and Jackson Agency warehouse that week. "They look great," he said, smiling down at the sneakered foot kicking the large haunched-over buttocks on the front of the shirts. "And I love the way the letters in the KICK look three-dimensional. ... What's that? ... Of course I know what a risk I'm taking." Milt was speaking to his old Brooklyn Tech High School buddy Abe Koppel, the owner of the Dixie Novelty Company in Atlanta. "That's why I want the first ten thousand shirts with no printing on the back. If they lose, I'll ship 'em out to my cousin Artie and let him sell 'em to the schwartzas in L.A. . . . Do I really think we're gonna win? . . . At least the first game. And with the big deal the Coach has made outta kickin' this newspaper columnist's ass on TV. . . . Yeah, I gotta bunch 'a kids lined up to scream KICK BUTT at the game. . . . The Athletics Director? I tried to talk to him but what can I say, a real goyishakopf. . . . And don't forget to fax me the figures on the three-color baseball caps, stadium cushions, and slurpy cups . . . Yeah, the quart size with the straws. Oh! and by the way, make the next batch of shirts eighty/twenty. . . . That's right eighty percent poly . . . And now that we got all that figyad out, what kinda break you gonna cut me on the next shipment. . . . Abby, c'mon now, who do you think you're dealin' with, Elmer Fudpucker? This is Milt Lee you're talkin' to."

CHAPTER 5

The week of August 30

'Six days to go," said Jet Jackson, handing his defensive scouting and personnel reports to Coach Star Sunday afternoon.

Tony leaned back against the blackboard in the conference room and looked over the computer print-out of stats on the Southwest Mississippi State Bearcats.

"Whadda you think, Jet?"

"I think you're right about running right at 'em. If we just keep hammerin' at their right side, they'll cave in by the third quarter."

KNOCK KNOCK

"Yeah, who is it?"

"Did you wanna see me, Coach?" Offensive lineman Arlo Plummer stuck his head through the door.

"Yeah I did—I'll catch you later, Jet."

"Okay, Tony."

"C'mon in, Arlo, sit down," said the Coach in a fatherly tone. "So what's goin' on?"

"Whadda you mean, Coach?"

"I mean, what's goin' on?"

Silence.

"Arlo, you and me have known each other too long to bullshit around. We're expecting big things from you this year, but for some reason you just ain't playin' up to potential. Now what's goin' on?"

"Nothin', Coach, honest."

"C'mon, you can tell me. You in some kinda trouble? Drugs? A girl? Your parents?"

"No, that ain't it."

"Well, what is it?"

"I guess I'm just tired of the way Coach Cossacky keeps ridin' me in practice, callin' me a pussy and—"

"Ahh, he screams at everybody."

"Yeah, but he doesn't call them faggots," said the guard, looking up into the Coach's eyes.

"It's not like he means anything personal by it, Arlo. He's just"— Suddenly Tony realized why Arlo had been so sensitive to Pete's comments. "I see," he said, noting the discomfiture in the young athlete's eyes.

"Yeah, that's right, Coach, I've been goin' through some changes lately, and—"

"I understand, honest I do," said Star.

"Really?"

"Hey Arlo, I wasn't born yesterday."

"You know I ain't the only one on the team who likes to experiment, if you know what I mean."

"I'm sure. And you're okay and everything?"

"You mean AIDS? Oh yeah, I'm always careful. Like you say, it only takes ten seconds to play it safe."

"Good."

"But I don't know how—"

"We're gonna get Cossacky to lighten up? I'll have a talk with him. In the meantime, Arlo, I gotta tell you we've decided to start White at your spot this week."

"I figured you would, but don't worry, Coach, you'll be putting me back in by the end of the game. White's good, but I can kick his ass all over the field any day."

"Now that's the way I like to hear you talk. I'll take care of Cossacky, and you can trust me, our conversation will be nobody's business but our own."

"Thanks, Coach."

"Now get your butt down to the weight room and get yourself a good workout."

• • •

"Five days left," yelled Boomer Cox to Chancellor Brewster on Monday morning. Boomer banked his Cessna 172 sharply to the right to get a better look at the new Carolina trucking depot his construction company was erecting beside the old Confederate cemetery on the east side of town.

"That's five days too many for me," said Brewster to his childhood buddy as they flew through the greenish-yellow smoke that was pouring from the stacks of the Dunning Electrical Parts factory and wafting over the JFK housing project. "Pshew, look at all those cars on I-660."

"Yeah, look at 'em," said Boomer proudly, nosing his plane westward toward distant Cullen County, where he and Brewster were thinking of purchasing a large parcel of undeveloped woodland.

"Maybe once the season starts, Dudley and the Committee will lighten up, eh?"

"Yeah, if we win." Boomer laughed. "Honestly though, Bill, I wouldn't let Dudley get to you. He didn't mean anything personal by what he said at that last meeting."

"President of the Board or not, I don't appreciate Dudley talking to me like I'm hired help. Hell, Dudley's the one who wanted to hire Star in the first place."

"I know. When Dudley gets frustrated he strikes at whoever's there. He's been that way ever since college. Hey, there she is, Billy Bob," said Boomer, changing the subject and pointing down at Morgan's eight hundred acre slice of pie-shaped campus. "You know it's just amazin' how this place has grown."

"Yeah it is." The Chancellor smiled as he ran his eyes across the three square blocks of hospital buildings, clinics and medical school research facilities built since his arrival in Metro.

"You oughta be proud of yourself, Billy Bob," said the contractor, who had made untold millions helping the Chancellor realize his vision of Morgan's greatness. "You've built yourself one of the finest medical centers in this whole dang country. The people of the Mid-South owe you a debt of gratitude."

"Well thank you, Boomer."

"And look at that new sports center. I got to admit it's a beautiful building, even if I didn't build it myself."

Brewster gazed down with satisfaction on the twenty-three million dollar sportsplex.

"You remember how the faculty complained about puttin' it up?"

"How could I forget?"

"And it probably never would'a gotten built if Felton Potts hadn't kicked in that extra two mil. It's funny the things those teachers of yours complain about. Why, that old gym was a disgrace."

Brewster nodded.

"And there she is, Billy Bob." Boomer dove down toward Fulsom Field and cast a rippling shadow across the playing field of the renovated Morgan football stadium. "Our first project together here at the school."

"Yup." The Chancellor grinned at his friend.

"For a coupl'a country boys from Texarkana, we've done pretty good."

"Yeah we have," agreed the Chancellor, who couldn't help, however, being slightly jealous of how much better his enormously wealthy buddy had done for himself.

"But that's what this country of ours is all about," said Boomer, pointing the plane's nose toward the glass and aluminum domes of the new National Hospital Company headquarters. "Doesn't really matter who you are or where you're from, long as you've got guts and determination."

"You're right," agreed the Chancellor, who once more had to wonder where all of his guts and determination would have gotten him without his father in law's help.

"Yeah, that's the beauty of a democracy like we got here in the U-nited States. Every one of us has the opportunity to pick himself up by his bootstraps and make something of himself. Why even a colored boy these days has a chance to win a scholarship like we did and get an education. Yeah, we got a lot to be proud of, Billy."

Yes, I guess we do, thought the head administrator, looking down over the endless acres of former forest and farm land—that had been turned into apartment house complexes, matchbox-sized subdivision homes, and shopping malls—all since the end of the Vietnam War.

"Look at all those happy, healthy, thriving people, Bill. Thirty years ago most of them would'a been stuck in some little hick town somewhere, unwashed and ignorant, hoein' soybeans and raisin' chickens, never knowin' the pleasure and enjoyment of modern civilization."

As they cruised beyond the thirty mile-wide umbrella of rust-colored air that hung over the urban center of Metro, out to where the people were still so ignorant that they preferred working on farms rather than in factories and office buildings, Billy Bob and Boomer slipped into the comfortable silence that is shared by the best of friends.

And it wasn't until fifteen minutes later that Boomer broke their reverie as he banked to the left and pointed out a large tract of hardwood forest along Little Arrowhead Creek. "There it is. Two thousand acres just waitin' to be turned into thirty-six beautiful holes."

"Twenty five hundred an acre still seems pretty steep to me."

"I know it sounds that way," said Boomer, "but mark my words, it's a money maker."

• • •

"And the following week," announced Professor Paul Fisher to the one hundred and fifty students sitting in his Communications 151 course, Minorities in Contemporary Media, "we will examine the portrayal of the Asian-American male in contemporary comic books."

"Scuse me, scuse me," mumbled the two hulking student athletes as they made their way to two seats in the middle of the last row of the lecture room twenty minutes late for their eleven o'clock class.

"And the week after that," continued the sallow, frizzy-haired professor, slipping his glasses back on his nose, "we will examine the portrayal of the mentally handicapped in contemporary situation comedies."

"Pssst," said Dewey Dobbins to a bearded graduate assistant sitting down the aisle from him holding a pile of extra syllabi in his lap, "you got a couple more of them sheets for DeVon and me?... Yeah, thanks man."

"And the next week of class we will look at the image of the Native American in music videos and television ads."

"I dunno," whispered Dewey to his teammate, "this course looks pretty tough to me. Look at all them books we gotta read."

"Those aren't books, Dew, they're articles," said 294-pound honors engineering student DeVon White, who was taking Professor Fisher's class to satisfy his social science requirement.

"Articles?"

"Yeah, magazine articles."

"Oh. Okay."

"As you can see," droned on Professor Fisher, "the emphasis in the course will not be so much on examining secondary source material as on your own personal interaction with the media. Now I expect everyone in the class owns their own television set?—Good—and DVD?—Uh huh. Now, are there any questions? Yes, Miss—"

"Brown. Will there be a midterm?"

"No, but in lieu of a midterm I will expect you to hand in a critique of two of the movies at the bottom of the page. Any other questions? Mr.—?"

"Goodall. Will there be a final exam?"

"Yes, Mr. Goodall, there will be (*groans all round*) a take home exam. In addition, I will also expect every one of you to hand in a project by the last week of class. I believe some of you may have seen the collages made by the members of our last class on display in the student center last spring. Are there any other questions? If not, I'll see you all on Thursday."

"What's a collage, DeVon?"

"You don't know what a collage is?" said the son of former Falcon running back, now Atlanta-based attorney Marcus White.

"Nope."

"A collage is . . . an artistic composition you create from—"

"Wha??"

"One of those things you make out of pictures you cut from a magazine and paste on a piece of cardboard."

"Oh yeah, I know what'cha mean," said Dewey. "I dunno, man, this course sounds rough. Maybe we oughta talk to the professor."

"If you want to, Dewey."

"Er, Professor—"

"Excuse me a moment, Miss Bullins," said Dr. Fisher to an eager, well-endowed coed in a micro-skirt and horn-rimmed glasses. "Can I help you?"

"I was just wonderin'," said Dewey, holding the Kick Butt cap he'd been wearing backwards on his head in his hand, "if you got mandatory attendance in this class."

"Well, not exactly, but —"

"Good, cause I—"

"Play on the football team??"

"Yeah."

"Then I'm sure Noweeta Hayes has spoken with you about our participation expectations in the Communications Department."

"Your what?"

"Relax, gentlemen," said the professor with a reassuring smile, "Miss Hayes and I have the situation under control, trust me."

"Oh, okay, thanks." Dewey put his cap back on his head and headed out the door of the lecture room with DeVon where a crowd of fraternity boys in Bermuda shorts and ball caps were waiting to pay homage to their heroes.

"Hey Dewey, what's happenin'? DeVon, slap me five! You guys have a good summer?"

"Yeah, man. How 'bout you?"

"Fan . . . fucking . . . tastic."

"Awright!"

"Four days left to go!"

"Yeah, and we're gonna kick butt on Saturday!" boasted the earringed Dewey Dobbins to his admirers. "Don't believe nothin' you read in them pre-season reports."

"Yeah, kick butt, kick butt, kick butt!" bellowed the intramural student-athletes to their champions.

"But I tell you what," said DeVon, looking at his watch, "me and Dewey gotta run. We can't be late for lunch."

• • •

"Ahhhh . . . yeah, that feels good."

"Like that?"

"Yeah, Savannah, that's . . . oooo, just perfect."

"Ohh, I'm so excited! Just three more days till the season starts."

Tom grunted and slowly, very slowly, moved his head an inch to the right and then an inch to the left.

"You musta pulled somethin', Mr. Hanagan," Savannah concluded as she stood behind his desk chair massaging his neck Wednesday morning.

Had he not been in such pain, the result of straining his back lifting weights on day three of his rehabilitation program, Tom might have appreciated the way Savannah kept rubbing, not altogether accidentally, her breasts up against the back of his head while she worked on his neck. As it was—"Thanks, that feels—ouch! a lot better"—he was happy just to have her knead his knotted muscles.

"Is there anything else I can do?" she asked, standing in front of his chair in her high heels, short black skirt and a cream-colored crepe blouse through which Tom could see the lacy front of her brassiere.

"Yes. You could get me a coupl'a Advils. They're in the bottom drawer right over there."

"Do you want some water with those, Mr. Hanagan?"

"Er—yeah, that would be nice," said Tom, recalling what the marriage counselor had told him about being lucky to be married to an intelligent girl like Jan.

"Here you go, Mr. Hanagan."

• • •

On Thursday evenings during football season, it was Tom's and Tony's custom to eat dinner together at the Time Out Bar and Grill—a sports bar three blocks from the stadium, with the best fried onion rings and coldest brew in town.

"Man, what the hell were you doing anyway?" asked the Coach after he and Tom had made their way through well wishers to their usual booth in the rear of the smoky bar.

"Lifting about a hundred pounds too much." Tom slid rigidly into his seat.

Star smiled. "I've been tellin' you you need more exercise."

"Right, Coach."

"You guys want the us'al?" asked their waitress.

"Hey Mabel, what's up, hon? Yeah, I guess we do." Tony looked at Tom.

"Yeah, but you can skip the onion rings for me."

"Okee dokee."

"Cutting back, huh?"

"Yeah."

"I've been tryin' myself," said Star, giving the high sign to an inebriated old well-wisher named Jim Bob Puckett who stumbled past their booth on his way to the men's room. "By the way, Rose bumped into Jan at the mall the other day. Jan told her the two of you have started going to some kinda—"

"Marriage counselor. Yeah, but you know, I think the guy's a homo."

"Really?"

"He sure acts like one. But if it makes Jan feel better, what the hell. Who knows maybe he can help." Tom dipped one of the fried chicken wing appetizers they'd just been served in ranch dressing. "One thing's for sure, I need to cut back on the hooch a little. And start losin' some weight too. That's why—ouch! I started workin' out again."

"You'll feel better in a coupl'a weeks. Keep it up, Tommy."

"There's only one thing that's gonna make me feel better," said Tom, turning serious, "and that's winning this game Saturday. You know what I mean?"

"Yeah I do. But I'm tellin' you not to worry."

"Not worry! What are you talkin' about, Tony? I got a meeting with Billy Bob's axe-man Edwards next week to discuss the budget and you're telling me not to worry?"

"It's not gonna do any good."

"Tell that to those boosters we ate dinner with Tuesday night. In case you hadn't noticed, they weren't exactly friendly."

"What can I say, Tommy?"

"No, what can *I* say when Brewster tells me the whole Board of Trust is complaining."

"People like to complain," said the Coach, cleaning the flesh off a chicken bone and tossing it on the plate in front of him.

"Yeah, but not like they've been doin' lately. I told you about Roscoe Barrett, didn't I?"

"That old racist?"

"Yeah, that old racist, but Clifton told me that Dudley Dunning's been saying the same thing–*Star's got more black boys on that team than anybody in the league and he still can't win.*"

"I've told you a thousand times, the talented white kids don't wanna play here—yet."

"I know, Tony, but I can't exactly tell Dunning that, can I?" Tom winced as he lifted up his beer glass. "Honestly, Tony, people are gettin' ugly. And maybe I'm talkin' outta turn, but, frankly, I don't see how we can win if, like everybody says, we don't start throwin' the ball. Have you ever thought about tryin' this Wallace kid out? Maybe he's better than you think."

"Tommy," said the Coach, suddenly lowering his voice and wiping barbecue sauce off his chin with his napkin, "can you keep a secret?"

"Of course I can," he said, leaning forward with a grimace.

"Awright then, but you can't tell nobody else in the whole world, Tom, nobody."

"Trust me, Tony, I won't tell a soul. What is it?"

"I mean nobody—not Clifton, Blake, not even Jan. Nobody!"

"Yeah, I swear, nobody. What is it, Tony?" said Tom, anxiously awaiting the revelation that he hoped might be able to save both his and Tony's jobs.

"Well," said the Coach, bending even closer to his friend, "I *am* planning on throwing the ball."

"Really?"

"That's right, Tommy, and you're right about Wallace, he *is* good. But I don't intend to use him until the third, maybe the fourth game. See, the way I figure it. . . ."

• • •

Twenty-four hours to go until game time, the Morgan faithful from all over the southland were arriving at the Magnolia Hills Country Club for the Camelot Kick-off gala.

"WATCH IT, HONEY!" yelled Tom Hanagan. Jan suddenly slammed on the brakes and he jerked painfully forward in his seat. "You almost rear-ended that car."

"Look, Tom," said Jan, who had been touching up her make-up in the car's visor mirror as they inched their way around the circular driveway of the moss-festooned, white-columned club, "if you want to drive, you drive—Oh, I'm sorry, honey, I forgot about your back."

"That's all right."

"But please, Tom, do me a favor tonight and try not to drink too much."

"Now wait a second, Jan," said Tom, cut short as two African-American doormen, dressed like hitching-post jockeys, opened their doors with big toothy smiles and hearty "Good ev'nins."

"Thank you," said Jan, sliding out of the Mercedes in a black knit chemise and string of pea-sized pearls she'd been given by Uncle Clifton on her 30th birthday. "Ready Tom?"

"I guess," said the Director, painfully pulling himself up to his full height and straightening his cummerbund.

"Jan, honey. Tom!" gurgled Clarissa Dunning, looking très chic in a gold-metallic cocktail dress and purple sapphire necklace. "Come ova' here and say hello to Dudley."

"Well if it idn't the beautiful Mrs. Hanagan," said Dudley, "and her husband."

"Hello, Dudley. How are you?" asked Tom.

"I'll tell you after the game tomorrow," said the short, salt and pepper-haired Board of Trust President, looking over his rimless glasses.

Tom wondered whether a knee in the crotch might make Dudley a little more responsive.

"Hello there, Mr. Gooch," said Tom, after Dudley returned to his conversation with Board of Trust treasurer Tyson Culpepper.

"'Lo, Tom," said Harlan Gooch, unenthusiastically extending his gnarled, liver-spotted hand.

"How are you tonight, sir?"

"Oh, pretty good, I guess," said the local supermarket mogul.

"Good."

"So whadda you think, Tom? We gonna throw that pigskin tomorra?"

"I wouldn't be at all—Hello, Mrs. Gooch," said Tom, bowing to the rugose daughter of the Confederacy, whose cadaverous breath nearly knocked him over. "I tell ya, Mr. Gooch, I think we're all gonna be surprised at what happens tomorrow."

"And how's my buddy Tom doin'?" boomed Buster Hooper, giving Tom an excruciating slap on his stiff back.

"Not too bad," said Tom after he had caught his breath. "How are you, Buster?"

"Hell, I'm always good, 'cept when I'm bein' bad," said the half-pint Texan, laughing at his own joke and proceeding to ask Tom and Milt Lee if they knew "what you call a white man on a bus with forty colored boys."

"I don't know, Buster, what do you call a white man on a bus with forty African-Americans?" asked Tom.

"Coach! Haw haw haw!"

"Coach!" Milt Lee guffawed. "I love it!"

"Tell you what, gentlemen," said Tom, feeling morally superior as he excused himself to go join his wife at the bar, "I'll see you later." But before he could make it across the parquet-floored ballroom, he was collared by Camelot Club President Blake Stevens—the only man in the room who was sweating more than he was. "Hey Tom, Felton here wants to know if Star's really gonna throw it tomorrow."

"I wouldn't be at all surprised, Felton," said Tom, after complimenting Felton Potts' chicken-necked wife Eula on how lovely she looked in her purple and gold checkerboard evening gown.

"Well, I sure as hell hope so," said Potts. "Now if it was me coachin' the team. . . ."

Fifteen minutes later, Tom finally caught up with his wife.

"Uncle Cliff's been looking for you," she said, momentarily tearing herself away from a conversation with the young and very pregnant wife of the Dean of the Business School about the joys of parenthood.

"Did he say what he wanted?"

"Something about seats for Senator Horton."

"I guess I better go find him."

"Yes, that sounds like a good idea." Jan looked with a frown at the cocktail glass in his hand. "I think he went out on the verandah."

Before heading outside, Tom stopped off at the bar for "one more."

"Double martini with a twist, Elwood."

"Yassa, Mista Hanagan. You doin' all right tonight, sir?"

"Not too bad." *And I'll be a hell of a lot better after I drink this,* he thought. *Maybe it'll even get this back of mine to stop hurting (glug glug).*

Tom straightened his tie, stepped out onto the verandah, and heard the hale and hearty voice of Senator Edward "Lil' Ed" Horton.

"Yes it has got to where it's hard to tell one political party from anotha' these days. . . . Pardon me? . . . Yes, I'll have the country ham," said the photogenic young presidential-hopeful to the black man in the white chef's coat and hat who was carving roast beef and ham at the end of the table.

"There you are, Tom!" said Clifton, motioning to him. "C'mon over here a second."

"Hello, Cliff, Chancellor, Mr. Cox."

"Tom, you know Senator Horton, don't you?"

"Yes, I believe we've—"

"'Course he does," interjected the senator. Like his bourbon-swilling, deficit-spending daddy, Governor Big Ed, Lil' Ed had also attended Morgan University. After graduating from Harvard, Lil' Ed attended Morgan law school for a year during which time Big Ed arranged for his son to enlist in the Army and do a tour of duty in Saigon, writing florid articles about patriotism for the *Stars and Stripes*, while he deflowered the WACS in his office.

"Tom, I was wond'rin if you might have a couple extra seats down near the fifty yard line?" asked Clifton. "Senator Horton likes to be where he can smell the sweat."

"I don't think that'll be any problem. How many do you need?"

"Three?"

"You got 'em," said Tom, "three seats, Section E, Row 1."

The Chancellor smiled at Tom—for the first time in several months—for taking care of the man who had helped him secure nearly a quarter of a billion dollars worth of federal money for Morgan University over the past decade. Then Dexter Brown and his Sound Machine, a black, twelve-piece, horn band in purple and gold tuxedos, began their second set.

"Now that's what I call music," said Lil' Ed, his eyeballs glued to singer Brandi Bottoms, as she began to shake her sequins to *Baby Love*.

"Yeah, that's my kinda music too," said the Chancellor, who for the record "appreciated all forms of musical expression," but in reality was particularly fond of what his momma called "trashy nigga music."

"Yes, we get Dexter here every year, don't we, Tom?" said Brewster proudly.

"Kinda takes me back to my ole college days," reminisced Lil' Ed.

"From what I hear, you were the terror of the Ivy League for a coupl'a years," said Boomer Cox.

"Oh, I don't know about that," replied the former Harvard quarterback, swelling with modesty. "I was never very quick on my feet, though I guess I did have a pretty good arm. Speakin' of which, you think your boy—what's his name?"

"Muggins?" said Tom diffidently as the Chancellor and Uncle Clifton tried not to frown.

"Yeah, that's it. You think he's gonna start to throw a little more this year?"

As the dance floor filled with pot-bellied boosters anxious to dispel any doubts about their waning virility by doing the Funky Chicken with their young girlfriends and third wives, Tom melted into the crowd and reappeared at the bar for one more "one more."

"Would you like me to make that a double, sir?"

"Yeah, you better," said Tom, thinking about what a good politician he would have made as he watched Elwood mix his drink. *Yeah, I should'a gone to law school like my old man told me. With his connections in the Teamsters' Union, I'd probably be a senator by now myself. Let's face it, if a numbskull like Horton can be a senator, it can't be very hard . . . not as hard as what I do anyway.*

And as if to prove how difficult his job really was, for the next two hours Tom ran from one end of the club to the other, huddling with rich alums, tackling questions from disgruntled boosters, and trying to score points with aggravated trustees. Then finally at 11:30 the entire party moved to the apron of the bandstand to cheer on a gatoring contest between a hyperventilating '75 DKE and a tachychardic '69 SAE, and Tom got to take a long overdue time-out.

"Oh God, that feels good," he said, easing himself gently down into one of the lawn chairs at the far end of the verandah, preparing to devour the pile of jumbo shrimp heaped on his plate. But as he swirled one of the prawns around in cocktail sauce and lifted it to his lips, Savannah McLane, looking delectably nymph-like in her purple chiffon dress, ran up to him out of the shadows and panted, "Mista Hanagan, please, you gotta save me! Milt Lee's been followin' me around for the last hour and he just won't leave me be."

"Here he comes now," said Tom. "Duck behind those bushes."

"Hey buddy, you haven't seen that little *sex*-cretary of yours, have you?"

"Yeah, Milt. I saw her go into the ballroom just a second ago."

"Thanks."

"Pssst. You can come out now, hon," chuckled Tom as Milt disappeared back into the building.

"Oh thank you!" said Savannah throwing her arms around Tom's neck and giving him a big kiss just as Mrs. Hanagan walked up with Noweeta Hayes and the Morgan PR Department's favorite token black couple, ex-basketball star, Dr. Otis Robinson and his attractive pediatrician wife Melba.

Mortified to find her husband making a public display of himself with his administrative assistant, Jan heroically held back her tears and flew off without uttering a word.

As Tom stood there with Noweeta and the Robinsons, and dumfoundedly watched his wife disappear across the room, he knew there'd be no way to explain what had just happened.

SECOND QUARTER

PENETRATION

...baseball represents to us our idealized selves, while football tells us what we really are....

MICHAEL ORIARD
Professional Football as Cultural Myth

CHAPTER 6

Saturday, September 3

An hour to go until game time, the barricaded streets around Fulsom Field are electric.... *Hey, get your programs here! Programs!* ... A detachment of motorcycle policemen roars to a stop on Stadium Avenue.... *Hot dogs! Hot dogs!* An ambulance with flashing blue lights pulls through the rear gate of the stadium. ... *Get your tee-shirts here! Kick Butt tee-shirts!* ... A kid in an Atlanta Falcons jacket steps up to sell you two stolen tickets on the forty yard line. ... *Twenty dollar, Mista ... Popcorn! Popcorn! Cold drinks here!* In the distance ... *BOMTiddiBOM* ... the thud of drums, the tinkle of glockenspiels ... In the air the scent of burgers, pizza, cigarette smoke, and auto exhaust ... Overhead, the Mid-South Conference pennants ripple and gleam in the breeze beneath halogen lights, beckoning the citizens of Metro to come, join in the spectacle, the pageantry, the celebration of the game.

In the Morgan locker room, the players, taped and wrapped, sit in jocks and tee-shirts waiting to suit up. Tedious and tense moments even for the veteran, the wait seems interminable to 297-pound true freshman, defensive tackle Bobo Thomas. As he sits down by his locker after visiting the john for the third time in twenty minutes, Bobo tries to do what his coaches and teammates have told him: visualize the faces of Bristol Banks and Art Simpkins—the men he is matched up against that night. But unable to focus on their beetle-browed visages, Bobo again thumbs through his game program, gazing approvingly at his picture on page eighteen and drooling over a pizza ad on the back cover. Too nervous to sit still any longer, he tries to strike up a conversation with linebacker Atilla Wilson who sits Buddha-like by the next locker.

"Hey Tilla, how you feel?"

"What you mean how I feel? I feel like kickin' some butt, little brotha'," says the linebacker, closing his eyes and resuming his meditation.

Then he tries stretching out on the floor like Dumptruck Hodges and Asswad King. But three minutes later Bobo's back up on his size nineteen feet looking for an empty bathroom stall. *Ain't nothin' to be scared of,* he reflects, returning again to his locker, the sour odor of nervous perspiration—so different from an active body's—filling his flared nostrils. *Ain't nothin' to be scared of.*

At 6:05 the Morgan assistant coaches in gold ball caps, purple polo shirts and khaki chinos, burst through the locker room doors.

"AWRIGHT, AWRIGHT, AWRIGHT!" bellows Pete Cossacky, marching up and down the lockers, making sure everyone is properly taped.

"LET'S GO! LET'S GO! LET'S GO!" bawls Wesley Woods, clapping his hands together, bantering with the players, who stand up, shake out their limbs and begin to buckle and lace themselves into pants and pads.

"What's the word, Symeon?" asks Jet Jackson, faking a punch to the fullback's stomach.

"Kick butt!"

"Awright! How 'bout you, Bum?"

"LET'S KICK SOME BUTT!" yells Craig Bumhoffer, slipping his shoulder pads over his head.

"Twenty minutes till special teams!" shouts Ed Tarmeenian, and as suddenly as they appeared, the coaches depart.

As the special team players clip-clopped through the tunnel from the Calhoun Complex to Fulsom Field, Chancellor Brewster and his wife, along with the Coxes and trustee Lamar Tubbs, were whisked aboard an elevator at the VIP gate and whooshed up seventy rows to the stadium's gigantic new press box. Constructed at a cost of more than four times the amount the University library had spent on books over the past ten years, the press box was one of the proudest and most renowned monuments of the Brewster era. Twenty thousand square feet, three stories high, the box had a 400-seat spectator gallery on the first level, twenty-four skyboxes on the second, and above that, a working press area with observation boxes and photo deck.

Although the Chancellor would have preferred going straight to the second level, where he and many of the Mid-South's most powerful and influential have their sky boxes, in the gallery below were arms that needed to be pumped and backs that wanted to be slapped.

"Hello, Harlan! How are you today?" trumpeted Brewster, stepping into the purple-carpeted gallery. "Delmore! I was afraid you might not make it after last night, har har. Of course we're gonna win tonight, Felton! . . . You can't believe what the polls say, Buster. . . . I think we're all gonna be surprised."

By the time Tom Hanagan walked into the gallery, the Chancellor had become thoroughly annoyed boosting the boosters.

"Hello, Chancellor, Mrs. Brewster," said Tom.

"Humph," grunted Brewster in the same icy tone that Jan had said "goodbye," when Tom had left her with Uncle Cliff and Aunt Inez in their 50 yard line seats.

"Where's Jan today, Tom?" asked the Chancellor's wife, Winnie, anxious to find out why Jan had left the kick-off social in tears.

"She's down with Clifton and Inez."

"You be sure to bring her up at halftime," ordered Morgan's first lady, "we didn't get much of a chance to talk last night."

"I'll be sure to, Mrs. Brewster," said Tom, who started to ask the Chancellor what he thought about the new electric Pepsi Cola sports information sign on University Drive when Brewster turned around and walked away.

Ten minutes before kick-off, stadium announcer Smokey Biddle crushed out his Lucky Strike, flicked on his mike, and greeted the swelling crowd: *Good eev-nin', lay-dees and gentlemen. Welcome to the op-e-nin' game of the J. P. Morgan Figh-ting Knights one hundred and eighth con-sec-u-tive season of col-lee-gee-it football! And tonight we are pa-leezed to welcome into the far-end-ly confines of Fulsom Field the Southwest Miss-siss-sip-pi State Bearcats.*

BOOOO HISSSS

As the fans welcomed their guests and Smokey informed them where they could find refreshments, lavatories, or a doctor—as well as what would happen to them if they were caught smoking, drinking, shouting obscenities or brawling—head twirler Wendy Witherspoon threw her baton in the air and led the Fighting Knights band onto the south end of the field.

HOOOORAY MORGAN!

"That's a fine looking girl, Elrod," said Brewster, cozying up to Wendy's father, a 20,000 dollar per year contributor from the New Orleans Camelot Club. Witherspoon swelled with pride as he watched his daughter high stepping across the 50 yard line in her glimmering gold tank suit.

"Yeah, she's the apple a' her daddy's eye, Billy Bob," said Elrod, his daughter calling to his mind a chorus girl he had recently spent the night with in Vegas.

In the locker room, meanwhile, Coach Star concluded his pre-game pep talk with a few words of inspiration from the venerable Vince Lombardi:

> ...I believe in God and I believe in human decency. But I firmly believe that any man's finest hour—his greatest fulfillment to all he holds dear—is that moment when he has worked his heart out in a good cause and lies exhausted on the field of battle—victorious.

"AWRIGHT NOW!" shouted Ed Tarmeenian. "WHADD'ARE WE GONNA DO TONIGHT?!"

"KICK BUTT!"

"I CAN'T HEAR YA?!"
"KICK BUTT!!"
"WHADDID YOU SAY?!"
"KICK BUTT! KICK BUTT! KICK BUTT!"

Five minutes to go, the fans began to stomp their feet up and down in the stands. Then the band blared out a fanfare, a cannon went off somewhere in the end zone, and the Morgan color bearer shot from the stadium tunnel followed by a dozen somersaulting cheerleaders—Coach Star—and the Fighting Knights!

HOOOORAY MORGAN!

While the band drew itself up for the National Anthem, Coach Carver checked in once more with the coaches on the field to make certain everybody's head phones were still working.

Then the team captains gathered at midfield for the coin toss—Morgan elected to defer to the second half—and the suicide squads lined up on the 40. As the crowd began to roar—LOUDER LOUDER LOUDER.... The referee started the clock, blew his whistle, and DeGama booted it—through the end zone! BEARCATS BALL, FIRST AND TEN from the 20.

Of the 60,231 spectators on hand, no one was more relieved—or anxious—that the game had finally begun than Tom Hanagan. He needed something good to happen. Rumors had been flying around Calhoun all week—disturbing rumors, the kind that always seem to have a way of coming true.

But hope springs eternal in every true sportsman's heart, and when Craig Bumhoffer dumped Bearcat halfback Ntume Hazard for a three-yard loss on the first play, Tom took it as a good omen for the new season.

HAZARD ON THE CARRY
A LOSS OF 3, SECOND AND 13

Then Steve Malenkovic collared fullback Raz Johnson at the line of scrimmage.

JOHNSON ON THE CARRY
NO GAIN

Butt Bowers almost intercepted one at the 24, . . . and Tom began to believe that Coach Star might actually have been telling him the truth about the Knights being better than people thought.

"Awright let's go, Big Purple!" screamed Tom, his sphincter relaxing as the punt return team came on the field, then suddenly puckering back up when Morgan deep man Cochise Cubbins fumbled the punt. "OH NO!"

As the officials dig through the pile of bodies on the Morgan 35, Tom felt as if he were going to be sick—until the referee stood up and threw his arm toward the Bearcat goal line. *MORGAN BALL, FIRST AND TEN!*

HOOOORAY KNIGHTS! GO! GO! GO!

"If we don't throw the ball, we're never gonna score," grumbled the Chancellor looking down from the skybox.

"I'm afraid you're right, Billy Bob." Boomer Cox took a gulp of bourbon and glanced over his shoulder at the USC-State game that was silently flickering on the TV behind them. "That score still the same, Lamar?"

"Yeah it is, Boomer," said the corpulent attorney, looking up at the screen, grabbing a handful of peanuts from the bar. "But we just got it back on our own 40."

Down on Fulsom Field, the Bearcats were again trying to find a soft spot in the Morgan defense. But to no avail. Three plays later the pigskin was again in the possession of the Knights, who themselves punted it away four minutes after that. And so the game went until the end of the first quarter when, with ten seconds left to go, Morgan cornerback Atilla Wilson intercepted a pass at the Bearcat 32.

HOOOORAY MORGAN! HOOORAAAAYYY!

"C'mon now, put it in there!" yelled Tom Hanagan, happy for an excuse to break off an annoying conversation he'd been having with Felton Potts about last year's disastrous basketball season. "Come on, Reggie! You can—damn!"

NUMBER 73 JONES ON THE TACKLE

SECOND AND TEN.
"Awright now, let's go, Purple! C'mon! C'mon!... Sheeeeze"
HARRIS ON THE CARRY FOR THE KNIGHTS.
A PICK-UP OF ONE.
"I tell you, Tom," said Willard T. Sanders, leaning forward and shouting in Tom's ear, "if we don't start passin', there's no way we're— now what the hell is Star doin'?!"

On third down, to the displeasure of every Morgan fan in the stadium, Coach Star, instead of passing, had Muggins run the ball to the center of the field to set up a forty-two yard field goal attempt.

"Well," said Boomer, lighting up a cigar, pressing his nose against the sky box window, "I guess we're gonna see if this Mexican boy Hanagan's been talkin' about is any good."

"We need to start passin'," grumbled the Chancellor, peering through his binoculars as DeGama measured off five steps from where Anthony Gentry knelt for the snap.

Then— hut hut— in a seamless motion, Cluck snapped, Gentry set, and DeGama sent it sailing. ... *It's high enough! It's long enough! It's ... GOOD!*

"YEA, FIRST BLOOD!" whooped Aunt Inez, dragging Jan to her feet and shaking a fist at the visitors' side.

But first blood doesn't always work to the advantage of him who draws it. Some opponents don't start to fight until after they've been hit—which is what Bobo Thomas discovered when Bearcats guard Bristol Banks—KABAM! gave Bobo an upper cut to the chin on the next play that laid the Morgan rookie out on the 35.
A PICK UP OF 13 ON THE PLAY
FIRST DOWN CATS!
As Bobo crouched on his hands and knees, birds tweeted inside his head like the ones he and his teammates had seen in the cartoons they'd watched earlier that morning in the Calhoun Auditorium. The referee blew a time out.

"You okay?" asked Stitches Stevens after he and assistant trainer Pat Pitouchi arrived at Bobo's side.

"I think so," mumbled Bobo, sitting on the ground, still reeling from his confirmation slap.

"Yeah, you're okay. C'mon now, get up."

HOOOOOORAYYYY!!

"Well, if that's the way they wanna play," growled Ed Tarmeenian, overjoyed at an excuse for escalating the violence, "let's give these motherfuckers a taste of their own medicine."

KAPOW!... UGH!... OOMPH!... OUCH!...
TWEET TWEET TWEEEEET!

UNNECESSARY ROUGHNESS ON THE DEFENSE!
FIFTEEN YARDS!

"Whadda you talkin' about?!" yelled Tarmeenian after Steve Malenkovic dragged the Cats' quarterback to the ground by his face mask. "I don't know what the hell's wrong with that ref."

"Me neither," said Star, who, like his defensive coordinator, knew that an opponent's use of unnecessary force must always be promptly countered by an equal display of unsportsmanlike conduct if the playing field is to be kept level.

But declaring open season can be dangerous. Overly aggressive players make big mistakes—like the one Morgan cornerback Zanzibar Jackson made on the next play when he came out of his zone to deck the wide receiver and let Raz Johnson run a screen pass right by him all the way down to the Morgan 13.

OOOOOOOOOOOOOOO

Stunned by Johnson's twenty-five yard dash, the din inside Fulsome suddenly diminished to a dull roar, which deteriorated into a discontented hiss three plays later when quarterback Tommy Bishop ran a bootleg in for six points.

As Ice Larsen made it seven to three, Morgan Provost Sam Edwards asked Dr. Lucius Thompson, head of the University Sports Medicine Program, if he'd heard anything about Dudley Dunning's recent meeting with Mel Beerbauer, assistant offensive coordinator of the Kansas City Chiefs.

"According to Dudley," said the surgeon, refilling his drink at the bar in the medical school sky box, "Beerbauer might be interested in the job here if the price is right."

"I don't think the money will be a problem," said the provost. "It's getting him to come we gotta worry about."

"Whatever the case," said the doctor, "if we don't find us a coach who's gonna throw the ball. . . ."

Unruffled by the Bearcats' seven quick points, Coach Star stuck to his game plan. And when the Knights took over the ball again at their own 20, he once more charged into the right side of the Cats' line. Like Grant at Vicksburg, Tony knew that with each butt of his bigger and deeper squad's heads he was slowly opening a breach in the defense through which his team would eventually be able to march at will. But the soundness of his strategy was lost on the Morgan fans. *THROW THE DANG THANG, THROW IT!* If the Knights couldn't score, the crowd at least wanted some fireworks.

But the most exciting thing seen in the air over Fulsom Field for the remainder of the second quarter was a bi-plane, which circled above the stadium towing an advertisement for Gooch's Grocery Stores.

"I don't give a damn what Star's got up his sleeve. If we don't start passin', we cain't win," growled Felton Potts, sticking his purple nose in Tom's face as soon as the whistle blew ending the half.

"That friend of yours got somethin' 'gainst throwin' the ball?" barked Buster Hooper, spraying crackers and vodka on the front of Tom's shirt.

And all that Tom could do was shrug his shoulders, shake his head, and tell them to "hold on till the second half. I think we'll all be surprised."

"That's what you said last year too," scowled Lelon Lipscomb, bumping up against Tom in the crowded gallery, drenching the sleeve of Tom's blazer with his drink. Tom could no longer restrain himself.

"Dammit! You oughta watch out where you're goin'!—uh—er—

Mr. Lipscomb, you don't wanna waste that good bourbon. Yuk yuk yuk."

But no face that Tom saw in the gauntlet he ran from the gallery to the restroom was as unpleasant as the Chancellor's. So irritated was Brewster by his team's performance that, when Tom stepped up beside him at the urinal and nodded hello, Brewster zipped up his pants and tromped off without uttering a word.

Lay-dees and Gentlemen!
The Purple Knights Marching Band!
While the Morgan Knights band paraded onto the field to per-form a tribute to Labor Day—which was odd since no one at the University had ever had a Labor Day off—head trainer Stitches Stevens and his crew went to work in the Morgan locker room, bandaging, bracing, and retaping. Thankfully, there were no injuries more serious than a broken finger, a handful of cuts and bruises, a hyper-extended knee and a pulled groin. Within five minutes the players were ready for Doc Willis to give whatever painkillers were needed. And five minutes after that, as the band chugged across the field to *I've Been Workin' on the Railroad*, the team, showing no signs of fatigue or despondency, huddled around the Coach.

"Awright," said Star calmly. "They got lucky once, but you guys played a good first half. They're getting tired. Stick to the game plan. Don't get flustered and we'll beat these bastards by three touch-downs."

"KICK BUTT!" shouted Symeon Smith, raising his helmet in the air.

"KICK BUTT!" echoed a hundred voices.

When the Chancellor walked back into his skybox after intermis-sion, he found Boomer and Lamar at the bar glued to the TV, watch-ing the State-USC game. Aggravated at having just spent thirty min-utes making excuses for his team, he grabbed the remote and turned off the sound.

"Hey wait a minute!" said Boomer.

"Yeah, it's the big play," said Lamar. "He's . . . got it! He's got it!"

"Hot dog!" shouted the Chancellor's associates, who had both wagered heavily on Morgan's cross-state rival.

"We did it! We did it!"

"Did we just score or somethin', honey?" asked Boomer's wife Betty, looking up from the couch where she and Winnie Brewster had just been discussing the virtues of live-in help and estrogen injections.

"Yeah, we just scored!"

"Twenty-one to 14! State's up by seven!"

Inside Fulsom Stadium, meanwhile, the crowd began to buzz after Morgan deep man Cochise Cubbins ran the second half kick-off all the way back to the 45.

LET'S GO, KNIGHTS! LET'S GO, KNIGHTS!

But seven plays later, five of which were runs at the right side of the Bearcat line, Pointer was back on the field to punt.

"Did you see that last play?!!" blurted the Chancellor.

"Yeah I did." Boomer shook his head and helped himself to another Swedish meatball.

The Mississippi offense, readjusted and remedicated at half-time, looked sharp when they took over the ball at their own 30. And nine well executed plays later, they stood on the Morgan 27, first and 10.

"I swear to God, Boomer, if they score, I'm gonna go down there and take over this team myself."

"I guess you couldn't do much worse, Billy Bob."

"You're damn right I couldn't."

But the Chancellor never got the chance to try. For when Bobo Thomas came to the line, after getting earholed by Bristol Banks on the previous play, there was blood in his eye. "I'z gonna kill the mothafucka," swore Bobo as he dug in, his ear still ringing from the wallop Banks had given him on side of his helmet. "I'z gonna kill 'im." Then they snapped the ball and Bobo jackhammered Banks in the groin with his knee and sent Bishop flying on the 34.

FUMBLE RECOVERED BY MORGAN!
FIRST AND TEN!!

As if awakened by the Ritalin that Bearcat trainer "Speedy" Smothers had distributed to his learning-disabled players at half-time, the hometown fans were suddenly buzzing, especially in the stands where Milt Lee sat with his two adolescent sons and a bunch of their loud-mouthed friends he'd brought to the game. Again and again the cry of KICK BUTT rose from their section. Barely audible at first.... *kick butt, kick butt*... the incessant chant was soon on the lips of a hundred, a thousand, then TEN THOUSAND.... *KICK BUTT! KICK BUTT! KICK BUTT!*

The crowd rose to its feet and Coach Star knew that the moment of truth had arrived. The Bearcat defense was ready to collapse. Still, one foolish mistake by his frustrated offense could be disastrous. So again he sent the Knights crashing into the right side of the Bearcat line...and again...and again..., and on the next play, the wall finally gave way when Reggie Muggins burst through the line on a reverse and headed for paydirt...30...20...10...*TOUCHDOWN!*
HOOOORAY MORGAN KNIGHTS!

"Thank you, Jeeezus!" yelled the Rev. Roy Nash, pumping his fists up and down over his head in the gallery beside Tom Hanagan.

"Yes, thank God!" Tom muttered.

"Well it's about time!" blustered Brewster as DeGama made it 10–7 Morgan's favor.

"Yeah it is," said Boomer, clapping his buddy on the back.

Inspired by the fans, the Morgan defense took to the field after the kick off and proceeded to drive the Cats back five yards in two plays. Then, on third and 15, safety Butt Bowers came blitzing in and laid a teeth-rattling hit on Bishop that jarred the ball loose on the 13.

FUMBLE RECOVERED BY D'AMATO!
FIRST AND TEN! MORGAN BALL!

Frenzied now with the scent of a kill, the Knights' offense once more charged back out and tore straight into the Cats' right side.

Then the left side. Then over center. *TOUCHDOWN! PURPLE KNIGHTS!*

As the Fighting Knights band struck up a funky version of *Happy Days are Here Again*, the Chancellor passionately embraced his wife Winnie.

"That's our boys!" cheered Boomer Cox. "I knew we could do it!"

And so they did. For the next twenty minutes the Knights gave their fans the revenge they'd craved for nine long months. Running at will through the Mississippi line, they systematically ground the Cats into the dirt, racking up 420 yards and four more TDs before it was over.

KICK BUTT! KICK BUTT! KICK BUTT!

When Coach Star trotted across the field at the end of the game to shake hands with Bearcat coach Dan Friendly, he felt something like pity for the gray-haired old field commander who, rumor had it, was going to be sacked at the end of the season. Though under no misconceptions about Dan being either honest or sporting, Tony nonetheless respected him for his twenty-five years of professional survivability.

"Good game, Dan."

"I don't know about that, Tony. But your guys look pretty sharp."

"Thanks."

In the Stadium Club where the Morgan faithful gathered to get drunk before, during, and after athletics events, there was, however, no pity for the vanquished. Raising a ruckus louder than the one in the Knights' locker room, the Camelot Club royalty were hooting and hollering with childlike abandon.

"Yahooo! Some game, eh Buster? . . . You betcha, Willard . . . How 'bout my boys, Felton? . . . Go purple! Go gold! . . . Well, Dud, whadda you think? . . .

Dudley hesitated a moment. "Not a bad game."

Circulating about the clubhouse, glad-handing every contributor he could, Chancellor Brewster noticed Tom Hanagan standing near the bar yakking with Roscoe Barrett.

"There you are!" blurted Brewster, walking across the room, pumping the arm of the man he was ready to fire an hour before. "Good game, Tom!"

It was nearly two in the morning before Tony Star and his wife Rose bid goodnight to the last revelers at their house.

"That's right, 120 Battery Road," said Star to the cabbie, pointing to Ed Tarmeenian, who was passed out drunk in the back of the cab. "And this one's 764 Jackson Pike," he added, nodding at Pete Cossacky, whose head was slumped on Ed's shoulder. "And here's twenty bucks and ten extra to help 'em to the door."

"Tank you, Coach! Congratulation on beeg victoree."

"Thanks, Akhmet."

"Well," said Tony, as he turned off the tape of the game that was playing on the VCR, and began to gather the beer cans strewn everywhere throughout the house, "I'm glad that's over."

"Yeah, me too," said Rose, emptying an ashtray full of cigarette butts into a plastic bag. "Those Bearcats had me kinda scared tonight."

"Naaa..."

"Yeah they did, Tony. I thought they'd never cave in. And the whole first half, Coretta Woods—you know she's due in two weeks—kept moanin' about not bein' able to pay for the new twins if we didn't win. It was drivin' me nuts."

"But you weren't really worried, were ya?"

"Well..."

"C'mon now."

"Cut it out, Tony, I gotta pick up this trash. Tony, I'm warning you....*giggle*...Tony."

CHAPTER 7

The week of September 4

When Tom Hanagan walked into the Calhoun Complex at 9:45 Monday morning, he felt like a winner. Not only had he worked out the kinks in his back—by avoiding exercise more strenuous than channel surfing—but the marriage counselor whose office he and Jan had just left had reprimanded her for behaving like a child over the weekend.

Maybe these marriage counselors aren't such frauds after all, he thought as he strolled through the glass doors of his office where Savannah McLane, dressed in gold tank top and purple micro-skirt, was anxiously awaiting his arrival.

"Mornin', Mr. Hanagan," she beamed, bounding up from her seat like a puppy to get him his coffee.

"Savannah—" he said, running his eyes over the curves of his secretary's body.

"Yes?"

"Call me Tom would you?"

"All right, Mr. Hanagan, I mean Tom," she cooed, handing him his mug with a smile.

"Now let's see, any calls?"

"Just a couple." Savannah shuffled through the papers on her desk. "Here they are. Mr. Barrett wants you to call him."

"Junior Barrett?"

"No, Mr. Barrett Senior. He said he'd been thinkin' things over and needed to set up a lunch with you."

"Good.... Good. And?"

"Ms. Brooks called again."

"Umm…" Tom was still feeling embarrassed about the other evening at the Hunt room.

"And Blake Stevens wants you to call about meetin' with Mr. Gooch for lunch this Thursday."

I wish Blake would handle that old windbag himself, thought Tom. "All right, Savannah, thanks. I'll be in my office if—"

"Oh, and this telegram came for you about an hour ago."

"A telegram?"

"I was going to call you on your cell, but Mr. Conner came in the office and—"

"No problem," he said, not altogether happy about Bill Conner cultivating a relationship with Savannah. *I've got to have a talk with that boy.*

Tom looked at the telegram, tore it open and saw it was from the NCAA. "I can't believe it!"

"What is it, Mr. —Tom?"

"I can't believe the NCAA is warning us about the conduct of our fans on Saturday."

Tom had feared there might be repercussions from a nasty brawl that had erupted between a gang of Mississippi State fans and several Morgan players and fans at a local Pizza Hut after the game. The telegram, however, had nothing to do with that donnybrook. Such outpourings of school spirit were after all quite common among fans of big-time college teams. What concerned the media-sensitive censors at NCAA headquarters was that the "*Kick Butt* cheer of the crowd might not have been in the best tradition of intercollegiate athletics."

"That's nonsense," said Tom, who all day Sunday had received congratulations about coming up with the *Kick Butt* battle cry. "I gotta call them right now." But unable to reach local NCAA representative Biff Wayne in Memphis (who was busy golfing) or Sammy Unger in Kansas City (also busy, on a two week trip to Sweden to check into the possibility of holding an international collegiate bowling tournament in Oslo next summer), Tom hung up the phone. *The hell with it. What am I getting upset about? Like that marriage counselor told us this morning, there's no sense worrying about things that are out of your control. Besides, there's no way I'm gonna tell our fans that they can't scream KICK BUTT if they want to. This is the first time in three years they've shown any spirit.*

As Tom sat back in his chair trying, as the counselor said, to "center himself," Savannah buzzed to tell him that Bobby Brooks was on the line again.

Tom paused a moment. "All right, I'll take it."

"Bobby, what's up? Thanks, it was a good game, wasn't it? . . . Yeah, we both knew it, didn't we? . . . That's right. . . . This week? . . . Ah, I'd love to, but I'm—the following Wednesday? . . . Let's see. . . . Yeah, I think that might work. . . . And about the other night, I'm really—"

BUZZ

"Hold on a sec, wouldja, Bobby? . . . "Charlie who? . . . Oh yeah! . . . Listen, Bobby, I'll call you next week. . . . Awright, bye bye. . . . Hey Charlie, how's our number one booster in Apaloochee. . . . What?! You're kidding! . . . No! That's fantastic! . . . O. J. Gore and Tiberius Brown both suspended from the team for our game this Saturday? Wait'll I tell Tony."

• • •

The J. P. Morgan University catalogue was not completely honest when it described the Crenshaw T. Fort Collegiate Study Center as "a multi-million dollar state of the art learning facility where each night of the academic year student athletes gather to receive supplementary instruction from a highly trained staff of professional educators." True, the center *had* cost two million dollars and was staffed by a team of four paid professionals, but it was *not* where Morgan student athletes gathered each evening during the academic year—least of all on Tuesday nights after practicing all afternoon and then watching game film with their coaches after dinner. Still, the Center was not completely empty on Tuesday evening.

There were five students in the facility at 9:15: Asswad King sitting in an audio-visual equipped carrel watching the Rev. Louis Farrakan deliver a speech on the emancipated role of women in Islamic society; Eddie Saxon, two carrels away from Mustafa, trying to read *The Diary of Anne Frank* for his remedial reading class while he listened to the new MegaDeath CD; and Pancho Arnez, in the booth to his left, writing a letter to Buster Hooper in Houston to tell him about his sister Angelita's tonsilitis.

> Dear Mister Hooper,
> I'm glad to see you at the game on Saturday. I'm hoping your wife and you are feeling good. I was very happy about the game too. Maybe I will see you at the game on this Saturday. I hope so.
> My mother told me she talked to you about Angelita. She is very very sick. I think her tonsil needs to come out and she doesn't have the insurance. So I am writing to you, like you said I should....

In addition, freshman Craig Bumhoffer and his teammate lineman, Laverne "Mongol" Harris, were being tutored in a small private study room by Dr. Barbara Sazlow, the head of the student-athlete tutoring program. Undaunted by her tutees' inability to comprehend the concept of an indirect object, she stood at a computer-generated board diagramming a sentence.

The girl / gave the ball / to the boys / in the gym

Pleasurably daydreaming as he watched Dr. Sazlow in her short skirt and clinging tank top, Craig Bumhoffer was at a loss when she turned around and asked him to name the direct object of the sentence on the board.

"Uhhh, uhhh…"

"I knows, Professor!" blurted out Mongol, waving his hand.

"Yes?"

"It's the ball."

"Good, Mongol! Very good," said Dr. Sazlow, who along with her jock-sniffing husband, psychology professor Louis Sazlow, had come to Morgan from Syracuse University after publishing a nationally acclaimed study on "Attention Deficit Disorder among freshmen ice hockey and basketball players." Accepted as warmly by the players at Morgan as they had been at Syracuse, Professor Sazlow and his wife were always ready to do whatever they could to help "da boyz."

"Now Craig, can you tell me what the indirect object is in this sentence?"

"It's uhhh…"

"I can, Professor," said Mongol again waving his hand in the air.

"All right, Mongol, but let's give Craig a chance."

"Gym!"

"No, Craig, that's a—"

"Object of the proposition."

"Preposition, that's right, Mongol. Very good. We really are coming along, aren't we?" Dr. Sazlow beamed at the muscular young man, her heart brimming over with the joy that a teacher finds looking in the face of an understanding pupil.

• • •

"Maybe you let me buy you cup of coffee tonight?"

"Ah, I don't think so, Stefan," said Jan Hanagan, toweling off her face Wednesday evening after aerobics class. "I've got a million things to do and—"

"You Amereekan women, really you make me laugh sometimes," said the handsome young instructor.

"Oh we do, do we?"

"Yes, with your talk of liberation and equality of sexes, and if someone asks a married woman like you out for innocent cup of espresso she runs as fast as she can the other way."

"Really, Stefan, that's not—"

"Yes?"

"All right." Jan smiled and stuffed her towel in her gym bag, "let's go have a cup of coffee—on me."

"Yes, and another cup of the Peruvian Highlands for each of us, please," said Stefan to Nadine Schwarz, the proprietress of the Bongo Mocha Coffee House.

"Do you really think I could, Stefan?" asked the Director's wife, leaning forward in her wicker chair.

"For sure, Jan." Mrs. Hanagan had insisted on dropping the formalities after they had been seated at their table under an old photo of Peter, Paul, and Mary. "Right now there's only three of us in troupe, but we plan to give, how you say, a recital, this spring."

"Oh, I don't know, Stefan, I'm not as young as I used to be."

"I know you can do it. I watch you in class each week. You are very graceful."

"You mean very out of shape, don't you?" she tittered, her voice blending in with the sound of Yusef Latif playing on the coffee house sound system.

"Don't be so modest, Jan," said Stefan, his ice blue eyes staring into hers through the steam rising from their coffee cups.

"Oh, well, I really think it's time I should be going," she said thirty-five minutes later, looking at her watch and starting to get up from her chair.

"Yes, it's gettink late." Stefan smiled. "But whatever you decide to do about dance troupe, give me call tomorrow and tell me if I should get extra ticket for Alvin Ailey Show."

"When was that again?"

"Next Thursday night." Stefan wrote his phone number on a paper napkin and gave it to her.

• • •

"I can't believe you were really worried," said Tom Hanagan to Dr. Lucius Thompson. Tom and Lucius had been gabbing for twenty minutes Thursday afternoon while a University maintenance man with a fractured ankle ground his teeth in pain in Dr. Thompson's waiting room. "Honestly, Lucius, I was never worried at all. . . . Gore and Brown? . . . Yes, they're both definitely out for the game. . . . Of course I think we have a chance with their two best players gone. . . .

Are we going to throw the ball Saturday? . . . Well, I can't say for sure, but I think we'll all be surprised."

BUZZ BUZZ

"I'll take it, Savannah. . . . Hey, Noweeta! What's hap'nin'? . . . Yeah, it is a beautiful day, isn't it? So anyway, what's cookin'? . . . Thaddeus Wilson again, huh? . . . He is a pain. . . . And being a minority member like he is, you'd think he . . . That's right. And not only does he take attendance, he demands that the boys take their exams along with the rest of the students. . . . I know, we've been trying to get rid of him for years. . . . It is a travesty. He doesn't even have a Ph.D. (Mr. Wilson only had an M.A. from Oxford where he had been a Rhodes Scholar.) I thought you were going to steer the guys away from his sections. . . . A scheduling conflict? Miller's not teaching the Gay Experience this term? How about Fisher's Contemporary Media? . . . At the same time as Urban Narratology 104? . . . Well, I'll talk with Wilson, but I don't think it'll do much good. . . . I know. . . . By the way, are you gonna be staying with us at the Marriott? . . . Oh really? You and Bill Conner are having cocktails with Dudley Dunning and Boomer Cox before the game? . . . All right, I'll talk with you later." *Cocktails with Dunning and Cox, huh . . . I think it's time Billy Boy started worrying a little more about getting his work done around here.*

BUZZ BUZZ

"Savannah, I wonder if you'd ring Bill Conner and tell him I need that women's program budget—he already gave it to you this morning? . . . You typed it up for him over the weekend? . . . Oh . . . Yeah, Bill really is on the ball, isn't he? . . . No, I'll get it later. I've, uh, gotta go see how things are going with the team. . . . All right, see you tomorrow. . . ." *CLUNK. Damn, that boy's ambitious!*

• • •

It took Tom and Tony forty minutes to make their way to their seats at the Time-Out Grill Thursday night. "Thanks, Jim Bob, appreciate that. . . . I told you we were gonna win, Charlie. . . . You betcha, Arvil, we're gonna kick some butt Saturday."

"So whadda you really think, Tony?" said Tom after they'd finally placed their orders and been served their fried mozzarella stick appetizers.

"Honest to God, Tommy, I don't know. Two weeks ago I wouldn't 'a given us a chance in hell, but with Gore and Brown out of the line-up, we just might be able to play 'em tough."

"You really think so?"

"Maybe. Ain't nothin' like disciplinary trouble to demoralize a football team—Yeah, Donna, thanks for the good word, hon. Keep your fingers crossed."

"I hope so. If we can just beat the spread, that should keep the boosters happy."

"Yeah."

"You should'a seen 'em in the gallery at half time last Saturday."

"Worried, huh?"

"That's not the word for it. Dunning, Brewster, the whole crowd mumbling and grumbling. 'Course I knew what you were up to all the time, and I told 'em as much."

"Atta boy, Tommy." Star raised his beer glass and toasted his friend.

"Here's to you too, Tony."

"And to kicking some butt in Apaloochee."

• • •

At four o'clock Friday afternoon the Morgan football team's chartered Delta L-1011 landed at the Apaloochee airport, where amidst a chorus of cat calls and jeers the team boarded buses and headed into town. As they passed through the cotton fields that surrounded the expanding suburbs of Apaloochee, Coach Star enviously eyed the tarpaper shacks that dotted the landscape.

Unlike most Yankees, who are appalled by the sight of rural shanty towns—though able to view their own inner city slums with equanimity—Coach Star knew that these boondocks where cotton had once been king were breeding ground for some of the best football players in America. As he looked through the bus window, he recalled the dilapidated row-house in Pittsburgh where he had grown up. And, strange as it may sound, he almost felt regret that his own sons would never have that same inducement to athletic excellence that he'd had.

Twenty minutes later, amidst another torrent of verbal abuse, the Knights filed through the doors of the Apaloochee Marriott. Never pleasant, being a visiting competitor at Apaloochee could even be dangerous, as it had been ever since the war-painted mound builders of the Apaloochee valley first hosted their murderous inter-clan ball games some thousand years earlier. So savage, in fact, was the Blue Wave team spirit that even Coach Star, accustomed to the rabid rivalries of Western Pennsylvania mill towns, had been taken aback when, two years earlier, he was awakened at three in the morning by a mob of Wave fans outside his window, setting fire to an effigy of him they had hanged from a lamp post and beaten with baseball bats.

Football was not just a game in Apaloochee; it was a religion. And like a medieval town whose center was its cathedral, it was around the University's gymnasium and stadium that the life of the surrounding area revolved.

A half hour after they had arrived at the motel, the Morgan coaches and staff drove to the visitors' locker room of Memorial Stadium to make sure the gear sent ahead by truck had arrived.

When they walked into the locker room—which had been painted pink after UA coach Al Crimen heard that pink was used in insane asylums and dentist's offices to pacify patients—Tony and his assistants were greeted by team manager Charlie Bumble and assistant trainer Pat Pitouchi. They had just finished laying out 100 helmets, 120 mouthpieces, 102 sets of shoulder pads, 198 uniform jerseys, 302 tee shirts, 120 jock straps, 320 pairs of socks, 320 pairs of shoes, 164 pairs of pants, 50 footballs, and two tons of other assorted athletic and medical equipment.

"You got those cooling fans ready to go, Charlie?"

"Yeah, these heat busters should keep 'em cool."

"How 'bout you, Pat? You ready?"

"All set, Coach," said the trainer as Stitches Stevens did a quick inventory of his medical supplies.

"You bring them extra tanks of oxygen?"

"Yessir, got 'em right here."

"Good."

"Awright, then, we'll be back at seven fifteen to work out. Weather report still the same for tomorrow?"

"High nineties, Coach. S'posed to cool down to the mid-eighties by game time."

"How's the field?"

"Pretty hard. They haven't been getting much rain down here either."

CHAPTER 8

Saturday, September 10

U.A. Coach Al Crimen had been waiting to hear from his athletics director, Dr. Jim Lee Hodges since 7 A.M. At 10:00, Jim Lee finally called to say he hadn't had any luck getting the new chancellor to rescind the disciplinary probation that the dean of students—who would be fired at the end of the year—had ordered for O. J. Gore and Tiberius Brown.

"Obviously Oglesbee don't know how thangs work around here yet," said Coach Crimen. "All the boys did was borrow a couple computers from a classroom. . . . How 'bout the Gov'ner? . . . In Washington? What the hell's he doin' there when we got a home game? . . . Awright. You dun good, Jim Lee, I'll holler at ya' after the game."

"No luck," said the Coach, turning to his offensive coordinator, Bill "Bum" Turner.

"We'll be all right, Al, watcha worryin' about?"

"Nuthin', I guess."

"If we can't kick Morgan's ass to Metro and back, we don't deserve to be coachin' here at Apaloochee."

"Yeah, I know, Bum, but I just wanna be sure Star don't sneak up on us like he did two years back—sonofabitch cost us the conference championship."

"Lightnin' don't strike twice, Al. No way Muggins is gonna get past our defense. All we gotta do is just keep hammerin' away at their left side and we'll be able to walk the ball in by the third quarter."

"How's Malenkovic?"

ısted fingers. And Einreich pulled his hamstring on
practice."

aid he looked okay last night." Willie Winters was a
...ber of the Apaloochee Stadium grounds crew whose job it was
to spy on visiting opponents when they worked out the night before
games.

"I dunno, Al, I think you're worryin' too much."

"Maybe, but how 'bout this Wallace kid they got?"

Al and his staff had received some unauthorized film of one of
Morgan's pre-season practice sessions from an airborne spy in Metro.

"No way they'll ever use him with Muggins healthy. Besides, the
kid's never played a single game."

"Yeah, you're right."

"C'mon, let's go downstairs and catch the rest of *Black Hawk
Down* with the boys."

"Here's ten and I'll raise you ten more," said Dudley Dunning, laying two ten-dollar bills on the table.

"All righty, Dudley," said Boomer. "Watchagot?"

"Kings over Jacks," said the spectacled financier, smiling as he
reached out to rake in the pot.

"Now, hold on, Dud, not so quick. Where I'm from"—Boomer
laid three deuces on the table with a big grin— "three of a kind beats
two pair."

"GODDAMMIT!" raged Dudley, throwing his cards down.

"I thought you had him too, Dud," said Lamar, puffing on his
cigar and leaning back in his seat.

"THAT'S IT FOR ME! I QUIT!"

"C'mon Dud, it's only a game."

"The only reason you play games is to win."

"You got a point there," concurred Lamar and Boomer, nodding
their heads.

"We'll be landing in Apaloochee in five minutes, Mr. Dunning,"
said the co-pilot of Dudley's Lear jet, poking her pretty face into the
cabin.

"All right, honey."

"You seem kinda jumpy today, Dudley. What's eatin' you?" asked Lamar, crushing out his cigar.

"Maybe I don't like goin' down to Apaloochee to get our butts kicked every year."

"We won the year before last."

"You know what I mean, Boomer."

"Yeah, I do."

"I hate losing."

"Who knows, maybe we'll win," chuckled Lamar.

"Yeah, just like we were gonna sign Kurt Neil." Much to Dudley's chagrin, Magnolia Hills Prep School tennis star, Kurt Neil, had earlier in the week turned down a full-paid scholarship at Morgan to attend the University of Florida.

"I was surprised about that myself."

"I'm not surprised about anything around here anymore, Boomer. I know you and Billy Bob are committed to Hanagan, but—"

"Now hold on a second, Dudley. You know I don't give a damn about Hanagan, and if Billy Bob were here, he'd tell you the same thing."

"It's time we got somebody in here who knows what the hell they're doin'."

"You're right about that, Dud, but just in case you forgot, we *are* 1 and 0."

"Don't make me laugh."

"C'mon buddy, cheer up." Boomer reached over and elbowed his friend. "It's a beautiful day. The girls are home in Metro shoppin' and we got eight hours before game time to see if we can't catch us some of those stripers Lake Apaloochee's so famous for."

Meanwhile, at the Fifth Quarter—the sports-bar/shrine where members of the press corps meet before and after UA games to drink, talk sports, and complain about what they got paid—Red

Carlisle and the voice of the Purple Knights, Morgan sports announcer Butch Sanders, were sitting at the bar drinking beer.

"Seven more hours till the slaughter begins," chuckled Red, ogling a buxom bartender as he talked with Butch.

"You never know," said Butch, looking up at one of the 200 pictures of legendary Coach "Boar" Baxter that lined the walls of the bar. "Star put it to Crimen two years ago."

"Believe me, Butchy boy, I know. Star's gonna get his butt kicked good and proper tonight."

"You know something, Red?"

"What?" said the journalist taking a drag off his cigarette.

"You got a bad attitude."

"Wha—"

"Just kiddin'. Hey Grover, what's the latest on Gore and Brown?"

"No go, Butch."

"Man, Crimen must be pissed."

"Yeah, he was bent outta shape when I talked to him this morning," said Red, "but it don't matter. He's got two other horses in his stable just as good."

"I dunno. Gore's a pretty big part of the offense."

"Yeah, maybe. So anyway, what's Star been sayin' about me?..."

At 5:00, after spending what seemed like an endless afternoon killing time, Tony Star stuffed the player profiles that lay on the bed into his briefcase and headed out the motel door to gather the troops for the ride to the field. Nothing on his mind but the game now, Star was startled by the voice of Jimmy Joe Wallace's father.

"Hey, Coach. How's it goin'?"

"Oh, Mr. Wallace." Star frowned.

"Well," said the quarterback's father, now joined by his wife, Billie Ann, "is he gonna play today?"

"I dunno."

"You don't know?!!"

"That's right," said Star, as an elevator full of stone-faced players opened in front of him and he hurriedly squeezed his way on.

• • •

"Jesus fucking Christ!" cursed Al Crimen two and a half hours later when his defensive coordinator Augie Burdle informed him that their starting left cornerback, Damien Putter, had just been rushed to the hospital with what appeared to be an attack of appendicitis.

"You sure it's his appendix?"

"That's what Doc thinks. He's been complainin' for a coupl'a days. I just hope it ain't busted. I'd hate to lose 'im for the State game."

"Shit!" roared the foul-mouthed, evil-tempered coach as he barged through the swinging doors that led into the Blue Wave locker room and was greeted with a cheer by his team.

"COACH CRIMEN! COACH CRIMEN! COACH CRIMEN!"

"AWRIGHT!" he yelled, regaining his composure, motioning for his Blue and White uniformed gladiators to quiet down. "Awright, men. Y'all know what's at stake today. The last time Morgan came down here to Apaloochee they gave us a whoopin'. That's right. In front of our parents, friends, classmates, and fans. And maybe I shouldn't oughta say it, but in all my days of coachin', I don't think I've ever suffered a more humiliatin' defeat.... But, gentlemen, I didn't come in here tonight to open up old wounds. No, I came here tonight to ask y'all to give me, this University, and all the citizens across this state the only thang that can ever make the wrong that's been done to them right: VICT'RY! COMPLETE, TOTAL, AND UTTA' VICT'RY!"

"Yeah, let's kill 'em!... Stomp 'em in the dirt!... UA number one!"

"All right now, boys, kneel down, Coach Turner's gonna lead us in prayer."

"Our Heavenly Father," began Bum Turner, a deacon in the local Free Will Baptist Church and head of UA Athletes for Christ, "we humbly beseech thee as we go forth into this con-test this ev'nin' that thou wouldst shield us from all danger and lead us in thy infinite mercy and powa' to the final and glow-rious victory over our

foes. We ask this in the name of the Father, the Son, and the Holy
Ghost. A-men."

"Awright now, let's go get some revenge!"

"REVENGE!"

"BLUE WAVE! BLUE WAVE! BLUE WAVE!"

"We certainly do appreciate your havin' us down for the weekend,
Tyson, don't we, Bill?"

"Yes we do," said Chancellor Brewster, taking his seat in the
Culpepper Corporation skybox.

"So what are you folks drinkin'?" asked Tyson Culpepper, who
had played tackle for Morgan in the late 50s before returning to the
family business in Apaloochee.

"I'll have a little white wine, thank you," said Winnie Brewster.

"And how 'bout you, Chancellor.... bourbon?"

"Yes, that would be nice."

"You want the us'al, Annebelle?"

"Thanks, honey," said the perky young wife of the treasurer of
the Morgan Board of Trust and owner of the largest pork processing
operation in the Mid-South.

"There you go, Billy Bob."

"Thanks, Tyson."

"Yeah, I'm gonna have to get me a sky box up at Fulsom too,"
said Tyson, smacking his thick lips together, "once I turn the business over to the boys (*glug glug*). But for right now I guess I can
content myself havin' one here at my wife's Alma Mater." Tyson's
third wife Annebelle had been a pom-pom girl in the UA Billion
Dollar Band.

Chancellor Brewster smiled politely.

"Yeah, it won't be long now till my two boys take over. Kinda
lookin' forward to it. They're smart as whips. Both of 'em Morgan
grads, you know. Joe-boy law school and Will the business school.
And how's that son 'a yours doin', Bill?"

The Chancellor hesitated a second. "He's fine, Tyson. Thanks for
asking."

"I forget now, what's he up to?"

"He's ah—teaching—teaching English at Appalachian State."

"Humm ... And how's that pretty daughter 'a yours?"

"One more year till she graduates from Radcliffe."

"I guess she musta got her brains from her momma, huh?... yuk yuk yuk. Jus' kiddin', Bill. Now, I wancha all to grab yo'selves a bowl a' that chili over there."

"Thanks, Tyson, but I—"

"Fix 'em up a bowl, Mosey," said Tyson to the bartender. "Here they come!" yelled Tyson as the Blue Wave came on the field and the skybox shook beneath their feet.

"You all right there, Winnie?"

"Yes, thank you, Tyson."

"Lookee there, Chanc'llor," boomed Tyson, who liked to give his guests a play-by-play description of the game whether they wanted it or not—which they seldom did after the first five minutes. "Looks like we're gonna be receivin' at the south end of the field."

"That it does," said the Chancellor, inwardly groaning with each word of Tyson's color commentary. Though it was not often that Billy Bob had to play the role of the fawning subordinate, Tyson Culpepper was someone whose favor he needed to curry. As treasurer of the Board of Trust and head of the University Finance Committee, Culpepper's approval was needed on all major University expenditures.

"Third and 17," announced Tyson, "Muggins is droppin' back to—no, he's gonna run it, oh, just short of a first down. Looks like we're gonna hafta kick, Bill. How's that chili?"

"It's—wonderful," said the Chancellor, helping himself to another spoonful of the over-spiced and greasy slurry.

• • •

"Okay you guys," said Ed Tarmeenian to the defense huddled around him on the sideline, "let's stick it to 'em!"

"Yeah! Kick ass!"

As Ed had anticipated, the Wave offense went right for the left side of the Morgan defensive line. But they were unable to gain more than a yard on either of the first two carries. Then, on third and 8, Crimen called a quick out to wide receiver Art Mumbley. But as Mumbley reached out for the pass and the crowd roared in expectation of a first down, Zanzibar Jackson and Larry Einreich jackknifed Mumbley between them, and sent him crashing to the astro turf.

"HEY, WHAT'S GOIN' ON HERE?!" yelled Al Crimen, whose own defensive backfield were known around the league as the "muggers." "Unnecessary roughness!" he shouted. His trainers ran out to tend Mumbley, who lay knocked momentarily senseless by the shock.

"Good hit," said Ed Tarmeenian, huddling with his defense at the sideline. "Good hit."

Two minutes later as the crowd roared its approval, Mumbley, his arms thrown over two trainers' shoulders, hobbled off the field.

"Anything wrong?" Al Crimen asked head trainer Luke Bellows after Mumbley was helped to a bench in front of Doc Dempsey.

"Nah, he's all right, just got knocked out for a second."

Stunned by the untimely loss of All-American Mumbley, Coach Crimen and the 80,000 Wave fans were even more shocked twenty-three uneventful minutes later when the first quarter ended with the score still 0 to 0.

"What the hell is goin' on?!!" raged Al Crimen at his offensive coordinator, Bum Turner.

"Don't worry, Al. They'll cave in soon." And as predicted, with six minutes left in the second quarter, JuJu Melons burst through the Morgan line for forty-eight yards. And on the next play Marcel Pitts catapulted across the goal line for six. After the extra point, it was Wave 7, Morgan 0.

HOOOORAAAAY BIG BLUE!

As the Blue Wave cheerleaders did flips to the Billion Dollar Band's rendition of "We Will Rock You," the crowd, hitherto quiet and apprehensive, set the Blue Wave rolling from one end of the stadium to the other, "GO WAVE! GO BLUE! GO BLUE WAVE!"

But the Knights were not to be written off so easily. Five minutes later they were on the Wave 31. First and 10.

"Well now, this is gettin' inter'stin'," said Tyson, laying down his chili and picking up the binoculars. "Whadda you think, Bill?"

"Could be," said the Chancellor, who, warmed by the bourbons he'd drunk and the possibility of his team actually scoring, had become more animated.

KNOCK KNOCK

"See who that is, wouldja, honey?" said the corporate butcher, his binoculars fixed on Coach Star talking to Reggie Muggins.

"Oh, what a nice surprise! C'mon in, Tom," gurgled Annebelle, letting Tom Hanagan into the skybox.

"Well, hello there, Tom, glad you could make it." Tyson turned his head to greet the husband of the niece of his mother's sister. "I'm glad Inez told you to stop up."

"Thanks for the invitation, Mr. Culpepper. Hello, Chancellor Brewster, Mrs. Brewster."

"Hold on, everybody, there goes Muggins, he's pitchin' out—No, he's dropping back to pass. He's got Lewis open over the middle.... Ohhh. Incomplete!"

"Darn it!" said Tom, stepping up to the window of the box as the ladies resumed their conversation.

"Now you get yourself som'a that chili over there, Tom. It's real good, idn't it, Chancellor?"

"Yes—great."

"We're playin' pretty good out there today, Tom. The Chancellor and I were just discussin' how well prepared they look. Here we go again, Muggins is droppin' back, lookin' right, lookin' left, he's got Dobbins open on the sideline, he's—INTERCEPTION! I'll be darned!"

Eight plays later, the Wave was another seven points closer to reaching *USA Today's* twenty-one point spread.

"So Tom," said Tyson, beginning to lose interest in the game, "what's the word on Jamal Jarvis?" Jamal was a highly touted Morgan basketball prospect from Apaloochee County who, unbe-knownst to Tyson and the Chancellor, had decided the week before to go to the University of Louisville.

"Ah, I'm afraid he's decided to take Denny Crumm's offer."

"He what?!" said the Chancellor, who had twice taken time out of his busy schedule to meet with the seven foot center.

"I'm afraid he's decided on Louisville," apologized Tom as Morgan deep man Cochise Cubbins caught the Blue Wave kick-off and tore out of the end zone to the 10, 20, 30. . . .

"Now that's not—go!" said Tyson as Cubbins all at once reversed field and broke two more tackles at the forty-yard line.

"Go!" chimed in Tom Hanagan, suddenly caught up in Cubbins' mad dash.

"Go! Go!" cheered the Chancellor, momentarily forgetting his anger over Jarvis.

"He's gonna go all the way!" shouted Tyson, "20, 15, 10, 5, TOUCHDOWN!"

"Hooray!" screamed Clifton Calhoun, flailing his purple pom-pom in the air, and feeling a pain shoot through his left arm and shoulder.

"Are you all right, Clifton?" screamed Inez in her husband's ear, noticing him grab his chest.

"I think so."

"You look a little peek-ed, dear. Yahooo!"

"I'll be all right."

"You're sure?"

"Yeah."

Inez smiled at Clifton and resumed cheering. But her euphoria didn't last long. Ten minutes later, Crimen's gladiators put another seven points on the board to end the half, leading 21 to 7.

HOORAY WAVE! YEAAAA!

Despite what Hollywood would have us believe, half time in the locker room of big-time college football games is seldom a time for outpourings of eloquent oratory. What most coaches have to say to their players as they are stitched and re-taped is quite pedestrian.

"You're pullin' too goddam slow, Dobbins."

"If you're gonna blitz, Atilla, make sure you get that sonofabitch."

"You look like you got fuckin' cement in your shoes, White."

But as the moment neared to head back to the field, Coach Star felt inspired.

"Awright you guys, now listen up! You played a good first half. I mean it. You did good. And you may not know it, but you got 'em scared. Trust me. You can win this game if you want to. You just gotta want it"—He thumped himself on the chest—"more than they do. Just stick to our plan, don't flinch, and we'll fly outta here winners. You understand?!"

Silence.

"I said, DO YOU UNDERSTAND?!!"

"YEA! GO KNIGHTS! KICK BUTT!"

Though the Coach's words doubtlessly helped to motivate the Morgan players, it was more being pelted with trash and heckled as they returned to the field that enraged them. Getting beat is one thing, having somebody rub your nose in it is another. And by the time the Knights huddled around Coach Star before the kick-off they were clamoring for blood. Gambling on the team's fury, Star decided to have DeGama drop a high blooper at the 20 yard line in the hope of forcing a turn-over. But as the ball fell out of the night sky into the arms of JuJu Melons, things didn't work out as Tony had planned— they worked out even better! For although Melons didn't cough it up, he got so banged up on the play that he had to be carried from the field.

"Jesus Christ Almighty, I can't lose Melons too. You sure he can't play?"

"Says it hurts to breathe, Al."

"What's Doc say?"

"He don't know yet."

"Go talk to him and see if he can't shake it off."

But no more than JuJu could shake off his fractured ribs could the Wave shake off the tenacious Morgan defense that held them to fifty-three yards and three first downs in the next thirteen minutes.

Unfortunately for Morgan, the UA defense proved equally grudging, until—with thirty seconds left in the third quarter—Muggins caught them out of position on a third and 4 draw, and scooted forty yards down the middle to the Wave 27.

GO MORGAN!!!! KICK BUTT!

"Whadda you think, Billy Bob?" yelled Tyson through the jabbering crowd of business associates that had come to his box at half time.

"May-be," said the Chancellor as a drunken Wave booster from whom Tyson purchased hog slops bumped into him.

"Here we go, everybody," shouted Tyson to the crowd. "Muggins has it, he's goin' round ... No, he's pitchin' it out to Ritter. He's goin' to the right—no wait, he's gonna pass.... He's got Lewis open at the 10! He's got it! He's still on his feet.... TOUCHDOWN!!!"

"YES!" blurted the Chancellor, pumping his fist in triumph as Lewis barely refrained from doing a penalizable bump and grind in the end zone.

Confounded by the unexpected TD, the crowd in Memorial Stadium became something to which they were unaccustomed, quiet—almost quiet enough to hear Coach Crimen reprimanding his strong safety Chaz Booker for being drawn out of his zone.

"BOOKER! WHAT THE FUCK WERE YOU DOIN'?!" lashed out the three time winner of the Mid-South Rotary Club's "Good Guy of the Year" award, spittle spraying the face of the shamefaced black boy in front of him.

As the Blue Wave band struck up the Fight Song in an attempt to drown out the chorus of Kick Butts that had suddenly risen from the visitors' side of the field, Tony, Ed and Jet pow-wowed on the 50.

"Whadda you think, Ed, Jet?"

"Let's go for it, Tony."

"Awright." Coach Star huddled on the sideline with his suicide squad. "We're gonna run the 86 and, Fernando, be sure to bounce it deep enough. Okay guys, let's get that ball back!"

The crowd rose to its feet for the kick-off, and the Purple Knights drummers beat a savage tattoo on their tom-toms. *BOM-Tiddi BOM-Tiddi BOM BOM BOM!* DeGama's arm dropped, the kamikazes took off, and the ball shot forward on a knee high line drive that bounced once on the 40 and came back to earth on the left hash mark of the 20 yard line. Executed perfectly, the onsides kick caught the Blue Wave off guard, and as Benito Bradley reached up to grab the ball, Hubert Dumpkins knocked him head over heels and ran down the fumbled pigskin with the same skill he'd used running down piglets on his pappy's farm in Picayune, Mississippi.

"We got it! We got it!" screamed Inez Calhoun, jumping up and down in her seat. "You sure you're feeling all right, Clifton?"

"YAHOOO!" shouted Buster Hooper, manhandling LouAnn, who wasn't quite sure what had happened.

"KICK BUTT!" yelled Milt Lee, almost loud enough for the Chancellor to hear him sixty rows above.

"You know, Billy Bob, I got a feelin' about this one," said Tyson, wrapping his meaty arm around the Chancellor's shoulder.

GODDAMMOTHERFUCKINCOCKSUCKINSONSOFBITCHES! were the only words Al Crimen could utter as he rushed on the field toward the nearest referee, flailing his arms trying to intimidate him into believing that Morgan had been offsides on the kick. Though he knew it wasn't true, with the momentum clearly swinging toward Morgan, Al wanted that twelfth man on the field. As the referee warned him to get back to the sidelines, the crowd rained curses and garbage on the Morgan players and fans.

BOOOOOO BOOOOOO HISSSSS!

When he huddled with his players on the sideline, Coach Crimen made it clear that if they didn't stop Morgan—and keep alive his chance of winning the $150,000 bonus he received at season's end for being Mid-South conference champ—there would be hell to pay. Or to put it more exactly, they could go to hell if they thought they were going to get paid that week.

But neither Al's rabble-rousing nor his threats could keep the

Knights out of the end zone. Fortune had donned a purple and gold uniform. Eight time-consuming plays later, Reggie Muggins with a great second effort ran in an off-tackle dive for another TD. After DeGama's extra point, it was 21 all.

Utterly befuddled, the crowd inside Tyson's sky box went dumb. As they stood in shock waiting for the last four minutes of what threatened to become a major upset, Chancellor Brewster's heart swelled nigh to bursting. *His* team, *his very own* Purple Knights had the number five team in the nation on the ropes. Unable to control himself any longer, he let out a war whoop of delight. "Awright now, get it back!"

"Yeahgetitback," slurred Bunny Culpepper, Tyson's drunk, disreputable, dyed blond sister, raising her highball glass on high, flashing the Chancellor a smile.

As if they had heard the Chancellor's order, the defense stood fast. Three times Wave quarterback Tim Battle tried to find a receiver and failed. And then after almost blocking the punt, Morgan took over on their own 35, with 2:43 left.

"Let's do it, boys!" boomed Billy Bob, tossing off the rest of his bourbon.

"Yealezdoit," echoed Bunny, feeling herself instinctively drawn to the Chancellor, captivated by the magnetic power that radiates from a winner.

Could it be? wondered 80,000 fans as Muggins came to the line and started to bark the signals.

"Yes! Yes!" the Chancellor shouted as Symeon Smith bulled his way forward for five. Then another three. And then, as Muggins dropped back and fired one to the sideline, Mongol Harris leapt up with linebacker Choo Choo James stuck closer to him than a Tri-Delt to an SAE at two in the morning, and came down at the 25 with the ball in his arms and yellow flags at his feet.

As a threatening roar of dissatisfaction erupted in the stadium, referee Clyde Beavers huddled with his back judge and field judge to decide who was guilty of what.

"Well, Delmore, whadda you think?" he asked.

"I dunno," said back judge Delmore Bugg.

"I dunno either," said line judge D.C. Diggins, yelling to be heard over the menacing crowd.

Clyde Beavers looked around at the howling faces of the frenzied multitudes, thought a minute, and ran to the middle of the field. The crowd went momentarily silent, then roared with approval as he began to walk fifteen yards against the Knights.

"We've been robbed!" raged Billy Bob, turning away from the skybox window in disgust.

"Don't give up yet," said Tyson. "Here comes that Mexican boy on to try one."

"C'mon, Fernando! C'mon!"

As Tom Hanagan stood on the sideline twisting his game program in a knot, he thought about the enormous outlay of time—and money—he had spent recruiting DeGama.

KICK BUTT! KICK BUTT! KICK BUTT!

Players like Fernando didn't come cheap. And with the new immigration laws in effect, it had taken months to arrange for him and his family—all twelve of them—to be allowed to reside in Metro while he matriculated at the University. But as the ex-soccer player gracefully skipped forward, reared back and sent it sailing—"It's high enough! . . . It's long enough. . . . It's gooood!!"—Tom knew it had all been worth it.

"We did it! We did it!" hooted the Chancellor, feeling Bunny Culpepper's surgically-enhanced breasts pressed firmly against him in the crush at the window.

"Yeah we did," said Tyson, "and only a minute fifteen to go."

Seventy-five seconds—not much time; but enough for future Oakland Raider quarterback Tim Battle to hit his wide receivers with two thirty yard strikes.

"Now that boy's got an arm," said Culpepper.

Forty-five seconds to go, the Billion-Dollar Band struck up the Blue Wave victory march. . . . The crowd rose to its feet. . . . Battle set them down. . . . handed off to Pitts. *WHAM*! Dropped at the line of scrimmage by D'Amato and Einreich. As a diminuendo of disappointment issued from the hoarse throats of the hometown crowd, Battle again took the snap and rifled one over the middle for Jones. *KABOOM!* Clobbered by Craig Bumhoffer just as the ball touched his fingers. INCOMPLETE!

"I don't know, Billy Bob, we just might stop 'em."

"Here they come, Tyson."

While the crowd held its breath, Battle conferred with Coach Crimen on the sideline, then he came to the line, rattled off the signals, and let one go for McCann on the 10—Broken up by Bowers! INCOMPLETE!

HOORAY MORGAN! KICK BUTT!

"We held 'em, Billy Bob! We held 'em!"

"Yeah we did!" gloated the Chancellor, once more feeling Bunny Culpepper's body against his at the window.

"Goddam overtime!" cursed Al Crimen as his kicking unit lined up at the 17. "There's nothin' I hate more than overtime."

Then, as 80,000 pairs of eyes turned toward the north end of Memorial Stadium, and another 6,000,000 ears bent toward their radios, Randy Brunt hiked to Tim Battle, who set it down for Ty McCay, who kicked it. IT'S UP! IT'S—DEFLECTED!!! by Morgan's Elijah Caroon. NO GOOD!

"*&^%#(*+(^%#@%&#@&*$! Offsides! They were offsides!" screamed Al Crimen, running onto the field—but to no avail. Unbelievable though it was, Morgan had defeated the Wave in Apaloochee, 24 to 21.

KICK BUTT! KICK BUTT! KICK BUTT!

CHAPTER 9
The Week of September 11

Tom Hanagan had been on the phone non-stop for two days. And Tuesday afternoon the calls were still coming in. "I told you so, Roscoe! Trust me. This is gonna be our year. Number one!"

"That's right, Harlan, numero uno! And I feel good about this coming Saturday too. . . . I SAID WE'RE GONNA WIN THIS WEEK TOO! . . . That's right, Mr. Gooch. And you have yourself a good rest of the week. I'll see you in Cambridge on Saturday—I SAID I'LL SEE YOU IN CAMBRIDGE ON SATURDAY!"

Click.

One more win, thought Tom, *and I'll have ole Gooch's five million, for sure.*

"I've got those season ticket figures you wanted, Mr. Hanagan."

Tom motioned to Savannah to come into the office. "How we lookin'?"

"Mrs. Mumphrey says she's sold 5,000 additional seats since Monday mornin'."

Tom looked at the print-out. "Awright!"

"And this just arrived for you, special delivery." Savannah handed Tom a manila envelope postmarked Lexington, KY. He tore it open and pulled out an oversized greeting card with a photo of a topless beach-bunny fanning herself with a copy of *Sports Illustrated.* "When you're hot," it said—Tom opened the card—"You're hot! Congratulations, Bobby."

Tom chuckled and handed the card to Savannah. "That Bobby, she's a crazy one, isn't she?"

Not that crazy, thought Savannah, handing the card back to Tom. "So, did Dan Anderson call back yet?"

"Yes, he needs to talk with you about Nathan Berry."

"Ring him for me, wouldja, hon?"

While Savannah went to ring Admissions, Tom turned up the sound on the television that was flickering across his office.

"And you're telling us," said Oprah, *a look of amazement on her face, "that you graduated from college without ever learning how to read?"*

"Dat's right, Oprah."

"And for four years all you did was play basketball?"

"Dat's right."

"Hey, what's up Dan?" Tom turned down the sound.... "Thanks. ... Yeah, *Sporting News* is gonna do a feature story on the game.... You bet. So what's up?... Sure I remember Nathan Berry, Callahan brought him in to meet me last spring. Smart kid, polite too. But his stats (Tom wasn't referring to Nathan Berry's SAT scores) just weren't there.... I know, but I don't think we can offer him any money over here.... No, we've got too many other kids, like that McGovern boy, who need help.... Okay buddy, and remember, call me if you need any tickets."

The Admissions Director hung up and threw Nathan Berry's application on the minority-student financial aid rejection pile, then he ran down his list of federal and state scholarships to see if there was any way he could find some additional non-Athletics Department assistance for Adonis McGovern, an academically challenged running back in whom Coach Star had expressed considerable interest at their last meeting.

After trying unsuccessfully to reach Jan and set up a time when they could both meet with Mrs. Grinder, the school principal, to talk about their oldest daughter's deportment problem—Erin had recently bloodied the nose of the little boy who sat beside her in homeroom—Tom headed off to the practice field to check in on Coach Star.

"Hey buddy!"

"What's up, Tom?"

"We are! Man, what a day!"

"Good, huh?"

"Fantastic."

"Awright! Bowers, Lewis, break it up! Save it for the Moccasins on Saturday. Reggie, run the 16 Blue series again."

"Yeah, Brewster called two times today to say how pleased he was with the way things are goin'. And get this, Tony, he said you did a brilliant job Saturday."

"I'm honored—NO! NO! NO! Dewey, you broke too soon."

"Everybody in good shape?"

"So far. Ritter's a bit banged up, but nothin' bad."

"By the way, did you hear about Red Carlisle?"

"No, what?"

"Picked up for driving under the influence last night."

"Serves him right."

"On Tubman Avenue."

"Humm."

"I guess ole Red was goin' to get hisself soma that brown suga'." Tom laughed. "So how you feel about Saturday?"

"Don't know, just don't know."

"You still plannin' on throwin' Wallace at 'em?"

"We'll see. THAT'S RIGHT! Dumptruck, spin off that linebacker. Let's do it again!"

"I hope so. His father has been calling me ten times a day."

"Is that all?'

"Sometimes I think the old man really is unbalanced. But anyways, I gotta scoot."

"Awright, Tommy, and by the way"—Star turned around and looked his friend in the eyes— "I'm proud of you."

"What?"

"You know what I mean, you're doin' a good job. Keep it up."

"Thanks, Tony." Tom beamed. Praise from Tony had always meant the world to Tom. Since childhood he had looked up to Tony like an older brother. *Yeah, I gotta admit*, he said to himself as he made his way across the practice field toward Calhoun, *Tony and Cliff were right. I was startin' to lose it. Thank goodness I finally saw the light. Just look what's happened already. I start to clean up my act and BINGO, I'm sittin' back on top of the pile.... Now if I could only get Jan to lighten up.*

• • •

Strength coach Brad Ballings left the Calhoun Complex early Tuesday afternoon to prepare for a dinner party at his newly redecorated downtown condo.

"Get away from there, Mrs. Whiskers!" he said, shooing his Persian cat off the dining room table as he tidied up an enormous arrangement of baby's breath, turtlehead and blazing stars that Rinaldo the florist had created for his party. "Bad widdle kitty cat," purred Brad, picking up the snow-white feline in his muscular arms and rubbing her soft fur against his cheek. "Now let's see, where will we put Arlo Plummer?... Humm... How 'bout next to Lance?... Yes, that's perfect," he said, pausing a moment to picture the handsome young lineman in his mind before placing a rainbow-colored place card in front of a crystal and china place setting that would have made the wealthiest Metro matron cluck with admiration. "And Mitch?"

At that moment, Brad's roommate Rob Williams walked through the front door with two loaves of French bread under his arm.

"Yoohoo, I'm home!" shouted the theater teacher.

"I'm in here, Rob!"

"Oh Brad, it looks just gorgeous!"

"Go take a look in the kitchen."

"Ooooh! Yummy!"

"Chicken a la regence with escargots maison and—"

DING A LING, DING A LING

"Who could that be?"

"I'll get the door, baby.... Brad, it's a Mr. DeVito for you."

DeVito, that stupid asshole, cursed Brad under his breath. "C'mere and watch the sauce, will ya, sweetie?" Brad slipped off his apron, flexed his muscles, and headed for the door.

"What are you doin' here, Al? I thought you said you'd be in town tomorrow."

"That's what I thought, but I'm goin' back to Miami early."

"And what the hell are you doin' here during the day?"

"Benny told me to deliver your order."

"All right, all right, pull the truck down around back."

"You need some help?" asked Rob as Brad walked through the kitchen down the stairs to the utility room and garage.

"No thanks, it's just the delivery man with the vitamins for the boys. I'll be right up, just keep stirring that sauce till it gets thick."

"Okay, honey."

When Brad opened up the garage door, Al was standing there with a large cardboard box in his arms that read "Fabrica en Mexico."

"Put the boxes over there."

"You better open 'em up and check 'em out. Remember what happened last time."

"Yeah, you're right." Brad tore open the top of a box and examined the contents. "Bulloxen, Dianabol—

"That was quite an upset on Saturday."

"Yeah."

"Think you can do it again this week?"

"Who knows?"

"I saw the Cottonmouths play last week. They're a good football team."

"Did you get the Lipoplex I wanted?"

"Yeah, it's in the other box. And from what I hear, you're gonna need that stuff this year."

"They're turning up the heat, huh?"

"That's the poop," said the drug deliveryman, tearing open a third box and rummaging around. "But don't worry, that Lipoplex works. It can mask anything. Oh, and before I forget, here's a little gift from Vinnie especially for you."

"Delatestryl! I'm touched. How much do I owe you?"

• • •

Dean Henry Robinson was sleepy. The chicken fried steak that he'd had for lunch, the stuffiness of his office, and Jo Ann Jenkins' unimaginative account of her date rape were glazing his eyes over.

"Yes, I understand," said Robinson, suddenly pulling himself up in his chair and straightening his bow tie, "but you said there were no witnesses?"

"Of course not," said the curly-haired sophomore from Little Rock who had come to the Dean to complain about Craig Bumhoffer raping her the previous night at the SAE house.

"But you admit that you went into the room with him?"

"Well, yes, Dean Robinson, but not so he could rape me."

"I realize that, Jo Ann, but rape is not only a very serious charge, it's also extremely difficult to prove."

"But that's what he did! He raped me! I asked him to let me go, he said no, and—"

"Now hold on a second. You admit that you'd been drinking, correct?"

"Yes."

"Drinking heavily?"

"Well—"

"And you know, of course, that you could be suspended from school for that."

"Well, er, I guess so, but—"

"Now I know how you feel, Jo Ann, I really do. And don't get me wrong, I'm not saying you shouldn't pursue your legal right to bring charges against Mr. Bumhoffer. Why, just last week, we expelled a young man for harassing a fellow student over her sexual orientation. All I'm trying to say is if I were you I would consider very carefully what I was getting myself into before I registered a formal complaint against Mr. Bumhoffer. Do your parents know about this?"

"Well, no."

"That's something else to think about. But whatever you do, I want you to know I'll stand behind you one hundred percent." The Dean rose from his chair.

"All right, Dean Robinson, thank you for your help. I'll think about it tonight and call you tomorrow."

"Good," smiled the gray-haired educational psychologist as the buxom young coed began to walk out. "And try not to let this traumatize you too much. Have you been to see the University psychiatrist, Dr. Moechus? He might be someone good to talk to.... Here's his number."

"Thank you, Dean Robinson."

"All right, Jo Ann, and remember to call me."

When he returned to his desk after seeing Miss Jenkins out, the Dean picked up the phone. "Margaret, would you ring Tom Hanagan's office please? . . . Hello Savannah, this is Dean Robinson, is Tom in? . . . *Strangers in the Night, la la la la la* . . . Oh, hello Tom, this is Henry.... Yes ... I just finished talking with Jo Ann Jenkins, and just between you and me, I think she's having second thoughts. . . . Of course I know how upset Mr. Bumhoffer must be about all this. But, as I was saying, my feeling is that after she thinks the whole thing over, she'll see the wisdom of letting the matter rest."

● ● ●

"I knew you'd want me to stop off and say good-bye before we left for Cambridge," said defensive back coach Wesley Woods as he stood in the doorway of Noweeta Hayes' office at 9:00 Friday morning, reeking of Macho brand sandalwood cologne.

"Good-bye."

"Now, is that any way to treat a brotha'?"

"Get outta here, would you, Wesley," said Noweeta, wheeling around in her chair to look for a file in the bookcase, atop which sat busts of Nefertiti and John F. Kennedy.

"And I thought you liked black folks, or maybe I jus' ain't good enough for you no more...."

"Look Wesley, you're really starting to get on my nerves," she said, turning back around to face him.

"That ain't what you used to say."

"Whatever may have happened between you and me is over."

"Oh I get it," he said, closing the door behind him as Noweeta rose from her chair.

"I want you out of here! Immediately!"

"Oh you do, do you, well, yassa, Miss Hayes, anything you sez. I'll be a good little nigga' and jus' shuffle on back to the cotton patch."

"Please!"

"Please what?! Fuck your brains out the way you want me to?"

"Go! Right this moment!"

"All right, Miss High and Mighty College Administrator. If that's the way you want it. But don't you think for one minute I don't know what you're up to."

"OUT!"

"Okay baby, okay," said Wesley, "but you can bet I'll be back."

• • •

The sun rose blood red in Cambridge on Saturday. And by game time, the mercury had climbed to a stifling ninety-seven degrees.

Fifteen seconds to go, Butch....

NOTHING ELSE HAS THE POWER!

NOTHING ELSE MAKES YOU FEEL SO ALIVE!

PEPSI

Three, two ... one, you're on!

Hel-lo, sports fans. This is Butch Sanders comin' to you on the Morgan Knights Radio network this afternoon from beautiful Simpkins Field in Cambridge, Mississippi, where we've got a capacity crowd on hand to watch the J.P. Morgan Knights play the Cottonmouth Moccasins. Boy, you can feel the energy in the air down here this afternoon, eh Rudy?

Yeah, and the heat too, said Butch's color commentator, former Morgan tight end Rudy Marrow, looking down from the press box at the 75,000-plus fans roasting like goobers in the muggy sun.

They were hopin' we might get a little rain here earlier this morn-

ing, but—here come the Knights back on the field! Boy do they look fired up!

Yeah, they do, Butch. In fact, Coach Star was telling me he's never seen a team this pumped.

"Tarnation, it's hot out here," complained Chancellor Brewster as he took his seat between Dudley Dunning and Boomer Cox in the front row of the visitors' section.

"It must be a hundred degrees," said the sweaty, red-faced contractor, fanning himself with his program. "I don't know why they ever changed this to an afternoon game."

"Maybe 'cause that's the best TV time slot they could get playing us," said Dudley irritably.

AND YOU HAVE OUR GUARANTEE
*WE'LL KEEP YOU WARM THIS WINTER
SINKS HEATING AND COOLING, A NAME YOU CAN TRUST!*

Just one minute now, and we'll be kicking off here in Cambridge, folks. And I gotta tell you, this one feels like it's gonna be a real humdinger.

It certainly does, Butch.

And a humdinger it was—for the first five minutes, during which time the Moccasins scored twice, first on an eighty yard bomb, and three minutes later on an intercepted Muggins' pass they ran all the way back. Then the humdinger turned into a ho-hummer, as the Mocs and Knights began a defensive tug of war in which neither team advanced the ball more than fifteen yards.

"Phew! I don't know how much more of this heat I can take," said a very hot and frustrated Chancellor Brewster as P.U. Pointer loped back to punt for Morgan with 6:04 left in the second quarter.

"Me neither." Boomer mopped the back of his neck with a handkerchief and thought how good it would feel to be sitting in an air-conditioned bar sucking down a cold one.

"Dudley's sure been gone a long time."

"Yeah, I think he went to get somethin' for his headache."

BEECHWOOD AGED BUDWEISER
IT'S ALWAYS BEEN TRUE.... THIS BUD'S FOR YOU.

Welcome back, folks, to this broadcast of Fighting Knights Football coming to you from sunny Cambridge, Mississippi where, with 6:04 left to go in the second quarter, the UM Cottonmouths are leading the Morgan Knights 14 to nothin'. I tell you what, Rudy, this has been one hard hittin' half of football this afternoon.

Yeah, it really has, said the color man, watching Morgan offensive tackle Eddie Saxon being hauled off the field on a motorized gurney. *They've been pounding away down there like they're playin' for the national championship.*

And nobody's been able to get much of anything done since the opening five minutes.

No they haven't, Butch, and it's not hard to figure why in this heat. Man it must be a hundred and ten down on the field.

Actually, it was only one hundred and four on the Morgan bench where Tom Hanagan, like the players, was having trouble staying focused on the game as he replayed in his mind the ugly scene that had taken place between Jan and him Friday afternoon before he left for Cambridge. "What the hell are you talking about, Jan. I always stay in Cambridge Friday night." "And I supposed that little slut from your office is going to be there too, huh?"

The players around him suddenly leapt to their feet to cheer on Ezekiel Lincoln.

He's at the 50, the 45, the 40, 35, ridden down by Dokes just outside the 30 yard line. Boy oh boy, that was a crackerjack move by Lincoln, Rudy.

Yeah, Zeke's been threatening to intercept one all afternoon, Butch, and he picked just the right time.

"Awright now!" yelled Coach Star, desperate to break things open before half-time. "Let's put some points on the board! And Reggie, whatever you do, don't cough it up."

"Okay, Coach," said the quarterback, buckling up his chinstrap, sweat pouring from his face.

WHEN YOU OR SOMEONE YOU LOVE NEEDS HELP, *HAPPY HILLS—A HOME AWAY FROM HOME.*

Here we go, Rudy, first and 10 from the Moccasin 35. . . . Muggins at the line, takes the snap, drops back, looks right. . . . Ooh! pounded to the turf by number 72 Ronnie Hill. Man, that was some kinda hit.

Yeah it was, Butch. Reggie's gettin' up real slow. Um um um, that Hill and Wiggins are some mean customers.

They don't call 'em the bookends for nothin'.

"That aspirin startin' to work yet, Dudley?"

"Yes finally, I think, Bill."

"Good. We'll get outta this sun in a coupl'a minutes and you'll feel better."

"I'll feel better when we start scorin' some points."

The Chancellor had begun to think maybe Red Carlisle's column was right about Morgan getting lucky the week before.

Then suddenly Boomer Cox was on his feet, as Ricky Ritter churned his way through the heat stricken Moccasin defense down to the 28.

KICK BUTT! KICK BUTT!

"Third and 2. C'mon Reggie, c'mon now, c'mon!! No! No! No!"

"You see what I mean?" Dudley glowered, as Reggie threw one away on the near side. "No pass, no score."

"You're right. We aren't gonna beat these boys kickin' field goals," grumbled the Chancellor.

But three points can make a world of difference to a scoreless team. And when DeGama reared back on the next play and made it, Morgan 3 UM 14, the Knights took something more than hope into the locker room at half-time.

As the Cottonmouth Band drew into the shape of a coiled snake for the hometown crowd, Tom Hanagan, with a laminated pass hanging from his neck, stood banging on the Morgan locker room door.

"Who the fuck is—Oh, c'mon in, Mr. Hanagan," said Pat Pitouchi, a bloody bandage dangling from one of his rubber-gloved hands and a forceps in the other.

"Over here, Tommy," yelled Coach Star, who was huddled with Stitches Stevens and Doc Willis in the corner with Butt Bowers.

"I'm pretty sure there's nothing broken, Butt," said Dr. Willis. "I'll give your foot another shot before you go out for the second half."

"Thanks, Doc," said the free safety, whose instep had been stomped by Moccasin tight end Glen Ivey on the Knights' last defensive series.

"How's Saxon doin', Stitches?" asked the Coach, headed in the direction of the bathroom stalls in front of which lay Eddie Saxon, his right knee swollen purple and four times its normal size.

"Don't look good, Coach."

"Ligaments?"

"Um hum. And a fracture too," whispered Stitches as the Coach knelt down over the hulking lineman, whom minutes before Pete Cossacky had berated for being a "fucking cry baby."

"You okay, Eddie?" asked the Coach.

"Yeah, I'm cool," said the tackle, beads of sweat dotting his pain-etched face.

"We'll get that X-rayed just as soon as the second half starts."

"Man, this place looks like a war zone," said Tom, as Star grabbed his clipboard and headed across the locker room toward Jimmy Joe Wallace.

"Yeah, Cheatem's boys ain't pullin' any punches today. But neither are we." Star smiled and gave the thumbs up to Capone D'Amato, who had broken Cottonmouth tackle Biff Eagles' wrist just before the end of the first half. "No, I ain't worried about injuries, Tommy, what I'm worried about is Hill and Wiggins." With only four first downs in the whole first half and possession time of under ten minutes, the Coach knew his defense was getting tired. Before they wore out completely, he was going to have to bring in his secret weapon. "You ready, Jimmy Joe?"

"Yeah, Coach, I'm ready," said Jimmy Joe Wallace, nervously chomping on a wad of gum and rocking from one foot to the other.

"And how 'bout you, Edwardo?"

"I'z ready, Coach," answered Jimmy Joe's main receiver Edwardo Holmes.

"Okay then. How much time we got left, Porky?"

"'Bout three minutes, Coach."

"Awright, guys," yelled the Coach over the hubbub. "NOW LIS-TEN UP!"

• • •

"Yes, I'll be sure to tell Winnie you were asking for her, Eula. . . . Scuse me, Harlan, scuse me," said the Chancellor as he found his seat, relieved to be back in the broiling sun after the icy reception he'd received from the Morgan Athletic Club members at halftime.

"Here, Billy Bob, have a sip a' this."

"Thanks, Boomer. Humm. Now that's some good tasting soda," said the Chancellor, feeling the cool gin and tonic sliding down the back of his throat. "Where did you get that?"

"Sam brought it down from the gallery."

"Thanks Doc," said the Chancellor, turning around and winking at Sam Edwards.

"My pleasure."

"How's your head, Dudley?"

"Better, I guess."

The first five minutes of the second half, as aficionados of the game will tell you, are perhaps the most crucial in the contest. The team that's ahead has an opportunity to give its opponent the coup-de-grace, and the team that's behind has a chance to make it a new game. For the Moccasins and Knights, it was neither. They started up just as they'd left off.

Nothin' doin' on that last series for Morgan, Rudy.

You're right, Butch. Looks like they're back on the same seesaw they were on the first half.

But I'll tell ya, Muggins has been takin' some mean hits.

He sure has, Butch. Reggie just can't seem to find daylight anywhere this afternoon.

"Damn, why don't we throw it," grumbled the Chancellor, refreshed enough by a cloud that had drifted between the stadium and the sun to be angry.

"Because we can't!" growled Dudley Dunning, counting his change to make sure the vendor hadn't short-changed him on the cokes he'd just bought.

BE ALL YOU CAN BE
IN THE ARRRRMY
SEE YOUR LOCAL RECRUITER TODAY

Here we go again, Rudy. UM's ball on their own 37. Dokes takes the snap, hands off to B.J. Poke, and he's wrapped up at the 38 by Bumhoffer and Bowers.

I guess that foot of Butt's must be okay, Butch.

The way he's movin' it couldn't'a been too serious—which it wasn't: just a hairline fracture, which, thanks to the doctor, he couldn't feel.

For the next twelve minutes the Knights and Mocs, like punch-drunk fighters, kept pushing each other around, unable to land anything solid. Finally, with 2:47 to go in the third quarter, Dokes hit Smith from his own 38 with a 26 yard pass that he ran all the way to the Morgan 11 before he was ridden out of bounds.

YEAAA MOCS! GO! GO! GO!

As the sunburned crowd shook off its torpor and got to its feet, Bobby Cheatem huddled with his players and exhorted them "to stick it in there!"

But the Morgan defense was no woozy Kappa Delt on Homecoming party night. On the first play Bumhoffer dragged halfback

Ronell Grits down for a loss of two. And on the next Malenkovic stopped Willie Griffith at the line. Then, on third and 12, Butt Bowers sent quarterback Dokes flying head over heels, and in the melée that followed, Malenkovic refractured his fingers clawing the ball out of Griffith's hands.

MORGAN BALL FIRST AND TEN!

Good golly, Miss Molly, that was some kinda hit Bowers just put on Dokes!

You could hear that one all the way up here, Butch.

I tell you, Rudy, these guys are playin' for keeps.

Yes they are, said Rudy as he watched the Morgan offense huddle with Coach Star and Jackson on the sideline. *And here comes Muggins and—*

No, wait a second, said Butch, grabbing his roster sheet. *It looks like Coach Star is sending in number 4 Jimmy Joe Wallace at quarterback. And yes, it's number 3 Tutomo Tongo in for Ricky Ritter, number 36 Cochise Cubbins in for Symeon Smith. And hold the phone! They're lining up in a pro set, Holmes wide to the left, Tongo in motion to the far side, Wallace with the ball, he's droppin' back to pass. He's got Tongo open down the middle, complete at the 28!*

Dumfounded by the wholesale substitution of the backfield and line, the UM defense was thrown into confusion.

"Who the hell is this guy?" screamed Coach Cheatem into his headphones.

"Jimmy Joe Wallace, number 4," said his defensive spotter from the press box.

"I know that, you idiot! Whadda we got on him?!"

"Nothin', Coach."

"Whadda'ya gonna do, Shelby?!"

"I dunno, Coach," mumbled the Mocs' defensive coordinator, Shelby Adkins, as Wallace hit Cubbins at the 37 for a gain of 15.

"Well, you better think of something, quick!"

"Why the hell didn't Star put this kid in before?" yelled the Chancellor over the roar of the crowd.

"Who knows!" hooted Boomer in amazement as Wallace hit Dewey Dobbins on the UM 35.

Rudy, this is just flat-out amazing!
Yes it is, Butch.
And here comes Wallace back to the line. . . . under center, takes the snap, rolls right, looks left, he's got Holmes open in the end zone. . . .
   TOUCHDOWN!
   HOOOOOOOORAY MORGAN! KICK BUTT!
As DeGama trotted off the field after making it Morgan 10 Mocs 14, the defense charged back on, determined to get the ball back for Wallace. And four minutes later, after almost blocking a punt on the Mocs' 37, they did. In the interim, however, Coach Cheatem and his staff hurriedly devised a new defense that called for Hill and Wiggins to play soft, take away the short yardage pass, and turn Tongo and Cubbins inside.

Their adjustments worked. Deprived of the short pass, Morgan's next drive sputtered out on the Moc 48. And for the first ten minutes of the fourth quarter, the game once again turned into a defensive deadlock. But then, with 2:13 left to go, on a third and 4 at the Morgan 40, Sean Dokes scrambled out of the pocket on a busted play, panicked, and let one go for Griffith—that Morgan safety Asswad King tore out of his hands!
   Ho-lee smokes! gulped Butch.
   That's King's second interception of the day, and it couldn't'a come at a better time.
   You're right about that, Rudy.
   GO MORGAN! GO MORGAN! KICK BUTT!

"What the hell are you motherfuckers doing?!!" roared Bobby Cheatem, tearing off his headphones and messing up his styled hair.

"Black cat sequence," said Coach Star calmly, sending the offense back on the field with 1:34 left on the clock, sixty long yards to go, and a totally inexperienced quarterback at the helm. No one really thought Wallace could do it—except his father, who had waited for this moment for nineteen years, ever since the obstetrician had held up his first born and he had seen it had a penis. "C'MON JIMMY JOE! YOU CAN DO IT, BOY! YOU CAN DO IT!"

WE WANT YOU TO REST EASY.
OSGOOD SECURITY AND ALARMS SYSTEMS
KEEPING YOU *SAFE FROM* THEM.
Well, Rudy, this has sure been a whale of a game here this afternoon. And now it's all up to Jimmy Joe Wallace.
I tell ya, Butch, this kid has shown a lot of poise, no matter what happens.
And here we go. Wallace sets them down, takes the snap, drops back to pass . . . and he's pounded to the ground by defensive end Cory Momos.
Back at the line, Morgan out of the no huddle offense, Wallace with the ball, fakes to Tongo, rolls left. . . . sees a seam down the middle, and slides forward across the 50 for a FIRST DOWN!

"Shelby, do sumpin'!" yelled Coach Cheatem, looking up at the clock.
But before the Moccasin coordinator could signal in a blitz, Wallace stepped up to the line, sent Cubbins in motion to the near side, and BINGO! connected with Dobbins over the middle for another first down.
"C'mon, Jimmy Joe. Git one fo' ya' Momma!"
KICK BUTT! KICK BUTT! KICK BUTT!

Back to the action here in Cambridge, one minute left. Moccasins 14, Morgan 10. The Knights on the 46, second and 10. Wallace in at quarterback steps to the line, takes a quick snap from Smith, rolls left, sees Holmes at the 9! He's got it!. . .TOUCHDOWN! MORGAN KNIGHTS!

"THAT'S MY BOY! THAT'S MY BOY!"

"SONOFABITCH! WHAT THE HELL IS GOIN' ON!" roared Bobby Cheathem.

MAN ALIVE! I can't believe it, said Butch as DeGama put Morgan on top 17 to 14.
    Yeah, this crowd is in shock here, Butch.
    KICK BUTT! KICK BUTT!

Twenty seconds left to go, a befuddled Bobby Cheatem huddled with his kick-off return men on the 50 and put it to them as simply as he could. "I got 5,000 bucks for anyone who can run it back."
    But the Coach might as well have offered five million. Fifteen seconds later Sean Dokes threw his third interception of the day. And five seconds after that it was all over: Morgan 17, UM 14.

Inside the Knights' locker room the players were in delirium. KICK BUTT! KICK BUTT! KICK BUTT! MORGAN NUMBER ONE!... Half-clothed athletes and coaches wandered aimlessly about, hooting, hollering, and dousing each other with beer.... HOORAAAYYY!... butting heads, slapping backs, pounding lockers ... COACH STAR! COACH STAR! ... And amidst the mayhem and madness Chancellor Brewster stood in ecstasy, savoring the sweet scents of sweat and beer, the adolescent exuberance, the moment of victory, of life-affirming triumph.
    "Yes! This is what it is," he reminisced, "to be young and victorious." And for a few moments Billy Bob felt the exhilaration that thirty-five years before had been his, when, like these young men, he had reveled in victory, standing on a bench in the locker room at Texas State University, clad in his jock strap, beer in hand, singing a paean to his Alma Mater.
    "Congratulations, Chancellor! Great game!"
    "Oh thank you, thank you."
    Everywhere you looked there were rapturous faces.... Next to the shower where Boomer and Dudley stood beaming, as a crowd of reporters inteviewed Jimmy Joe Wallace. ... by the training tables

where Butch and Rudy were taping the Coach's wrap-up show . . .
beside the water fountain where Chancellor Brewster had just
pushed his way through the crowd and was hugging Tom Hanagan.

Yes, everywhere you looked there was happiness. . . . except on the
face of Reggie Muggins.

CHAPTER 10

The Week of September 18

"Yassa, that was one heck of a football game."

"Yes it was, wasn't it?" said Chancellor Brewster, his eyes still blinking from the flashbulbs, his heart still pounding a day later to the drums that had greeted the victorious players as they deplaned in Metro.

"Newspap'a said we oughta be in the top twenty."

No, there was no question, ruminated Billy Bob. *No matter what the second raters and almost-rans of this world might say, nothing beats winning.*

"Yassa, you got a lot to be proud of, Chanc'ler. Looks like dere's a big crowd here today." Lamont turned the Fleetwood into the long driveway that led up the hill to the River Bend Baptist Church, a capacious, white stucco house of God, with soaring white columns, pastel windows, and a newly renovated steeple that rose high above a half acre of administration buildings, Sunday school classrooms, and athletics facilities.

"Yes, it does look like a full house," said the Chancellor, who made a point of never arriving early for the 10:30 service.

Lamont pulled to a stop in front of the front porch steps, and Brewster saw his wife waving to him. Winnie and the other ladies on the Living Waters Gymnasium Fund-raising Committee had cooked—actually reheated—the ham and biscuits that Lamont and his wife Geneva had made for the seniors' brunch after the early service.

"Yoo hoo! Billy Bob!"

"Hello dear," said the Chancellor, who was no sooner out of the car than he was surrounded by a crowd of glad-handing, back-slapping brethren who wanted to share their belief that this was going to be the Knights' year. "Keep the faith, Lester."..."God willing, Duncan."

Saved by the bell five minutes later, the Chancellor and Winnie were escorted to their customary seats—third pew from the back on the aisle—by Deacon Edwin Adcock. "That was a fantastic game, Chanc'lor," whispered the tall, somber deacon, handing them that week's church bulletin as the congregation rose to join the choir in *Onward Christian Soldiers.*

Unlike many successful Southern Baptists of his generation, who had either converted to the more socially acceptable Presbyterian or Episcopal sects or given up the faith altogether, the Chancellor and his wife had remained true to their birthright religion. Although skeptical of nearly all the "revealed truths" to which the Baptist clergy claimed access, Billy Bob continued to have faith in the church—as he did education—as an agent of social change. Had not the great Dr. Martin Luther King, Jr., after all, been a Baptist preacher?

The congregation took their seats after the hymn and the Chancellor acknowledged Roscoe Barrett's congratulatory wink with a knowing smile. Then the grave, gray and grandiloquent Reverend Dr. Elmo Goodpasture rustled to the lectern to read the Old Testament Lesson.

> In the wilderness prepare the way of the Lawd
> Make straight in the desert a highway for owa God
> Ev'ry valley shall be lifted up
> And ev'ry mountain and hill be made low
> The uneven ground shall become level
> And the rough places a plain. . . .

Isaiah 40:3–4 was one of the Chancellor's favorite passages. The former dean of the theological school, the Rev. Dr. Rupert Chism, had recited it at the groundbreaking ceremony for the Felton Potts Sports Center. Yes, thought Brewster, a smile of satisfaction on his lips, *I have been about the work of the Lord: lifting up new labora-*

*tories, classrooms and hospital buildings—making J.P. Morgan a light
to the world: a beacon of equality and justice!*

Three prayers, two hymns, and one lengthy reading from Paul's
Letter to the Colossians later, the Rev. Roy Nash—whom the Rev.
Dr. Goodpasture had invited to speak on behalf of the Living Waters
Fund-raising Committee—strode up to the pulpit of the purple-carpeted, perfume-impregnated church, and began: "My dear brothas
and sistas, I have come here this mornin' to speak with you about a
subject that is of the gravest importance to every member of this
congregation, and every other congregation in this city." While the
Rev. Nash pleaded for funds to build a new gymnasium, the Chancellor's mind drifted back ... *to the scene in the Morgan locker room
the afternoon before.* . . . "And let us not forget, brothas and sistas,
that it was on the playin' fields of church-affiliated colleges and universities, and in the gymnasiums of campus YMCAs across this
nation that our great tradition of intercollegiate sports first took
shape." ... Then Billy Bob remembered *the pep rally out at the airport.* . . . "Yes, our commitment to ath-e-let-ics is a tradition that we
as Christians have cherished for hundreds of years. . . ." *and the
phone ringing off the hook with people calling to congratulate him.*
. . . "For if we do not give our children a place where they can escape
from the sin and depravity of this world, a place where they can
enjoy the good clean pleasures of sports. . . ." *No doubt about it,* the
Chancellor nodded, *to the victor go the spoils.* "Drugs, teenage preg-
nancy, violence in the schools—there's trouble everywhere you
look. And there's no escapin' it. No, not even here in our own community (*cough cough ... flutter flutter*), which is why, my friends, I
want you to consider how little the cost, but how great the blessin'
to our young people, if instead of comin' home from school in the
afta'noon, and sittin' down to listen to the latest piece of satanic
rock-and-roll music, or watchin' the newest pornographic music
video on the television, they could gather for Christian fellowship
with their friends in a new state of the art gymnasium. Three million
dollars may seem like a lot of money; but if you think about it,
which I'm sure you will, with the help of the One from whom all

blessings flow, I know you'll find it in your hearts to help us reach our goal and begin construction of this sorely needed facility."

• • •

"What a day!! What a beautiful day!" chortled Tom Hanagan, who hadn't felt better on a Monday morning in three years.... *Hell, in ten years, since I first met Jan,* he thought, *the year Carolina went to the Liberty Bowl.... No, there's nothing like winning. Brewster sure was singing a different tune at that meeting this morning—"Tom, I think it's time to start moving forward on Star's new contract."—No kidding, numbnuts!*

BUZZ BUZZ

"Yes, Dr. Redman ... Well thank you.... Yes, it was a great game. ... What? ... Jan cancelled our appointment tomorrow?! ... No, she didn't mention it to me.... She thinks you're on my side? ... That's ridiculous.... You're right.... No, I don't mind at all.... Whatever you can do will be appreciated. And by the way, if you need any tickets...."

Damn that Jan. Everything's comin' up roses and she's acting like a spoiled child. Hell, she's been out every night the past two weeks, and when she's home she's colder than ice. I know I haven't been a model husband, but—

BUZZ BUZZ

"Yes?"

"Mr. Acres from WBUX is calling."

"I'll take it. Hey Mort! What's hap'nin, big guy? ... Yeah, it was quite a game, wasn't it? ... Well thanks for saying that, Mort, but I can't take all the credit.... Well, that's true.... But anyway, what I needed to talk to you about is next season.... That's right, but at this point, buddy, I think we're gonna have to wait and see what everybody else.... I realize that.... But ... Whoa! Whoa! Hold on a second, Mort, you're talkin' to me now, not my sports information director.... That's all right...."

As Tom listened to the sales pitch of the man whom he had begged to continue broadcasting Morgan games less than six weeks ago, Savannah walked into the office with a note to tell him that Roscoe Barrett was on for lunch.

"Wait a second, would you, hon?... Yeah, I know you've done a great job for us, Mort...." As Savannah stood in front of his desk beaming at her victorious boss, Tom leaned back and shamelessly ran his eyes up and down her body. "I'm just gonna have to think about it, Mort." *Is she hot for me or what?* he thought. *I can smell the hormones in the air. That's human nature for you. Everybody loves a winner.* "Okay, Mort, we'll talk again soon.... No, I'll call *you*.... All right, bye bye."

Tom hung up the phone and rocked forward. "You know what, Savannah, you are looking *good* today."

Savannah blushed to the color of the blush painted on her cheeks.

"That Bill Conner is a lucky man to be escortin' you around town. I saw the two of you at the game on Saturday. He's bein' a good boy now, isn't he?" asked Tom, joking in earnest.

"Well, yes," she said coyly.

"And treatin' you right?"

"I suppose."

"Whadda ya mean, you suppose?"

"It's just he acts so—immature sometimes."

Oh man, wouldn't she just love for me—Whoa! What am I thinking? Control, Tommy! CONTROL.

"Oh well," said Tom, picking up a piece of paper in front of him, "he'll grow up."

• • •

"So what's the damage on the boys?" asked Coach Star Tuesday morning.

"Not too bad, Tony," said Ed Tarmeenian, his arms draped over the back of the crushed velvet couch in front of the Coach's desk. "Bower's foot is still pretty sore and I'm not sure about Lincoln's back. But besides that—"

"How about Malenkovic?"

"You know how it is with fingers, Tone."

"Yeah I do," said Tony, flexing the misshapen knuckles on his left hand.

"And Saxon?"

"Gone."

"For the season?"

"Yeah, Jet said that Stitches told him there's nothin' left of that left knee. And from what I hear, even Doc Thompson doesn't think there's much he can do."

"Poor fucker."

"Yeah, and I don't think Saxon's exactly been an academic over-achiever."

BUZZ BUZZ

"Yeah, Peaches, I'll take it. What's up, Chipper?" Chip Mulligan, an old acquaintance of Tony's and Ed's from the Pittsburgh Steeler days, had called to read an article he'd written about Morgan for *Sporting News*.

"Hottest team in the South. . . . Not too early to start thinking about a Bowl. . . . Great coaching staff. . . . Of course I love it," said Star after Chipper had finished his article. "Yeah, Eddie's sittin' right here. . . . Okay, I'll be sure to. . . . You're comin' to the game Satur-day? . . . Great . . . Okay, buddy, thanks for the call."

"You know, Tony, two weeks ago that sonofabitch wouldn't'a said hello if he'd passed us on the street, and now he's our long lost best friend."

"Hey, that's entertainment." Star shrugged.

"Thank God there's still a couple of us that ain't completely full of shit."

Star smiled.

"Speaking of which, I talked with Tomachek last night." Steve Tomachek was an Atlanta-based sports attorney and agent who spe-cialized in getting athletes and coaches in and out of old and new con-tracts. "He says if we was smart we'd start lookin' around right now."

"Yeah, I know, he called me last week too. But I been so swamped I haven't had a chance to call 'im back. Besides, I think we oughta hear what Tom's got to say first, don't you?"

"I guess so, Tony, but with things goin' like they are we should really be shopping around. I know how you feel about Hanagan, but we gotta think of ourselves first. Brewster and his buddies might be smiling now, but you know as well as I do that we don't mean shit to any of these rednecks. You're laughing, but it's the truth. You know how Brewster was talkin' at the beginning of the season. I mean, this is the land of opportunity we're livin' in, and if we don't take it while we can, we could wind up gettin' screwed."

"You're right."

"I'm tellin' ya, Tony, you and me are a great team, don't be stupid and let your loyalty to Hanagan blind you to the facts of life. Oh, and before I forget" — Ed lowered his voice — "Milt Lee called to tell me he sold every one of those tee-shirts and sweats, and he's got 30,000 more on the way."

• • •

"Thank you, Stefan, it was a wonderful performance," said Jan, looking at her watch later that evening. But I really think I should be going."

"But it's only nine-thirty and you haven't eaten yet."

"I know. I'll just pick up something on the way home."

"Jan, can I ask you question?" Stefan paused at the bottom of the stairs in front of the B.J. Clower Auditorium. "Are you afraid of me?"

"Afraid of you? Don't be ridiculous, Stefan, I just need to get home. It's Tuesday night, and my housekeeper's been there since seven o'clock this morning."

"And? —" he said, pouting like Jan's youngest.

"All right, Stefan, if it means that much to you, let's go."

"Yes, waitress, the Chablis is mine, thank you. I didn't know Sonia Wizlowska had studied in Moscow."

"Oh yes, I dance with her many times." Stefan raised his wine glass. "And now what shall we toast?"

"Let's see, how 'bout to dance?"

"Yes, to dance, to life, to you, Jan, the most beauteeful woman in all Metro."

"You're laying it on a little thick, Stefan, don't you think?" Jan laughed.

"No, it's true, you are," he said as the waitress reappeared from behind a fern and served them their fettucine. "Why would I lie to you, Jan? In my country, when man thinks woman is beauteeful, he tells her how he feels."

"Even," she said, taking a bite of her pasta, "when she's married?"

"You think like American male, Jan. Just because woman is married or over thirty doesn't mean she can't still be beauteeful."

"No, it doesn't," she agreed, buttering a piece of French bread which Stefan had torn from the loaf and handed to her.

"A woman doesn't begin to be truly beauteeful until she is—"

"As old as me, right?"

"You're being unkind. I'm tellink you truth. American men think of women as—how you say, sex objects. The younger the better, the less work they have to do to relate."

"Well, that's certainly true," said Jan, picturing Savannah McLane in her mind.

"To me a woman without character, without soul, is nuthink—a silly child, someone who only another child could be interested in."

Jan munched on a crust of bread and looked into the flame of the candle on the table, thinking about her husband.

"They are like stupid little boys."

"Yes, Stefan," she said, raising her eyes to meet those of the handsome dancer, "they are."

• • •

"You sure Bow Wow said (*snorrrt*) this stuff was pure, Tootie?"

"He said he jus' got it in from Miami this mornin', Reggie."

"He's lyin' (*snorrt*) and you're a dumb ass for buyin' it."

"Man, I jus' did what you told me. I know how you like chillin' on Wednesday night."

"You don't know shit, Tootie. Here, you have the rest of this."

Reggie Muggins threw himself back in the red velveteen armchair that sat beneath a poster of Snoop Doggy Dog in his off-campus apartment.

"I know one thing, Reggie. You in a bad mood," said the football player's sidekick, leaning over the glass-topped coffee table snorting another line through the gold-plated coke straw that Reggie had given him along with a matching pinky ring for his twenty-first birthday. "You even chased Teeny away today."

"What if I did," said the quarterback, flipping through the channels on the TV with the remote control.

"You been bent outta shape since you got back Saturday night." Tootie got up to get a bottle of Boone's Farm that was chilling in the refrigerator. "And we both know why."

"That Wallace ain't shit. And everybody's actin' like he's Dan Marino or somebody."

"Yeah, they was talkin' all about him on the news tonight. Hey, der he is right now." Tootie pointed to the screen where footage of Saturday's game was being run while Joe South interviewed Coach Star.

"*Well Coach, Jimmy Joe Wallace sure looked impressive on Saturday, didn't he?*"

"*Yeah, he did, but he wasn't the only one who turned in a great performance.*"

"*That's true, Coach. But how 'bout it, is Wallace gonna start on Saturday?*"

"*I don't think so. As far as I'm concerned, Muggins is still our number one quarterback.*"

"Like hell I am," growled Muggins, flipping the remote to the Disney channel where a suburban housewife was being raped by a masked intruder; then to CNN where a recently paroled sex offender was holding four second graders and their teacher hostage with an Uzi; and finally to *The Letterman Show* where the diamond-studded, former football star, now film actor, Alonzo Washington, was extolling the virtues of Hollywood, professional sports, and capitalism. "That Coach Star's a lyin' mothafucka."

"Yeah, he is—man, dig that ring on Lonzo. I hear he's been goin' out with one a' them Kennedy bitches."

"Speakin' of which, where's Nateesha and Yolanda?"

"They said they'd be here as soon as they could, Reggie."

"Er, excuse me, nurse, could you tell me how to get to Room 1208?"

"Sure. Take a right at the end of the hall, then a left, then another quick right and a left, and you'll see it. By the way, that was a great game Saturday, Coach."

"Thanks."

Coach Star approached Eddie Saxon's room and saw the light of a television flickering through the half-open door. He stepped closer to listen if anyone was awake inside and heard someone sniffling as if they'd been crying. Not wishing to intrude, Tony turned around and was about to leave when he was met by a maternal-looking old black nurse carrying a tray with a large dish of chocolate ice cream, a Diet Coke, and two sleeping pills in a small plastic cup.

"Lordy be, if it ain't Coach Star himself."

"I was gonna stop in and say hello," said Star, nodding toward 1208, "but I think there's somebody in there with Eddie."

"Ain't nobody in there but Mista Saxon. Everybody went home 'bout a half hour ago."

"I thought I heard somebody in there."

"I don't know what you heard, but I know Mista Saxon's in there alone."

"Say, how's he doin' anyway?"

"Why don't you go in and ask him yourself. Lemme see if he's decent." Nurse Price pushed open the door and entered the young athlete's room. "Here's that ice cream you wanted, baby, and you got a visitor to see you too. Coach Star's out in the hall."

A moment later, after hearing Eddie blow his nose, the Coach entered the room and took a seat in the chair next to the bed where the former starting right guard lay, his left leg stretched out in a cast attached to a stirrup dangling from a pulley.

"So how you feelin', Eddie?"

"Not too bad as long as I got this." The sandy-haired, red-eyed ex-athlete forced a smile and showed Coach Star the push button switch that released morphine drip into his IV.

"Yeah, I know how it hurts," commiserated Tony, smiling and knocking on his own knee. "But in a coupl'a months you'll be on your feet, good as new."

"You really think so?" asked the 295-pound child.

"I know so."

"That ain't what the docs say."

"Hey, whadda they know? If you want it bad enough," lied the Coach, "there's nothin' you can't do."

"I guess you're right." Eddie shifted painfully in the bed.

"Well," said Star, after making small talk for fifteen minutes about the weather, pennant races, and the miracles of modern medicine, "I guess I better get goin'. I got a lot a work to do."

"Yeah, I know, Coach. Thanks for comin'."

"I guess the guys'll be up to see you tomorrow."

"The nurses can't wait," joked Eddie.

"Hang in there." Star punched Eddie on the arm and turned to go.

"Hey, Coach."

"Yeah."

"Kick some butt for me this Saturday, wouldja?"

As Tony squeaked off down the hall in his custom-cushioned Nikes, Eddie Saxon felt the pain returning to his mutilated knee and reached for the button on his drip. Then the morphine coursed into his blood and he felt better, until Jay Leno broke for a commercial and Eddie saw two perfectly formed models frolicking in the surf together, while the announcer extolled the virtues of health, vigor and Ocean Mist deodorant soap. Tears then filled his eyes. Though Eddie had never bothered to read any of his class assignments, he could read the writing on the wall. He knew that his football days—his days to live the high life and enjoy all the wonderful things American society lavishes on the young, strong and healthy—were over.

• • •

"OHHH YEAAH! WE DID IT! WE DID IT!" yelled Tom Hanagan, beside himself with joy. His old Tar Heel fraternity brother, Bill Dugan, who now worked for NBC Sports, had called to tell him that Morgan's name had come up at their weekly meeting! One more win, and NBC might consider broadcasting a Knights game as their regional game of the week. The thought of an extra million dollars made Tom literally break out in a sweat. And if that weren't enough, just after hanging up with Dugan, Blake Stevens called to tell him that Harlan Gooch had ordered his attorney to start drafting a bequest to the Athletics Department.

Tom walked around his office in a state of nervous excitement, thumbs hitched under his braces, humming a combination of *I Feel Good* and *Everything's Coming Up Roses*. He passed by the liquor cabinet and all at once felt extremely thirsty.

What the hell, it's almost four-thirty, a little pop wouldn't hurt, he said to himself. And he went over to the trophy case and poured himself a little one.

As the Grey Goose hit his belly, he heard his phone buzz. "I got it, Savannah.... What? Sold out! You're kidding me! AWRIGHT! I knew those ads would work. And only five hundred seats left for Homecoming? Yabba dabba do!"

Twenty minutes later, after trying to reach Jan and remind her he would be home late—*Damn, she's always busy*—Tom poured himself one more little one and stepped into his waiting room. Savannah was tidying up her desk for the following morning. She looked up at him when he walked in and smiled. "You know what, Tom?"

"No, what?"

"You look *good* today."

A playful look came over Tom's face. "Good?" he asked.

Savannah smiled coyly. "You know what I mean," she said. "Happy."

• • •

"What a day! Hey Tony?"

"Yeah, nice day," said the Coach when Tom arrived at the field twenty minutes later. "You're not gettin' off fast enough on that dive, Plummer. When I say fire out, I mean it."

"Guess who I just got off the phone with?"

"I dunno, Tommy. Let's go, Dewey, hustle up!"

"Bill Dugan at NBC."

"Yeah?"

"They're thinking about us for the regional game of the week."

"Really? That's great!"

"I thought you might think so," said Tom proudly. "If we win this one, we're a shoo-in."

"Yeah, if—," Star shook his head as Muggins threw one two feet over his receiver's head. "Muggins, c'mere a minute, wouldja?"

As Tom stood there on the sidelines, the late afternoon sun shining on his face, the warm autumn breeze tousling his hair, he was sure he'd never felt better in his entire life. Here he was, 3 and 0, director of one of the biggest and classiest athletics departments in the country. A grown man still playing kid's games and getting paid over a quarter of a million dollars a year to do it. *Yeah, I really am a lucky guy,* he thought. *Not as lucky as Terry Bradshaw or Joe Montana, maybe, but compared to the rest of the people in the world....* It was impossible now for Tom to believe how wretched he'd felt three short weeks before; now that everything was working out the way he wanted, the way he'd planned, the way it should.

"I was afraid this would happen," grumbled Star, rejoining Tom on the sidelines.

"Muggins is upset about Wallace, huh?"

"Yeah, and we're gonna need him. NO. NO. NO, Ritter! You're getting off too slow!"

"You know what, Tony?" said Tom.

"No, what?" said Star, his eyes riveted on the field.

"You need to relax."

Star turned to face him and Tom grinned boyishly at his friend. "It's what you've been telling me."

Star didn't smile. "We've been very lucky these past two weeks, Tommy."

Tom shrugged.

"I'm not kidding. The Raccoons are tough customers. And Dim Haley's one of the best coaches in this league."

"Yeah, but—"

"But nothin'. One dislocated shoulder, one broken leg, and poof, there goes the season."

"You're right about that. But so far, so good."

No response.

"Well," said Tom, "I gotta run. I'm meeting Bobby Brooks for cocktails."

The Coach eyed his friend.

"Don't worry, Tony, everything's under control. I'll meet you at the Time-Out at 8:30."

Tom had reluctantly let Bobby talk him into picking her up at the Marriott. And at 6:15, he walked into the hotel and dialed her room. Not back yet. He sat down at the bar in the lounge and ordered a martini, and ten minutes later felt someone sneak up from behind and slip their hands over his eyes.

"Guess who?"

Tom smelled Tabu and knew.

"Sorry I'm late." Bobby flashed Tom one of her loveliest smiles. "Come on up and mix me one while I freshen up."

"Ah, maybe I shouldn't—"

"Oh for God's sake, Tom, come on."

"The vodka's in the fridge," said Bobby, stepping out of her heels as she closed the door to the hotel room. "I'm gonna jump in the shower a minute." Before Tom could object, she disappeared into the bathroom.

Now, having drinks in a hotel room with a young woman he wasn't married to was not a new experience for Tom—in fact, he and the present Mrs. Hanagan had enjoyed cocktails at the Courtyard in Raleigh more than once when there was still another Mrs. Hanagan.

Maybe that's the reason Tom began to feel so uncomfortable. *If Jan ever knew I was here*—Tom shuddered—*it would be all over. I know her.*

"That was a helluva game Saturday."

"Did you say something, Bobby?" he asked, pouring the vodka over the ice in the glasses.

"I said that was one helluva game Saturday," called Bobby from behind the half-opened bathroom door.

"Yeah it was, wasn't it." Tom took a long drink and began to pace.

"Honey, could you do me a favor?" He stopped walking. "In the bag on the bed there's a bottle of body lotion. Could you slip it through the door?" Tom walked over to the bed and found the lotion in her bag beside a box of cigars and a pair of black lace panties. He reached through the door with the bottle.

"Listen, Bobby, maybe I should go downstairs and wait."

She turned off the shower. "Lands sake, suga', I'm not gonna try to jump your bones, honest."

Tom thought a moment and went over and sat down.

"And I'll tell you anotha' thing." Tom heard the faucet turn on and off. "It's about time people started givin' you the credit you're due. Let's face it, you're the one who's responsible for what's been happenin'."

"I don't know if I can take *all* the credit," said Tom modestly.

"A smart goodlookin' guy like yourself, hell, you'd probably be successful at anything you tried."

The thought had occurred to him.

Then suddenly the bathroom door opened and Bobby stood there, her beautifully tan body barely concealed beneath a skimpy satin kimono. "Is that my drink there, lova'?"

"Ah, yeah," said Tom a lump starting to form in his throat.

"I hope it's a strong one."

Tom reached out to give Bobby her drink, and as she took it, her kimono fell open. . . .

CHAPTER 11

Saturday, September 24

KICK BUTT! KICK BUTT! KICK BUTT!

KICK BUTT! KICK BUTT! KICK BUTT!
There hadn't been so much excitement at Fulsom Field since Doc Fulsom's team won the conference championship in 1956.

GO KNIGHTS! GO KNIGHTS!

In a world stripped of all that is sacred by science and commerce, 65,000 fans were on hand on this warm autumn evening to watch the Cinderella story come true.

KICK BUTT! KICK BUTT! KICK BUTT!

Never had school spirit run so high. The campus police had actually had to break up a pep rally the night before when a mob of drunken and disorderly students nearly set fire to Alumni Hall with a flaming effigy of a raccoon.

BOM Tiddi BOM Tiddi BOM BOM BOM!

"Well, Billy Bob," said Boomer Cox, leading everyone in the skybox in a toast to his friend, "here's to your health and to victory."

"To victory and health."

"And to regional telecast revenue," said Brewster, clinking his glass against Tom's. The Chancellor had just found out that Tom had swung a last minute 200,000 dollar deal to have the game broadcast locally.

"I can't believe it," said Abe Koppel, surveying with delight all the Kick Butt merchandise the fans were wearing.

"I told you!" yelled Milt Lee in his friend's hairy ear as DeGama's kick-off sailed through the end zone. "And if we win tonight, we'll move twice as much product for Homecoming."

KICK BUTT! KICK BUTT!

"You remember what I told you, Kelvin?"

"Yassa."

"Awright then," said Raccoon head coach Dim Haley, snapping the wire of the headphone set like a whip, "Go git 'em!"

As the teams came to the line, Aunt Inez and Uncle Clifton, who had been feeling "kinda puny" all week, joined the crowd in a rousing *BIG D* chant. And on the first play from scrimmage, Raccoon halfback Hardee Mimms got flattened by Bobo Thomas behind the line.

"Yeah, mothafucka!" growled Bobo, who had learned by now to talk trash with the best of them.

"I always knew this here Star had what it takes," said Harlan Gooch to Camelot Club Exec Blake Stevens.

"Yes, you did, Harlan," agreed Blake, conveniently forgetting the brow-beating the supermarket mogul had given him about Coach Star a month earlier.

"We got 'em on the run already," whooped Buster Hooper, slapping Felton Potts on the back.

I believe you're right, brotha."

BLOCK THAT PUNT! BLOCK THAT PUNT!

"Awright now, Reggie, be cool and remember what I toldja, if the play gets busted, eat it. We can't afford any turnovers. You got it?"

"I got it, Coach," said Muggins sullenly.

"Awright!" yelled Coach Star as the Morgan offense took over at their own 37. "This is gonna be our night!"

KICK BUTT! KICK BUTT! KICK BUTT!

But ten minutes into the first quarter, it was obvious that Cinderella was going to have a hard time getting her foot into the slipper. Red Carlisle had been correct: the Raccoon front four were giving Morgan more than they bargained for. But rather than risk an interception, Coach Star stuck to the ground. Though even that wasn't failsafe, as he found out three plays later when Mongol Harris fumbled a pitch-out and Raccoon linebacker Rinaldo Spriggs picked up the loose change and ran it all the way down to the Morgan 18.

UGGHHHH!

Backed up inside their own 20, the Morgan defense, however, hung tough. And after two bone-crunching tackles by Thomas and Einreich, and a near interception by Lincoln, they forced the Coons to settle for three.

WE WANT WALLACE! WE WANT WALLACE!

"I don't know what Star's waitin' for," muttered the Chancellor. "We oughta get Wallace in there."

"You're right, Billy Bob," concurred Boomer, clipping the end off a Macanudo.

"You got another one of those with you?"

"Sure do."

The Chancellor languidly ran the cheroot under his nose and was about to light it up when he heard a knock on the skybox door. *Jesus Christ! Paul Fisher and his wife.* Having forgotten that he had invited the new school of education dean up to see him—an offer he never intended Fisher to take him up on—Brewster was momentarily non-plussed. But he soon fabricated a smile and invited the anemic-looking professor and his unattractive spouse into the box.

"Come on in, Paul," he said, slipping the Macanudo into the inside pocket of his purple sport coat. "Glad you could make it. And this must be—"

"Mona," said the sociologist's wife in her metallic Chicago twang.

"Well, I'm pleased to meet you," said Brewster, introducing the Fishers around, wondering as he did if perhaps he hadn't made a mistake in his choice for the dean's position. Like many men and women, his opinion of a person was based in large part on what their mate looked like. And looking at Paul's frumpy wife, Brewster felt there must be something more wrong with the jock-sniffing sociologist than just the fact that he was your normal academic type.

"Well now, you tell Mose what you want to drink and come on over and take a look at the game."

"Gee, this is really fantastic," drooled Fisher, looking down where the ant-sized Raccoon offense had just run a reverse past its own 43.

"Here, try these." Boomer handed Fisher a pair of binoculars.

"C'mere Mona, honey, take a look at this."

"Chancellor Brewster tells me you're a regular sports fanatic," said Boomer.

"Oh yes."

"You look like you mighta played a little ball, eh?" lied Boomer.

"Varsity basketball at Oberlin," said the teacher proudly, making a motion as if he were shooting a foul shot.

Chancellor Brewster came up and threw his arm over Fisher's shoulder.

"Dr. Hayes and I were just talking about you yesterday."

"Really?" said Fisher. "Well, I certainly enjoyed working with her on our new communication major."

"And Noweeta enjoyed working with you too. She said the two of you pretty much saw eye to eye on everything."

Fisher nodded.

"Like for instance putting old Thaddeus Smith out to pasture."

Fisher looked puzzled.

"You did tell her you were going to ask Smith to retire, didn't you? Hey, look at that! We just intercepted!"

WE WANT WALLACE! WE WANT WALLACE!

"Oh no, not Muggins again," said the Chancellor along with 55,000 other angry Morgan fans.

BOOOOOOOOO! WE WANT WALLACE!

Now, as education psychologist Lou Sazlow would have told you—if you asked or maybe even if you hadn't—negative reinforcement is invariably deleterious to the performance of athletes. And for the past fifteen minutes, whenever Reggie Muggins touched the ball, he heard a stadium full of disgruntled fans screaming for Wallace. No wonder, then, that after being booed for getting dumped for a three yard loss he got confused on the next play, ran out of the pocket, and POW! coughed up the ball on his own 49.

BOOOOOO! HISSSS!

"You okay, Reggie?" asked Coach Star, lifting his headphones off one ear.

"Yeah, I'm okay," said the mortified quarterback, too embarrassed to be surly.

"Don't let those assholes in the stands get to you. You're doin' all right."

But Reggie knew that he wasn't. His game was off. He just couldn't seem to get in the rhythm. He'd had the same problem all week.

Luckily for Morgan, Ed Tarmeenian's well-oiled multiple defense made it equally difficult for the Raccoons to get their rhythm, and had it not been for a field goal the Coons scored after Muggins' fumble and another three-pointer they kicked before the end of the first half, the Knights would have gone into the locker room tied, not down 6 to 0.

The Morgan faithful were not particularly friendly as the Chancellor and his party made their rounds at half time.

"I don't know why they don't put that Wallace boy in, do you, Bill?" "You sure Star knows what he's doin'?"

"Tom! C'mon over here a minute, wouldja?" said Brewster, flagging him down.

"Yes sir. . . . Hello Mrs. Brewster. Mrs. Cox. Mr. Cox."

"What the hell is Star up to?!"

"Up to?"

"You know what I mean. Why doesn't he put that Wallace boy in and start scorin' some points?"

Tom shook his head. "I've been wondering the same thing myself."

"Well then, why don't you go tell him to put Wallace in?" blustered Willard T. Sanders, who three weeks ago would have been content to see Morgan trailing only by six.

"If we're gonna be in a Bowl at the end'a this year, we gotta start playin' like it," growled Dudley Dunning. "I'm gettin' tired of always playin' catch-up."

"That's right! . . . You said it, Dudley! . . . Exactly my thoughts."

As the second half was about to get underway, Tom sidled up beside Coach Star on the sidelines and asked him if he was thinking about playing Wallace.

"Hey buddy," said Star, slipping on his headphones, "remember our rule, no questions during the game."

"Yeah, I'm sorry, Tony."

Then *KA-POW!* . . . the second half was underway.

WE WANT WALLACE! WE WANT WALLACE!

"I can't believe it! I just can't believe it! It's him again!" stormed the Chancellor. "Where did I put that damn cigar?"

As Reggie Muggins pulled himself off the ground after being dropped for a five yard loss—Teeny McAdoo's heart went out to him. She could tell that Reggie wasn't himself. He'd barely acknowledged her presence when she'd caught his eye. What's more, he hadn't shown up for the Cinema Guild movie, as he did without fail, on Thursday night.

WE WANT WALLACE! WE WANT WALLACE!

"I don't know what he's up to myself," said Raccoon offensive coordinator Spanky Smuthers. "Maybe that Wallace kid's hurt."

"Yeah, maybe, but I don't trust Star," said head coach Dim Haley as he watched his punt return team take to the field.

A thousand miles away, meanwhile, Dr. Tilford D. Stinson, President of the University of Cosmopolis, and his athletics director, Edward "Howdy" Morrison, were also watching the Morgan game.

"Well, Tilford, whad'da you think?" said Howdy, who had stopped watching the drubbing his Cosmopolitans were taking seventy-five rows below and tuned in the Morgan game by satellite.

"I tell ya, Howdy, I'm thinkin' that with our organization and backin', Star just might be able to do great things down here."

"I think you're right, Tilford," said the gray-haired athletics director, refilling his drink at the bar. "And bein' a Yankee like he is, I think he might get on better with this new breed of boys we got playin' for us." The "new breed" Howdy Morrison was referring to was the increasing number of African-Americans on the team (eight-five percent) who were coming from the increasingly urbanized areas of their increasingly industrialized state.

"Yeah, ole Booger' jus' doesn't seem to be able to relate with the players anymore, does he?"

"No he dudn't. From what I hear, Star was born in the slums himself. He can relate. And if I'm not mistaken, he'll go where the money is."

"'Less he's dif'rent from everybody else in this business." Dr. Stinson grinned.

"I guess the next step is for us to get in touch with ole Hamilton Pigg and tell him what we've been thinkin'."

"Yup."

Back at Fulsom Field, with three minutes to go in the third quarter, neither the Knights nor the Coons had come within striking distance of each other's goal since the beginning of the half.

"What in the name of hell is he waitin' for?!" boomed the Chancellor, who had lost count of the bourbons he had consumed. "This is ridiculous!"

"Billy Bob, it's him!" hooted Boomer, pointing to the field as Jimmy Joe Wallace, Edwardo Hayes, Tutomo Tongo, and the guinea pigs trotted on the gridiron to a roar of approval.

LAY-DEES AND GENTLEMEN
NOW COMING IN TO PLAY FOR MORGAN....

"Well it's about time!" said Dudley Dunning, turning around in the Dunning Corporation skybox to check on the two industrial real estate developers from Guadalajara he was entertaining for the weekend. "Y'all havin' a good time?" he said, winking at the two buxom, former 4-H'ers who had arrived at half time from the Daisy Mae Escort Service to party with his guests.

Jimmy Joe brought the Knights to the line and Coach Haley conferred with his defensive coordinator to make sure their alternative defense was in place.

"Don't worry, Dim, they ain't gonna pull no fast ones on us."

No fast ones, true, but Morgan was able to mount a balanced, time-consuming drive that looked as if it might go all the way—until Tutomo Tongo dropped a third and 7 pass on the Coon nine-yard line.

OOOOOOOOO

Fourth and 7 from the 38. Amidst pounding drums, rattling seats, and 60,000 screaming voices, Coach Star conferred with his kicker.

"Well, Fernando?"

"I t'ink I get it, Coach."

"You sure?"

"Sure, maybe."

Noting the uncertainty in the young Brazilian's voice, the Coach decided to go for broke and try a fake field goal pass to tight end Dewey Dobbins.

An intelligent and gutsy call, which might have succeeded, had not the ball-holder, Anthony Gentry, thrown the pigskin three feet over Dobbins' head.

BOOOOOOOOOO

"WHAT THE HELL IS STAR DOIN'?!!"

"Beats me, Billy Bob." Boomer shook his head in disbelief.

As a buzz of hostility swept through the stadium, Dim Haley huddled with his offensive squad and told them he was "beginnin' to get flustrated," which his players knew could mean anything from running five miles of wind sprints on Monday to having their automobiles repossessed. "Now let's git to work."

But Ed's "hit men" were a stone wall. On first down, they upended Mimms at the line of scrimmage. On second, they dumped Watkins for a three-yard loss. And as the Coons came to the line on third and 10, Tom Hanagan began to do something he hadn't done in a very long time—pray. *If you just let us win this one—*

Tom had felt guilty ever since he'd left Bobby's hotel room Thursday night. And even though, like our former chief executive, he technically hadn't committed adultery with Bobby, he couldn't help but think that maybe his activities had something to do with his team's lackluster performance. *What goes around comes around,* he thought, trying to sort out his feelings. *But it'll never happen again, I swear.*

But whether it was Tom's soul-searching or Ezekiel Lincoln's lucky unwashed socks that determined what happened next is uncertain. What can be said for sure, however, is that when Cedric Amos got blind-sided by Bobo Thomas on the next play, Morgan wound up with the ball!

BOBO! BOBO! KICK BUTT!

As tears of humiliation and pain welled up in Amos' eyes, a red mist of rage gathered before the eyes of Coach Haley. Not accustomed to seeing an opponent get back up after his boys had knocked them down, Deacon Dim, who regarded each game as a cosmic struggle in which God bestowed victory on the more righteous team, was literally palpitating with fury. "Boys," spake he, casting his burning eyes upon the terrified players, "y'all are gettin' me angered . . . *real* angered."

KICK BUTT! KICK BUTT!

Meanwhile, Wallace, on two quick outs to Dobbins and Cubbins, moved the Knights to the Raccoon 48. Then on second and 7 from the 45, he found Tutomo Tongo on the 31 for another first down.

"You can do it, Jimmy Joe! You can do it!" burst out Tom Hanagan, swept up into the passion of the moment, happy, like 60,000 other people in the stadium, to exchange his real cares and worries for the mock anxiety of a football game.

KICK BUTT! KICK BUTT!

The play clock began to tick and Wallace set them down, took the snap and dropped back. . . . looking . . . he sees Holmes in the end zone. TOUCHDOWN! MORGAN!!

"That's my boy! That's my boy!" screamed Jackie Joe Wallace, whirling his sportcoat around over his head in a rapture of joy that, had he died that moment, would have spirited him off to football heaven: that beautiful emerald gridiron in the sky where the likes of Knute Rockne, Red Grange, and Pudge Heffelfinger spend their days scrimmaging with heroes like Jim Brown, Walter Payton, and OJ.... (Oops! Strike that!)

KICK BUTT! KICK BUTT! KICK BUTT!

As the Knights lined up for the point after, Dim Haley called on the heavenly host to smite all unclean foreigners and Yankees like Fernando DeGama and Coach Star. But sometimes even the prayers of prophets go unheeded. Five seconds later DeGama split the uprights and put the Knights on top 7 to 6.

KICK BUTT! KICK BUTT! KICK BUTT!

Two long minutes to go, the Morgan cheerleaders grabbed their bull horns and began to lead the fans in a frenzied chorus of Big D!

As they lifted their voices to the heavens, no one's voice was louder than Clifton Calhoun's. "DEFENSE!" sang out the ex-trustee, swaying back and forth, waving his hands in the air—when a bolt of pain shot through his chest, so intense that it dropped him to his knees.

"Clifton! Are you all right?!"

No answer.

"HELP!" screamed Inez Calhoun, her voice drowned out by the crowd as the Raccoon deep man crossed the 5, the 10, the 15, 20, 25, 30, and was finally ridden down by Butt Bowers.

DEFENSE! DEFENSE! DEFENSE!

"Help! Please! Somebody get a doctor!" wailed Inez, cradling the ashen head of her husband on her lap.

HOORAY MORGAN!

"Clifton! Clifton honey! Talk to me!" she screamed as Amos again took the snap on second and 10, looked left, looked right, set himself, and— *INCOMPLETE!* on the 35.

DEFENSE! DEFENSE! KICK BUTT!

• • •

"Step back, everybody! Step back, please!" ordered a team of paramedics, pushing through the irritated crowd.

"Hey, watch where you're goin'. He's just drunk!"

While the medics strapped an oxygen mask over Clifton's face and lifted him onto a stretcher, Amos, out of the shotgun, rolled left, and POW! was nailed by D'Amato.

YEAAAA MORGAN! KICK BUTT!

Fourth and 15. Fifty-two seconds left. Coach Haley called his last time out.

"Look out! Look out! Comin' through! Look out!"

"Oh Clifton, honey!" babbled Inez, running next to the stretcher down the entrance ramp.

Then the Coons lined up, the paramedics slid Clifton into the back of an ambulance, Amos took the snap—saw Watkins at the 40, and let it go.... *INCOMPLETE!*

HOOOORAY!!! WE'VE DONE IT! IT'S A MIRACLE!

"Clifton, honey, can you hear me?" shouted Inez as the ambulance turned on its siren and pulled through the press box gate. "We did it! We won!"

CHAPTER 12

Later that night

*R*ING RING . . . *RING RING*
"Yeah, who is it?"
Sugar pie, honey bunch, you know that I love you.
Can't help myself, I love you and nobody else.
"Hey, turn that down a minute!" yelled Coach Star across the dining room to Wesley Woods, who was standing next to the CD player drinking a malt liquor, gabbing with Pat Pitouchi.

"Okay Coach!"

"Yea! We did it! Number one!"

"Who is it?" yelled Star into the receiver of the phone. "Oh Jan, yeah, this is Tony. What's goin' on? . . . He's here somewhere. . . . Are you all right? . . . What? Oh my God . . . Yeah, I'll get him. Hold on."

"Yeaaa Knights! Kick Butt! Hey, run that play back again, Porky," burped Pete Cossacky, standing in front of the television swaying drunkenly back and forth, a piece of pizza dangling from one hand and a beer can in the other.

"Anybody seen Tom?"

"No, I ain't," said Jet Jackson, who was kicked back in a La-Z-Boy, sipping on a highball, swapping yarns with Stitches Stevens.

"Anybody here seen Tom?" Star popped his head into the kitchen where the coaches' wives were standing around talking about the pre-holiday sales at the River Bend Mall.

"I thought I saw him on the deck with Wyatt," said Coretta Woods, looking exceedingly pregnant.

"Thanks," said Star, heading into the dining room where Ed

Tarmeenian, who was having trouble standing, was spreading mustard on a ham sandwich and his shirtsleeve.

"Heywazgoinonbuddy?"

"What's up, Eddie?"

"You are," said Ed, poking a gnarled forefinger in Tony's chest. "Wedidit, brother, wedidit! Slapmefive!"

"Yeah sure, Eddie," agreed Star. "You seen Hanagan?"

"Waitaminit!" said Ed, throwing a beefy arm over Tony's shoulders, pulling him so close that their foreheads touched. "You'n'me we're buddies right?"

"Yeah—"

"I mean realhonestogod nobullshit friends, right?"

"Yeah, yeah."

"Good, I juswannabesure. I love ya, Tony."

"I love you too, Eddie," said Star, finally breaking free from his drunken friend's grasp and opening the deck door. "There you are!" he said, calling to Tom. "Jan needs to talk with you, right away!"

"Is anything wrong?!"

"Yeah, it's your Uncle Cliff. Here you go."

Stop in the name of love
Before you break my heart
Think it ooooover

"Hello, Jan? ... *KICK BUTT! KICK BUTT! YEAAA!* ... Are you there? ... Honey, this is Tom. ... No, I'm not drunk! ... What did you say? ... Oh my God! ... At the ball game? Why didn't you call me before? ... You just found out about it yourself? ... Intensive Care? ... Okay, I'll be right there."

Tom screeched out of Coach Star's driveway just as the cell phone jingled in the pocket of Hamilton Pigg's bathrobe a thousand miles away.

"Ham Pigg here," said the national president of the Cosmopolis Booster Club. "Hallo Howdy ... Yessum, I was jus' gettin' ready to call you back. Hol' on a second, wouldja?"

When we get behind closed doors

And she let's her hair hang down

Honey, could you turn that music down a minute?" said the sixty year old billionaire to his twenty-three year old wife, who was sitting in her satin nightie on the bed brushing her long blond hair. "Yeah, I left the game afta' the first fifteen minutes." Pigg snapped his fingers for his wife to get him his lighter for his cigar. "It was flat out embarrassin'... Thanks, honey... I've been sayin' we need a new coach fo' a while.... Star?... I saw him on the news tonight, that was quite an upset.... How's that?... Yeah, I do kinda like him.... And I think you're right, a Yankee like Star might know how to handle these.... Me too," said the oil man, swishing around the brandy in his snifter, smiling down at his wife who had just sat down on the floor in front of him and rested her chin on his knee. "Don't worry, ev'ry man's got his price." Pigg chuckled and looked into his wife's upturned face. "You know how these football coaches are, they're all a pack'a ho's.... Yeah, I'll get on it immediately.... You're right, this is gonna be tough on Booger, 'specially with his wife bein' sick and all, but you know how it is, you gotta win if you want to keep your job.... I'll call ya Monday.... All righty... Well honey," said Hamilton Pigg, blowing out a big smoke ring as his wife fumbled to untie his silk robe, "I think we're gonna get ourse'ves a new coach here in Cosmopolis."

CHAPTER 13

The Week of September 25

'Hey Tony! Did Peaches tell you? . . . That's right, we did it, buddy! The big time! College football spread of the week in *Sports Illustrated!* I just got off the horn with Stone. And he wants the lead photo to be of Wallace with a caption under him that reads *Morgan Kicks Butt.* . . . Yeah, it's fantastic! . . . This is it, Tony! I told you we'd do it! Ain't no lookin' back from here. . . . Let me make a few calls and I'll stop down."

BUZZ BUZZ

"Yes, I'll take it, Savannah. . . . Jan honey, how is. . . . Oh, thank God! . . . And nothing showed up on the tests? Pshew, Cliff sure gave us a scare. . . . No, I don't know what we'd do without him. . . . Listen, dear, I think I can get out of here early tonight if—Oh, you're going to dinner with the girls again? . . . But—Okay, bye—Hey wait! Jan, Jan. . . ."

Dammit, I wanted to tell her about Sports Illustrated. *But what the hell, she doesn't care anyway—wrapped up in that stupid job of hers. It's all she ever seems to think about anymore.*

BUZZ BUZZ

"Who? . . . Tell him to hold a minute," said Tom, leaning back in his chair, fingers hooked under his suspenders, savoring his moment of glory. *Yeah, I really have done it. Put this school back on the map. Now maybe a few of these rednecks around here will start to appreciate old Tommy for the genius he is. Ah, the hell with these morons. Things keep goin' the way they have been, I'll have a job at a really topnotch school. Who knows, maybe even move over to the pros.*

BUZZ BUZZ

"Oh, I forgot, sure, put him through. Well if it's not my old buddy, Dudley. Good news travels fast, doesn't it? . . . That's right, *Sports Illustrated*. And I—have I heard from NBC yet? No, but I'm sure it's gotta be at least a million. . . . Yes, I was going to let Buddy do the—I know Lamar used to . . . I realize that, but—whoa! time out, Dudley. I think I know what I'm doing around here, don't you? *BUZZ BUZZ* . . . Hold on a sec, wouldja Dud? . . . Who is it? . . . Yeah, I'll take it. Well, hello there, Roscoe . . . Yes, it was quite a game, wasn't it? . . . I told you so. . . . Of course, we're gonna. Listen, could I call you back in a minute? I've got Dud Dunning on the other line, I'll get right back. . . . Yeah, I promise. *CLICK* . . . Dudley? . . . Sorry for the interruption, but like I was saying, I've always considered you one of the best businessmen in this whole—county. And as such there's no way I'd ever try to tell you how to run your electronics company or pharmaceuticals firm. On the other hand, sports is my business, and although I appreciate your suggestions I figure I wouldn't have this job if I didn't know what I was doing, don't you agree? . . . *Silence* . . . Dudley? . . . There you are. But, anyhow, what matters right now is getting this *Sports Illustrated* spread wrapped up. . . . Yeah, I spoke with Wexler this morning. Of course *Sporting News* is interested. . . . That's what I've been saying all along. . . . Uh huh . . . Listen, Dudley, I'm kinda busy right now. Why don't I just give you a call back when I hear something. . . . All right. Bye bye." *CLICK.*

BUZZ BUZZ

"Savannah, honey, you wanna ring the Chancellor for me again? . . . *De de de da da, blue skies, nothin' but blue skies from now on.* Not back yet. Humm, I thought Noweeta said they were doing lunch today. What's that, hon? . . . Ahh, tell Miss Brooks"—Tom thought a minute—"maybe next week."

• • •

"And the fourth president of the United States was?—"

"I don't know," said Reggie Muggins, slamming his fist on the arm of his chair in exasperation Tuesday night.

"Well, you better know," said Teeny, "cause it's gonna be on the test tomorrow morning."

"The hell with that stupid test." The quarterback threw himself on his dorm room bed. "It's all a bunch of booshit anyway."

"You know, Reggie, sometimes you act like such a baby. I don't think you even looked at that old test I gave you."

"I been too busy."

"Yeah, too busy runnin' around with Tootie Ruggles, doin' God knows—"

"What I do with my time is my business."

"Is that so?" said Teeny, who had walked over to the Athletics Dorm in the rain to help Reggie study for his history exam. "Well then, maybe you should just study for this test by yourself."

Teeny stood up and started to put on her raincoat and Reggie instantly regretted flying off the handle. But his pride, rubbed raw by the events of the past three weeks, prevented him from apologizing. Instead, he silently stared off, as the one person in the world he cared about gathered up her things and, with tears welling in her eyes, walked out the door.

While Reggie lay in his room sulking, halfback Tutomo Tongo, basking in the afterglow of Saturday's victory, sat in the Learning Center pouring over several equations that his tutor, Dr. Barbara Sazlow, had given him to figure out while she went to call her husband at his office in the Lyndon B. Johnson Education building.

"Lou, this is Barb, I think I'm gonna be running a little late tonight," said the dark-haired instructor, telephone balanced on her shoulder as she fished through her grocery bag sized pocketbook looking for her lipstick. "No, don't bother," she said, standing up and adjusting her miniskirt, popping a Certs in her mouth. "I'll just eat when I get home. There are some blintzes in the freeza. I'll see you later."

When she returned to the study room, Dr. Sazlow was pleased to see that Tutomo had correctly multiplied the fractions she had left with him.

"That's great, Tutomo," she said to the beaming barrel-chested athlete from Guam.

"Gee, thanks, Dr. Sazlow. I don't know what I'd do without you."

"Oh thank you, Tutomo. Listen, it's getting kinda late. Why don't we call it a night and tackle percentages again next time."

"Sure, whatever you say," said the muscle-bound athlete.

"You need a ride, Tutomo?"

"Nah, it's only two blocks. . . ."

"Ah, c'mon," she said, throwing her pocketbook over her shoulder, her eyes momentarily lingering on the bulge in the crotch of Tutomo's tight jeans. "I'll be glad to take ya."

"Gee, thanks (*slurp slurp*) for the burger and fries, Barb," said Tutomo, sucking on the straw in his milkshake as she slowly pulled her black Volvo to a stop in the dark shadows of the maples that lined the road leading to the top of Battery Hill Park—a small hogback overlooking downtown Metro on which Yankee occupation forces had placed a battery to protect the railway depot during the Civil War.

"My pleasure, Tutomo," she said, turning off the lights and turning to face the athlete. "I like you, Tutomo."

"I like you too, Dr.—I mean Barb (*slurp*)."

"You know what I mean when I say I *really* like you?" she asked, looking her tutee straight in the eye.

"Yeah, I guess so. You really like me. And I really like you."

"No, you're jus' tellin' me that cause I'm your teacher," said Dr. Sazlow.

"No, I mean it."

"Really?"

"Really."

"Like whadda you like about me, Tutomo?" she asked, reaching out to turn down the radio, her hand brushing his thigh.

"Ah . . . ah."

"Do you like my . . . nose?"

"Yeah."

"And do you like my hair? I like your hair," she said, running her fingers through his kinky locks.

"Yeah."

"And do you like my lips?" She touched his lips with the tip of her crimson lacquered index finger.

"Uh huh."

"And do you like my breasts?" she asked, reaching over, grabbing one of his hands and pressing it to her breast.

"Yeah (*pant pant*)."

"And I betcha you'd like my pussy too, if I showed it to you."

"Yeah, yeah, yeah," nodded the panting setback.

"But you've got to promise me if I let you see it, you won't tell anybody."

"I promise, I promise."

"We could both get in a lot of trouble if you told anybody."

"Not me, honest."

"Well then, I guess I can show you." Dr. Sazlow lifted up her miniskirt, under which she was wearing no panties. "You like my pussy, Tutomo?" she said, sliding her hand up the athlete's thigh, undoing the button of his jeans and yanking down his zipper.

"Lou, I'm home!"

"Down here, Barb," huffed Dr. Louis Sazlow, climbing off the Nordic Trac in the den of their cluster home. "What took you so long?"

"I got stuck going over some figures with one of the guys."

"You look tired," panted the doctor, grabbing a towel to mop his bald head and furry gray chest.

"Yeah, I am," said his wife, throwing herself in a chair with her legs akimbo.

"That's a tough job teaching those boys."

"Yeah, but it's got its rewards."

"You're right, honey." Sazlow reached for his glasses, which sat on the bookcase next to a trophy the basketball players at Syracuse had given to him and his wife. "If somebody doesn't care about these boys, they'll wind up right back on the street where they came from."

"You're right, Lou, and it's for sure the coaches and athletics directors don't care about them."

"You're right, it's criminal the way they use these kids."

"Yeah it is, Lou. By the way, did you save me a blintz?"

• • •

The Chancellor had just finished thumbing through the Morgan spread in *Sports Illustrated* for the tenth time Thursday morning. He was whistling something that sounded like *King of the Road* while he putted golf balls in his office, polishing up his game for the meeting of the National Association of Independent College and University Administrators in Washington the following week. *Trailers for sale or rent, rooms to let, fifty cents....*

BUZZ BUZZ

"Yes, of course I'll take it. Hallo, Sambo," he said to Provost Sam Edwards. "That's right, college game of the week in *Sports Illustrated*, we can't do much better than that now, can we? So, what's on your mind this beautiful Thursday mornin'? . . . No, Sam, I haven't had a chance to look at those figures you sent me, I've been too— Third quarter health care profits off by 17 percent?! . . . Psychiatric hospital occupancy down by a third . . . No, that's not good. And your figures take into account the down-sizing of the registered nurse force? . . . You're right, the Board's not gonna like it. But they've got to understand, we can't keep growing at the same rate we have. Truth is our outpatient clinics have been doing too good a job with this preventive medicine. Seriously though, we need to talk about this after I get back from DC. . . . Well, all right, Sam. And don't you forget about that barbecue we got coming up after the Homecoming game.... Okay, I'll holler at you next Thursday."

BUZZ BUZZ

"Sure, Nita, put him through. Lamar, what's goin' on? . . . Front page, that's right.... Yeah, we've got a lot to be proud of. So what's the word on Commissioner Plunkett?—What?! I thought he told

you we could burn our waste at the Hargrove County facility indef-
initely? ... I know there's an election coming up, but—they're only
gonna let us burn there until January and then reconsider it? There's
no chance Plunkett could lose the election, is there? ... Hum. But
just in case, a little campaign contribution couldn't hurt.... One TV
spot is probably all it would take. I tell you what, why don't you call
Dudley and let him know what the score is. We don't need anything
getting in the way of this biological terrorism research deal with
Uncle Sam. ... Yes, I'm planning on meeting with General Ridley
when I'm in Washington. ... That's right, maybe even catch a Redskins game while I'm up there. Awright, Lamar. Now don't forget to
call Dudley."

No game scheduled for Saturday, Coach Star dined with his family
at home Thursday evening.
　　"You wanna beer, Tony?"
　　"Yeah, thanks, hon." He threw *Sports Illustrated* on the kitchen
table and sat down.
　　"It'll be about a half an hour till the lasagna's done." Rose closed
the oven door and wiped her hands on the apron she was wearing
over purple sweats.
　　"How's Junior feeling?"
　　"I dunno. He's been throwin' up all day."
　　"Did you call Dr. Reynolds?"
　　"Not in on Thursdays."
　　"How 'bout Schwartz?"
　　"In Myrtle Beach, but his nurse said there's some kinda flu goin'
around."
　　"Huh."
　　"Just let me bring Chris some more ginger ale." Rose smiled.
"Then you can read me the whole story."
　　"Awright, baby."
Star leaned back in his kitchen chair, took a sip of his Bud Lite,
and was suddenly overcome with exhaustion. Spent by the excite-
ment of his nationally touted success, which he still wasn't sure he

should ascribe to luck or talent, like a general who has carried the first day of a great battle, he was elated but anxious.

"I think he's feeling better," said Rose, tousling her husband's hair as she scuffled back into the kitchen. "And how 'bout you? You look worn out."

"Shooo, I am." Tony grabbed his wife around the waist and pulled her down on his lap. "I'm so wound up I don't know whether I'm coming or going."

"Yeah, it's real exciting, isn't it?" Rose flipped through *Sports Illustrated*. "Look, there's your picture! You should'a told me!"

"Not very good, is it?"

"Whad'da'ya talkin' about, you look like—"

"Robert DeNiro?"

"Well, maybe not DeNiro, but listen to this. *And when the dust had settled Saturday evening in Fulsom Field, it was the better-coached team that emerged victorious.* I'm glad somebody's givin' you the credit you deserve."

"You like?"

"I love it!" Rose gave him a kiss on top of his head. "You've done it again, you big galoot!"

"Yeah, I guess so."

"Whad'da ya mean?! The trouble with you is, you're too modest."

"Not modest, Rose, just careful."

"Careful, shmareful, you're a great coach, and everybody knows it. Did that Hamilton Pigg guy call you back?" Rose got up and headed for the refrigerator.

"Yeah, he did."

"Well?"

"They want me."

"You're kidding!" She wheeled around with a bag of pre-cut carrot and celery sticks in her hand. "How *much* do they want you?"

"Five hundred and fifty a year base salary."

"Tony!!"

"And with my TV show and perks it adds up to about twice that."

"That's fantastic!"

"Yeah, we'd be livin' high on the hog down there, but—"

"But what?"

"There's some things about the deal I'm not sure about."

"Like what?"

"Like for one thing he wants to know my answer right away."

"Uh huh."

"And for another he wants me to keep the son-in-law of the President of the University as my defensive coordinator."

"So?"

"So, that means I can't bring Eddie. And without him—"

"You'd still be where you are—hold on a second, what did you say, Chris?" she yelled.

"I dunno, Rose."

"I do. You're the one who's responsible for what's happened here, just like you were at A. State. You know it's true, honey—I'm coming, Chris!"

"Yeah, maybe," said Star as Rose walked out of the kitchen. "But Ed is a hell of a defensive coach. And what's more, he's my friend."

Rose scurried back into the room a moment later.

"Chris wanted to know if he could have some lasagna." She laughed. "Just like his old man."

"And then there's Tommy to consider too."

"Whad'da you mean, *TOMMY*! You know as well as me there's only one person Tom Hanagan cares about, and that's Tom Hanagan."

"I guess."

"Has he given you that new contract yet?"

"Not yet. But we just haven't had time to sit down. He says Brewster's ready."

"And?"

"You can't blame Tommy for—"

"For what? For not giving enough of a damn about his so-called best friend to have taken care of business months ago. You got a big heart, Tony, and I love ya for it, but think back a few weeks. You remember how Tommy was talking then?"

"Yeah I know."

"I'm sorry, Tony, I don't mean to bitch, I'm just sayin' $550,000 a year for—"

"Four years. I know what you're sayin', Rose. This is a dog eat dog racket."

"Everything is these days, Tony. Here, put some o' this diet Cheese Whiz on your celery sticks, it's very low in calories. You know, Tony, the days of looking out for your friends in this world are gone. It's every man and woman," she said, stealing a celery stick out of his hand, "for herself."

• • •

It was the first Friday night the players had had off since August. Arlo Plummer was out with Brad Ballings, Norm Summerfield, and Mitch Pomfrey at the Silo, Metro's Wild West theme gay nightclub.

"Too bad Rob's not here tonight," said Norm, trying not to get crushed in the throng of sweaty dancers that had just come off the strobe-lit floor. "He always gets a kick out of Miss Kitty's girls."

"Did you say something?" asked Brad, who was eyeing a cute young barfly in a black Stetson and armadillo skin boots.

"I said, too bad Rob's not here," said Norm. Rob was directing the opening of *Victor Victoria* at his high school.

"Yeah, it is," said Brad, his eyes still riveted on the rear end of the desperado dancing in front of him.

"So did you like the show tonight, Arlo?" asked Norm, almost getting knocked off his feet by a giggling two hundred pound cowpoke reeking of Macho cologne and gin.

"It was pretty funny," said the offensive lineman, who had been shyly exchanging glances with a long-haired hombre at the bar.

"Yeah, the girls are always a scream." Norm ordered himself another shooter. "Keep the change, honey. Hey, I wonder what's keeping Mitch so long." Mitch had left fifteen minutes earlier to smoke a joint in the car.

"He's been gone a while," said Arlo. "Maybe I better go check on him."

"Maybe you should. There's been some trouble around here lately with the locals," said Brad, smiling at an outlaw in a fringed vest and bolo tie who had just passed him.

As Arlo pushed his way through the drunken crowd milling around outside the wagon wheel-lined entrance to the club, he was accosted by several heterophobic gunslingers who mistook him for straight.

"Hey big boy, you got a light?"

"Sorry, I don't smoke."

"Yoo hoo, superman, where's Lois Lane?"

Unable to find Mitch out front and feeling that something was amiss, Arlo set out for the car. When he turned down the dimly-lit alley where Norm Summerfield had parked, he saw three drunk skin-heads prowling around Norm's Lincoln laughing and cursing. Inside the car sat a terrified Mitch Pomfrey desperately trying to honk the horn Norm had been meaning to get fixed.

"Git outta there, you lil' cocksucker," yelled one of the punks, hammering on the roof of the parked-in car.

"You're gonna hafta git outta that car sometime, faggot," threatened another, taking a swig off a bottle of Southern Comfort.

"Yeah, git outta that car! We ain't gonna hurt you—too much," cackled the third member of the threesome who were on weekend leave from Fort McArthur.

"Git outta there, faggot!" said the leader of the pack, brandishing a bloody fist he had cut on Mitch's tooth when he punched him in the mouth.

"Please! Leave me alone!" sobbed Mitch from inside the car, holding a handkerchief to his bloody mouth, frantically leaning on the broken horn.

"Git outta there, you fuckin' little queer," ordered Private Ernie Peeby, who, as he leaned over and pressed his face against the windshield of the car, suddenly felt Arlo Plummer's brawny shoulder hit him square in the back, shattering his nose on the windshield. As the private slid off the hood of the Lincoln into a semi-conscious heap, Arlo jumped to the left, and POW! knocked helicopter repairman

Corporal Dwayne Jenkins unconscious. Then he whirled to his left to make it a triple-header, and discovered that the platoon leader with the bloody fist had taken off down the alley and deserted his comrades.

"Oh Arlo, thank God you're here!" sobbed Mitch, opening the car door and slowly climbing out on rubbery legs.

"You all right?" asked the lineman, looking at the bloody handkerchief Mitch was holding to his mouth.

"I think so."

"Here, let me see that." Arlo reached out to remove the handkerchief from his mouth.

"No, don't!" screamed Mitch, pushing the football player's hand away. "Don't touch me! I'm positive."

CHAPTER 14
Sunday, October 2

Chancellor Brewster arrived in Washington for the fall meeting of the National Organization of Independent College and University Administrators at 9:05 Sunday morning. Five hours later he was sitting in RFK Stadium watching the Redskins and the Cowboys.

"I don't know how you did it, Grady."

"It wasn't easy, Bill," said Assistant Under-Assistant Secretary of Education Grady Peckers. "Tickets to Skins games are harder to get in this town than aircraft carrier contracts."

"I bet," said the Chancellor, one hand wrapped around a plastic cup of beer, the other around a wiener.

HOOORAYYY! SKINS! GO! GO! GO!

"I'm just glad I was able to do my ole boss a favor," said Grady, who had served as an assistant to Chancellor Brewster when he was upgrading Yale's computer systems in the early eighties.

"And I appreciate it. There's nothing that beats a professional football game."

"You're right about that, Bill. Course you've been watching some pretty good ball in Metro this year yourself."

"Well—"

"Don't be so modest. Number 18 in the nation with a big spread in *Sports Illustrated* and *Sporting News*. You should be proud of yourself."

"If you put it that way."

"Honestly, you've done wonders there at Morgan. You've put the school on the map."

"I guess you could say that," said the Chancellor, glancing at the plastic wrapped gladiators on the field who, like himself, were at the top of their game.

YAHOO REDSKINS!!

"Hey, look who's over there, Bill," said Grady as the Redskinettes began to do an exotic-dancer bump and grind in front of them. "It's General Tommy Franks."

"Where?"

"Right there," he said, pointing to a gangly-looking man with a big nose and ears who, with his buzz cut and Hawaiian print mufti, could have passed for an Alabama chicken farmer. "And there's Tom Delay with him. And I'll be darned if that's not Ted Kennedy two boxes behind them with—yup, Jesse Jackson!"

"And are those two young women Mr. Jackson's daughters?"

"I don't think so, Bill. And I'll be, look who's down there."

"Is that really—"

"Yessiree. Monica Lewinksy . . . and Joe Lieberman. Wow!"

"I guess you're right about everybody coming to the game."

"Oh yeah, whenever they get a chance. But it's not surprisin' when you think how most everybody who's anybody in town played ball when they were in school."

"I never thought about it, but you're right," said the Chancellor.

"Let's face it, most successful men in America, and I'm talkin' *really successful,* got their start on the playing field. It makes sense. Natural born leaders and all that stuff. Team players. Why, most every president this century who's been worth a darn was some kinda ball player. Heck, even ole Woodrow Wilson was a college coach."

"You're absolutely right."

"'Course," said the former SMU free safety, as Troy Aikman was brought to the turf with a spine-tingling tackle, "there's a lot of smart and talented folks who have never been athletes, but by and large the real movers and shakers in this world are old jocks like you and me. . . . Oh look! There's Bill Clinton with, I'll be darned, Muhammad Ali and Gerry Ford!"

• • •

The high point of the Chancellor's visit to the Capitol did not, however, occur until the final night of the OIUCA meeting.

He had spent two delightful days talking football and software with the presidents of Miami and USC over rack of lamb at Nicola's; reflecting on faculty diversity and football with the presidents of Stanford and Harvard over filet mignon at Lion d'Or; and jawing about federal aid and basketball with the head administrators of Howard and Fisk over coffee and donuts in the Hilton Coffee Shop.

Suddenly he found himself being nominated for president of the OIUCA by former ice hockey All American Dr. Seymour Pudd of Dartmouth College—*HOORAY!!*

"I don't know what to say," said Brewster as he stood at the podium and embarked on a fifteen minute panegyric on intercollegiate sports, democracy, the abiding value of education administration organizations, and, of course, the threat of international terrorism.

• • •

On Wednesday afternoon, Tom Hanagan was Bo Hanks' special guest on his local *Sports Talk Show.*

"Great to have you with us today, Tom."

"Thanks, Bo. It's a pleasure to be here."

"This has certainly been an amazing year for your football team. Here we are in week six of the season. The Knights are 4 and 0, ranked number 18 in the nation. You've just had a big spread in *Sports Illustrated* and *Sporting News.* You're tied for number one in the Mid-South and 14 point favorites to beat Tech this Saturday. Wowee! How do you explain it, Tom?"

"Well, number one, hard work. And number two, the great support our program has gotten from the people of this wonderful community."

"The what?!" blurted out Tony Star as he pulled his Cadillac into the parking lot of the Marriott Airport Hotel.

"You know, Bo, without everyone pulling together, the fans, the alumni, the boosters, the press, the administration, not to mention the coaching staff and players, none of this would have happened."

"What a crock," said Star, pulling his key out of the ignition.

As he got off the elevator on the seventh floor of the hotel several minutes later, Star was ninety percent sure he was doing the right thing. He'd thought about it all week. Rose was right. It was time he started looking out for number one. The only reason J.P. Morgan's Fighting Knights were national news was because of him. *Hell, I've had to fight Brewster, the boosters, the press, every step of the way. And Tommy, he's my pal, but—*

KNOCK KNOCK

"Hey, Tony! Come on in," said sports attorney Mike Tubo, pumping Tony's arm and giving him a slap on the back as he led his old Pitt Panther teammate across the room toward a table on which sat a pile of documents, a bottle of J&B and a cellular phone. "You wanna drink?" said the chunky, balding attorney whose Armani suit, Gucci loafers, and Rolex testified to his jurisprudence.

"No thanks, Mike."

"You sure?"

"Yeah, I gotta a long night ahead of me."

"Big one comin' up this weekend, huh?"

"Yeah, and Tech's better than people think."

"You're right. That Liberia Lewis is an animal. Nine tackles and two sacks last week."

"And Jones ain't a bad quarterback either. So how'd it go?"

"Great," said the lawyer, who had met with Hamilton Pigg atop the Pigg Towers in Cosmopolis earlier that morning.

"And did he go for the incentive package?" asked Star, picking up the three inch-high contract.

"To the dime—an extra 250 for a conference championship, and 200 for a major Bowl. And he also gave me the contracts for your TV and radio show. Seems he and a friend own the station."

"Figures."

"Yeah, the guy's worth more money than the national debt. Everybody says he's the reason they can't get the border with Mexico closed. Pigg's makin' too much money off the cheap labor."

"Nice guy."

"Actually he ain't bad, kinda ossentatious though."

"What?"

"Ossentatious. You know what I mean. Kind of show-offy, with the cowboy boots and hat and everything. But he's a straight shooter."

"What about Eddie?"

"Nope, he's not backin' off on that. President Stinson's son-in-law stays as defensive coordinator."

"Damn."

"Ah, he ain't so bad. He's smart enough to stay out of the way."

"So whadda you think, Mike?"

"I know you'll like it down there, Tony. They got a lot 'a talent on the team right now. It's a great area to recruit. And from what I can tell, they're a no-bullshit operation. Nothin' like these assholes up here—Tommy excluded, of course."

"I think you're right." Tony tossed the contract back on the table.

"Oh, and there's one more thing," said Tubo, pulling another thin typewritten document from his snakeskin attaché case, his diamond studded ID bracelet dangling over his hairy wrist. "Pigg says he needs you to sign this as soon as possible."

Star took the paper and frowned.

"It's just a letter of intent, promising that if you get a better offer from another school before we get all the details of the contract worked out, Cosmopolis reserves the right to make a counter offer at ten percent higher than the other offer and bind you to the deal."

"That don't sound bad."

"Not to me either. And all they want us to give them for their guarantee is the right to renegotiate the contract at a figure no less than twenty-five percent lower than their original offer if you should somehow turn out to have a losing season, and they should still want to hire you."

"I don't know if I like that."

"Me neither, Tony, but, like Pigg said, it'd be hard to ask the

Board of Regents for the kind of money they're payin' if you showed up on their doorstep with a losing record. Besides, the way you're goin'—"

"I guess so. But I tell you, Mike. I'm gonna hafta think about all this."

"I figured you would. Take your time. You got a week or so. But if you want my professional opinion"—the thirty-five grand incentive that Pigg had offered Tubo to get the letter of intent signed in ten days was making him more persuasive than ever—"I'd go for it. You sign this letter and you'll be sitting pretty even if somebody else comes along with a better deal."

"That's a point."

"And besides,"—Tubo winked—"it sure would be nice to know where you're goin' so you could take a bunch of good recruits with you. I saw your recruiter Stult in the airport at Dallas, and he told me the players have been running after him. Said you had two Pepsi Players of the Week ready to sign."

• • •

RRRRRRRR! RRRRRRRR!

"STEFAN! SLOW DOWN!"

RRRRRRRR! RRRRRRRR!

"WHAT?" yelled the smiling young Russian over his shoulder as he wheeled his Honda 450 around one of the hairpin turns that led up to the top of Battery Park.

"I SAID, SLOW THIS MOTORCYCLE DOWN IMMEDI-ATELY!" yelled Jan, her arms clutched tightly around Stefan's trim waist.

"Oh, okay!" Stefan backed off the throttle and coasted to a stop near a large, graffiti-scarred cannon at the top of Battery Hill. "You weren't scared, were you?" he asked, grinning devilishly.

"Petrified," she said, taking off her helmet. "I thought you said we were going out for lunch not our funeral."

"I'm sorry," he smiled, revealing his strong white teeth, "you aren't too angry with me, I hope."

"Not too angry, I guess." Jan brushed herself off and walked over to a stone bench that overlooked the city.

"What a beauteeful day!" gurgled Stefan.

Yes, thought Jan, *it is a beautiful day, and what's more, I'm actually enjoying myself for a change. . . . and maybe it's foolish of me, but—*

"What are you thinkink, Jan?"

"Oh . . . just what a lovely day it is," she said, looking into the eyes of the young man for whom she had begun to feel more than just brotherly affection.

"Let's dance!" said Stefan, suddenly whisking her off her feet.

"Whoah! Hold on a minute, Stefan."

"No, let's not waste another minute," he said, lifting her over his head and whirling her around.

"Hey, who do you think I am, Ginger Rogers?"

"No, you are much more beauteeful than Geenger Rogers." Stefan let her slide slowly down through his powerful hands. "Jan—"

"No," she said, feeling his warm breath on her face.

"Don't you want me to make love to you, Jan?"

"Please, Stefan—" she trembled.

THIRD QUARTER

INTERFERENCE

The rise of the sports metaphor in American life is among the most significant cultural developments of our age. The ubiquity of the metaphor may now have reached the point where sports is the metaphor for what we mean by American life.

STANLEY ARONOWITZ
Foreword to Choosing Sides

CHAPTER 15

Friday and Saturday, October 7 and 8

"That's a pretty sight, ain't it, Tony?" said Ed Tarmeenian from his seat across the aisle. "Kinda reminds me of Pennsylvania."

"Yeah it does, Eddie," said Coach Star, looking joylessly out the bus window at the scarlet and gold foothills of the Appalachians. Star had called Mike Tubo earlier that morning to tell him he'd decided to accept Pigg's offer. And he felt terrible.

"Just look at dem cows." Ed put his fingers in his ears like a pair of horns and started mooing. "Poor cows gettin' ready to go to slaughter, just like these bastards we're playin' tomorrow, eh Tony?"

"No doubt." Star laughed.

"Yeah, we're gonna make hamburger outavem," said Ed, grinding his fist in his palm, confident that the outcome of the game would be decided, as most football games are, by which team has the bigger bodies — little knowing that Saturday's contest would be decided by bodies microscopically small.

Jimmy Joe Wallace had been feeling queasy since the team's plane left Metro. And as the bus began to ascend Pioneer Mountain to Stumpsville, he suddenly ran to the rest room, tore open the door, and vomited once . . . twice . . . three times.

"You okay, Jimmy?" asked Porky Watson, poking his head in the lavatory door and immediately pulling it back out.

"I'm sick, Porky," groaned Jimmy Joe, the remains of a Spanish omelet dripping off the end of his chin.

"You want me to get Doc?"

"No, I'll be—" (*RETCHHH!*)

"You okay, Jimmy Joe?" asked Doc Willis, opening the door a moment later and seeing the quarterback on his knees hugging the commode.

"I don't—" (*RETCHHH!*)

"You think it's something you ate?

"I don't know.

Humm. Nobody else seems to be sick, thought the doctor, and then he recalled that Dr. Wright, head of the student infirmary, had said something to him on the golf course Wednesday about an outbreak of stomach virus on campus. "You haven't been around anybody who's been sick lately, have you, Jimmy Joe?"

"Naw, I don't think so," he began to say, all at once remembering that the co-captain of the cheerleaders Sue-Ann Raskell, with whom he had spent the wee hours of the morning Tuesday exchanging body fluids, had called last night to tell him she was feeling sick to her stomach.

"Hey, what's goin' on?!" said Coach Cossacky, poking his head in and out of the john.

"Jimmy Joe's sick," pronounced Dr. Willis.

"He's just got a case of nerves, Doc. You'll be okay, Jimmy Joe."

But when the team filed off the bus at the Stumpsville Ramada Inn forty-five minutes later, Jimmy Joe was feeling no better.

"Maybe he'll be all right by tomorrow," said Star, zipping up his coat while the driver unloaded their bags.

"If he ain't, we could be in some big trouble." Jet Jackson blew on his hands. "'Cause Muggins ain't been worth a shit all week."

By the time the Knights got out under the lights of Pioneer Field for evening practice, the temperature had plummeted another ten degrees.

"Damn, it's cold." Star bobbed up and down as he watched his players go through their warm-up.

"Yeah, and it's s'posed to rain all day tomorrow," said Ed, his breath visible on the damp evening air.

"Welcome to Stumpsville, boys," said Coach Wesley Woods,

throwing a ball to second string quarterback, Anthony Gentry, "coldest dang football stadium in the entire sunny south."

The East Tennessee native knew what he was talking about. Pioneer Field, known throughout the Mid-South as the Ice Box, had been built by the WPA in the '30s. Wind-whipped, weather beaten, situated on the wrong side of a marshy mountain top, the drab, 40,000-seat, concrete horse-shoe was the work of a government architect who had obviously never been to a football game in his life. But the ugly arena was not without its compensation for the home crowd. At least once each season, the old concrete stadium played host to an upset over some sunny, overconfident team that blithely sauntered up from cotton fields to be ambushed on the tundra. And this year the Techies, at 3 and 1, were more dangerous than ever.

Just what we don't need, thought Star, looking up into the murky sky. Though not given to superstition like many athletes, he had started to have bad feelings earlier in the day when he broke his St. Christopher's medallion while showering. And now with Wallace sick and Muggins looking useless—*Nah, get over it,* he said to himself as Ed began to run the defense through their paces, *you've already beat two of the best teams in the nation. Of course that was with Wallace. But we don't need to throw to beat these guys. We can run 'em into the ground like we did last year.*

"Whad'da you think, Eddie?" he asked as the Knights wrapped up their workout and headed to the locker room.

"Whadda ya mean, wha'do I think? We're gonna kick these hillybillies' asses tomorrow and get the hell outta this place before we all freeze to death."

"How 'bout you, Jet?"

"We're lookin' pretty good. Plummer's hand is still sore where Doc stitched it up. And Smith's heel is botherin' him again, but besides the fact that Muggins doesn't seem to know what the hell's goin' on, we're all right."

"You think we oughta start Gentry?"

"Could be. But if we do, that might really be it for Muggins."

"You think it would help if I talked to him again?"

"Who knows. Let's just hope Doc can bring Wallace around."

• • •

As the weather report predicted, by breakfast on Saturday morning a cold, joint-stiffening drizzle had begun to fall. And by 11:00, when the Knights made their way through a motel lobby full of cheering boosters and media to board the buses for the stadium, a freezing rain was coming down in sheets.

GO KNIGHTS! KICK BUTT!

"Tom, have you heard any more about the status of Wallace?" asked Chancellor Brewster, who had arrived via Lear Jet and limousine an hour earlier with Dudley and Boomer.

"No I haven't, Bill." Tom smiled and waved at the Sports Central camera crew who were there to cover the game.

"I sure hope he's gonna be well enough to play," said Brewster solicitously.

"Here he comes now." Tom stepped forward and gave Wallace an encouraging thumbs up as the pale and drawn quarterback shuffled past at the end of the column with the trainers.

"Are you okay, Jimmy Joe?" asked his mother, elbowing through to talk to her boy.

"I dunno, Maw."

Humm, said Tom to himself, *he doesn't look good.*

Not good at all, thought the Chancellor.

"Sick as a dog," whispered Dudley under his breath to Boomer.

"I wouldn't worry, Bill," said Tom. "And before I—." Tom broke off his conversation with the Chancellor to go shake hands with Rollie Burroughs of *Sports Illustrated*.

"That was a fantastic spread, Rollie. . . . I know you do. . . . Wallace? Nah, he'll be fine!"

"Now what was I saying?" said Tom, returning a moment later to the Chancellor's side. "Oh yeah, I think I can maybe get you guys some seats up in the press box if you like."

"Yes, that might be nice," said Brewster, looking out the window at the teeming rain.

"Just don't leave here till you talk with me. Hey Willie Black-stock!" yelled Tom at the *Sporting News* journalist. "Slap me five, brother! Yeah, those photos were great!"

"Well, Bill," said Dudley Dunning, looking at the Chancellor over his rimless glasses, "I guess us *guys* better go into the lounge here and get a drink while we wait for Mr. Hanagan."

An hour later, when the last of the raincoat-clad, umbrella-toting supporters finally made their way onto the buses taking them to the stadium, Tom and Blake Stevens collapsed on the grimy sofa in the motel lobby and gave each other a double, over the head high five. "Are we hot or what, buddy." Then Tom remembered he'd forgotten to find out about the press box seats for the Chancellor. "Damn! We gotta get over to the stadium pronto!"

By the time he and Blake arrived, the small press box was full. But fortunately for the Chancellor and the other 40,000 people at Pioneer Field, the rain had stopped and turned into cold, foggy mist.

GIVE ME A P! GIVE ME AN I!
AN O! N! E! E! R! S! PIONEERS!
YEAAAA!

"Bill! There you are. Listen, I'm working on those seats for you," said Tom after he had threaded his way through the crowd to where the Chancellor and his friends sat huddled drinking lukewarm coffee.

"Thanks, Tom," said Brewster, taking a hot dog from Boomer. "I think the rain's let up."

"I'll keep working on it. I'm sorry."

"That's all right," said the Chancellor as the Stump Jumpers, a local gospel-singing group, began a barber-shop quartet version of the National Anthem.

Then the referee signaled that the Pioneers had won the coin toss and it was time for the game to begin.

HOT DOGS! HOT COFFEE! HOT PRETZELS!

"You want another cupacoffee, Billy Bob?"

"Yeah, I think I just might, and another dog too."

"How 'bout you, Dudley, you want anything else?"

"No, I'm all right, Boomer," said the industrialist, peevishly pulling up the collar of his trench coat and clapping his hands together.

DEFENSE! DEFENSE! DEFENSE!

• • •

"Okay now, Reggie, remember what I told you. ATTITUDE!"

"Yeah, I got it, Coach."

"Awright, go to it!" said Star, sending him in with a slap on the rear to take over at his own 28.

BIG D! BIG D! DEFENSE!

"Muggins looks worthless," said Ed Tarmeenian, stepping up beside the Coach after the quarterback nearly fumbled on the first play.

"Yeah, you're right," said Star, signaling in the next play.

Fortunately for Morgan, the Tech offense didn't look much better when they took over the ball three plays later on their own 37. The poorly drained field was so muddy that the players were having trouble standing, much less getting first downs. And so it was, the pigskin passed from one team to the other with neither scoring until the end of the first quarter when Pioneer tailback Jessie Rickles lost his footing in the end zone and was hauled down for a touchback. MORGAN 2 TECH 0.

HOORAY MORGAN! KICK BUTT!

"Well, it's about time!" said Dudley Dunning, opening up a green and yellow striped umbrella.

"Let's go, Knights!" yelled the Chancellor, who, thinking he would be sitting in the press box, had neglected to bring an umbrella and was now holding a soggy game program over his head. "You get that umbrella at the souvenir stand?"

"Yup. I did, Billy Bob, the very last one," said Dudley, watching as Mustafa Lewis ran the Pioneer kick-off back to the 32.

The rain became more intense. And the players, at times nearly invisible in the haze, slogged their way through the mud for another fifteen minutes, unable to put any more points on the board. Then, with three minutes left in the half, on a third and 8 at the Pioneer 38, Einreich blitzed through the Tech line and stripped the ball from quarterback Jordache Jones.

"Let's go now! Let's go!" said Tom Hanagan as loudly as he dared in the overcrowded Pioneer press box. Tom had been hoping that his team would make a strong enough showing to move into the top ten before his upcoming meeting with Brewster and the Athletics Board. He was planning on asking for an additional three quarters of a million dollars to cover contract negotiations with Coach Star and the rest of the staff. Unfortunately it was beginning to look as if the Knights might not even beat the spread.

"Look at that fucking rain!" said Tech saxophonist Luke Lowery, gazing out from under the tunnel at the field. "We're gonna get soaked."

"Everybody ready? Charlie? Luke? Cheryl?" asked Pioneer band director Dr. Wallace Murdock.

"All ready!" said clarinetist Cheryl Clower, rolling her eyes at Lowery. "No way I'm doing this again next year," she said. "I don't give a damn if they take my scholarship away or not."

"I know what you mean," said Lowery.

"And don't forget," said Dr. Murdock, "this afternoon we're doing *America the Beautiful* right after *Bad Bad Leroy Brown.*

DEFENSE! DEFENSE! DEFENSE!

Third and 10 two gainless plays later, Coach Star had Muggins move them to the middle of the field for a field goal attempt. Then the Coach ran the clock down to twenty-three seconds, took his last time out and sent DeGama in to try for three. As the pigskin sailed through the uprights, the Morgan fans let out a half-hearted whoop and ran for cover, leading the Pioneers by a disappointing five points.

194 · KICK BUTT

"Bill! There you are!" said Tom Hanagan when he finally found the Chancellor and company shaking themselves off like wet spaniels in front of a pizza stand by Entrance D. "They've got room for you in the press box for the second half."

"Oh really," said Brewster, eyeing his dry Athletics Director while he shook out his raincoat.

"Ow! Ow! Ouchhh!"

"I hope that heel ain't torn," said Stitches Stevens, working on the chaw in his cheek at the same time as Symeon Smith's swollen ankle. "Yeah I'm comin', Atilla. . . . Here, let me get a look at that wrist, Steve."

As invariably happens on cold, wet days, the players had twisted, turned, and hyper-extended bones, ligaments and tendons in directions they were never meant to go.

"What's wrong with Smith?" asked the Coach, pulling a dry shirt over his head.

"Maybe his Achilles tendon."

"Jesus. And Wallace?"

"He says he's feelin' a bit better. That IV the doc's got him hooked up to seems to be workin'."

"Yeah, I think you're right," said Pioneer head coach Larry Scales to his offensive coordinator Delwood "Bo" Stamps.

"Trust me, Larry." Bo spit a gob of tobacco in a trash bucket. "That Smith boy of theirs is through for the day. I saw that pop Roberts gave him. He's lucky he can still walk. And if I ain't mistaken, King is hurtin' too. Rodney dang near took his head off there at the end of the half. If you ask me, I say we stick to our first half game plan."

"Sounds good to me. You're all set, Billy?"

"Yeah, we're ready," said Billy Ervins, the defensive coordinator. "We got the news back on Wallace. Still no go. I think we can hold 'em, Coach."

"Let's do it, gentlemen."

As the Tech offense came to the line at their own 34 after the kick-off, third string Pioneer receiver Dwayne Stubbs, his clean brown and green uniform already soaking wet in the freezing rain, got up to cheer on his teammates. Just two more quarters, thought the 160-pound theatre arts major, shivering from the cold and collision of the players on the field. Then I can get out of this uniform, take a hot shower and start partying. I don't know why I let myself get roped into this another year, he said to himself, looking guiltily over his shoulder where his father, Pioneer great "Stubby" Stubbs, and Dwayne's twenty-eight year old trophy stepmother were cheering on their team. "GO TECH! GO TECH! GO! GO!"

"Can I get you anything else?" asked Tom, who had just squeezed past a reporter in the press box, his hands full of soft pretzels and Coca Colas.

"No, I'm okay. How 'bout you fellas?"

"We're fine, Billy Bob," said the Chancellor's companions, happy to be out of the rain, though uncomfortably packed like sardines in the smoky and drafty press box.

"They get that men's room fixed yet, Tom?"

"Not yet, Dud."

"Now look, Reggie," said Coach Star ten minutes later on a third and 12 from his own 42. "Don't do nothin' foolish."

"Okay, Coach," said the quarterback, raindrops dancing off his helmet.

But on the very next play, as he dropped back looking for his receiver in the fog, Muggins got submarined and fumbled the ball. *HOORAY PIONEERS!*

Afraid the tide might be turning against them after Tech picked up two quick first downs, Star sent Porky Watson to get Jimmy Joe Wallace.

"And tell him to get his ass out here. QUICK!"

GO TECH! GO TECH

"Whadda you think, Eddie?"

"We'll stop 'em, Tony, don't worry," said Ed, water dripping off the ends of his Fu Manchu mustache.

But on the next play quarterback Jordache Jones managed to find his tight end for ten. And on the play after that, he slipped through the arms of two tacklers and splashed his way down to the Morgan 23.

PI-O-NEERS! PI-O-NEERS!

"What the hell is goin' on?!" hollered Ed, moving his players in and out of man-to-man coverage in a desperate effort to force a turnover. But the Pioneers weren't to be denied. Four minutes later, although being stopped short of the end zone, they drew within two points of the Knights on a twenty yard field goal.

HOOOOORAY TECH! GO! GO! GO!

"What's the word on Wallace?" asked Star as soon as Porky arrived back from the locker room.

"Doc says he can have him ready in ten minutes."

"Ten minutes! We only got two minutes before the end of the third quarter!"

"That's what he said."

Star turned to his offensive coordinator. "What do you think, Jet?"

"You wanna try Gentry?"

"Maybe we should."

"He couldn't do worse than Muggins."

"Gentry!"

"I'm comin', Coach," said the third string quarterback, laying down the football he'd been tossing on the sidelines.

"You ready?"

"Yeah, I'm ready," said Gentry, blowing on his freezing fingers.

"Awright then, go to it! But watch out for Lewis!"

Anthony Gentry ran onto the field, huddled with the team and—Tom Hanagan was stricken with terror as he recalled twenty-five years earlier when he'd fumbled that crucial snap on his own 18 against Duke.

"Tom, you told me that Wallace was feeling better," said the Chancellor.

"I thought that's what Tony said. But I guess I must'a been wrong."

"That's not the first time today that's happened," quipped Dudley, watching as Gentry was thrown for a three-yard loss.

"I think I'll go downstairs and find out what's goin' on," said Tom, feeling a chill wind blowing through the press box.

"That sounds like a good idea," said Brewster.

"Scuse me, excuse me, comin' through."

"Well, if it ain't Tom Hanagan!"

"Hello, Red," said Tom, sidling his way toward the press box door.

"I hope you didn't bet too much on this game," said the red-faced reporter, malevolently smiling for the first time in weeks.

"Not too much, Red," said Tom, recoiling from the whiskey on Red's breath.

"Good! 'Cause I'd hate to see you lose your money! . . . har har har."

Unable to move the ball any better with Gentry than Muggins, two minutes later P.U. Pointer punted it to the Pioneers, who in turn bogged down at their own 43.

And so it went for the next ten minutes until with 7:43 left in the fourth quarter Jordache Jones scrambled out of the pocket on third and 8 and hit Willie Winfield with a twenty-six yard pass at the Morgan 49.

YEAAAAAAA TECH! GO! GO!

"You fucking moron!" raged Ed Tarmeenian at his second string cornerback Chaz Winston. "What the hell were you doin'?!! Never never never move out of your zone. For nothin'! You understand?!!!"

"Yeah," stammered the mortified juvenile.

"Wha'did you say?"

"Yassa, Coach, I understand."

"That's what I thought. Now sit your dumb ass down on that bench and think about what I toldja. You could'a cost us the game!"

"I'll have a cup of coffee, black with no sugar," said Dudley Dunning, standing at the concession stand after finally relieving himself.

"I'm sorry, sir. We ain't got no coffee left."

"I can't believe you're out of coffee!"

"It's a fact," said the bulldog-faced concession stand attendant, stomping her feet to keep warm.

"Well then, how 'bout some cocoa?"

"We got any cocoa left, Charlene?" yelled Millie to her pregnant and equally overweight co-worker.

"Nope, we ain't, Millie."

"I'm sorry, sir, we ain't got any cocoa left neither."

"What the hell kind of place is this?" huffed Dudley, stomping off toward the VIP gate.

"You know, Charlene," said Millie, turning around to flip over some burgers, "sometimes I just cain't figger these rich folks out."

"Me neither, Millie," said Charlene, grease from the grill splattering her apron. "Seems like to me, with all the money they got they could find somethin' more int'restin' to do on Saturday afternoon than come out here into the freezin' colt rain to watch a football game."

"Or at least they could watch it at home. You know with that new dish Radney's got he can git near ev'ry football game in the world right at the house. "That'll be twelve dollars and forty-five cents, sir. Thank you kindly."

PI-O-NEERS! PI-O-NEERS! HOOORAYYY!

"What's all that racket?" said Millie as the stadium overhead shook and rattled beneath the stomp of ten thousand feet. "Sounds like we musta scored or somethin'. . . . Here's your change, sir."

Indeed Millie was right. After driving the ball down to the Morgan 20, Vince Swill kicked his second field goal of the day and put the Pioneers on top 6 to 5.

HOORAY, TECH!

"You get that arm warmed up?"

"Yeah, I'm ready," said Wallace, bobbing up and down to keep warm in the driving rain.

"You're sure?"

"Yeah, I can do it, Coach," said Jimmy Joe, still feeling a bit dizzy as he stood next to Star on the 40 yard line.

"Okay, but watch out for Jones and Simmons."

"Okay."

"Awright, no huddle Black Cat 2 series."

LADIES AND GENTLEMEN
NOW COMING IN AT QUARTERBACK…

A wave of excitement rippled through the press box.

"It's him!" said Tom.

"Yes it is!" said the Chancellor as Jimmy Joe hit Tongo for ten yards on the first play from scrimmage.

KICK BUTT! KICK BUTT!

Then he rifled one to Harris for a quick six and to Tongo for another first down. Tom smiled at the Chancellor as they watched Tongo churn forward for six more.

"I told you, Dudley," said Brewster.

"Let's go, Morgan!" yelled Boomer, forgetting where he was as Wallace hit Holmes on the Tech 20 for another first down.

"We got 'em now, eh Tommy," said the Chancellor.

"Yes sir!"

But as the Knights lined up, third and 1 on the Tech 11 with forty seconds left, Morgan rookie Bradford Bibb jumped off sides.

"YOU DUMB MOTHERFUCKER, BIBB!" roared Coach Star. "Time out! Time out!"

Thank God it's almost over, thought Mrs. Lydia Scoggins, rubbing together her gloved hands in anticipation of a warm dry house and a glass of sherry.

"You gotta stop 'em now, boys!" blubbered her thick-jowled, bespectacled husband. Dr. Doyle D. Scoggins, president of Tech.

"This sure is excitin', isn't it, Lydia?" prated Kathy Lee Purdee, the perennially perky fifty year old sorority-girl wife of provost Parnell Purdee, not sure what was actually happening on the field.

"Oh yes," said Lydia, all too painfully aware of what was going on, having attended at least three hundred games with her husband. Years ago she had discovered, after reading several books on the subject, that he knew nothing about the game.

"I betcha they try a quick pass over center," declared President Scoggins.

"A slant pass to the halfback on the weak side," said Lydia.

"Awright, Jimmy Joe, blue sky-2," said Star, confident the slant pass to Mongol Harris on the weak side would catch the Pioneers off guard—which it did. But, unfortunately, as Harris stretched out to grab the perfectly thrown spiral, he lost his footing and the ball sailed out-of-bounds. INCOMPLETE.

HOOORAY PIONEERS!

As the Morgan faithful grumbled at having to settle for a field goal—wondering if winning by only two would hurt their national ranking, Coach Star huddled on the sideline with Fernando DeGama.

"No problemo?" asked Star, throwing his arm over his kicker's shoulder.

"No problemo, Coach."

Star gave DeGama a slap on the butt and sent him out on the field. Then they set up.... Gentry took the snap.... Fernando skipped forward—slipped in the mud! and shanked it—WIDE TO THE RIGHT!

YAHOOO PIONEERS! YAHOOOOO!

As DeGama gripped his knee and writhed on the ground in pain, Chancellor Brewster's jaw dropped like the market on Black Tuesday.

"Oh my God!" gasped Tom Hanagan, suddenly feeling as if he were going to be sick. "We've lost."

CHAPTER 16

The Week of October 9

"Thompson operates on Smith's Achilles tendon tomorrow," said Coach Star, plopping down in his desk chair Sunday morning.

"Don't worry, we'll get by without him, especially if Wallace stays healthy."

"That's a big 'if,' Ed. We shouldn't'a lost that one yesterday."

"You're right. But they got lucky."

"Yeah, maybe. But I'm worried."

"Hey, what's wrong with you, Tony? You been actin' weird all week."

"Ah, it's nothin', man. Forget it."

"If you say so, but I'm tellin' you, we really need to get serious about gettin our asses outta this place. You know what I mean?"

"I haven't given up on Hanagan yet."

"The hell with Hanagan. I talked with Tomachek again last night. He says now's the time to start shoppin' around, while we're still on top."

"I know."

"So?"

"Just give me a coupl'a more days."

"We can't wait much longer."

"Let's just get this next game outta the way, then we'll mess with Hanagan and Tomachek."

"Okay," said the defensive coordinator, lifting his hulk off the gold couch. "On a happier note, I talked with Milt Lee this morning."

"Yeah?"

"Over 60,000 shirts in one week. You know how much bread that is?"

RING RING

"Coach Star here—ah, just one second, I gotta take this call, Eddie."

"Awright, Tony, I'll meet you down in the tape room in a half hour."

"Good. And close the door on your way out, wouldja? Hello Mr. Pigg. . . . No, not too bad . . . What's that? . . . Yeah, Pioneer Field is a tough place to play. . . . That's right, Mike and I are gonna go over the details this week. I should have it back to you by the—middle of next week, sure. . . . All right, sir, have a good day."

• • •

Though the players returned to Metro Saturday night in a state of depression, by Monday morning most of them were back in good spirits. And why not? The young usually rebound quickly from misfortune. Besides, the loss had done little to tarnish their glory in the eyes of the local press, boosters, alumni, parents or classmates. Tied for second place in the conference, with a pair of pushovers coming up in the next two weeks, the players who were still healthy were enjoying the fruits of their success.

On Monday morning, for instance, after watching the conclusion of *Deep Throat* in Prof. Fisher's Gender Issues course, Mongol Harris went to his mailbox and pulled out a letter from Law School Dean Ben Carlucci informing him of his early acceptance to Morgan's prestigious law school, quite an honor for a 2.1 GPA human development major who had scored 110 on the LSAT.

Then there was the phone call Dewey Dobbins—who had slept through his nine and ten o'clock classes—received from Felton Potts inviting him to dinner on Sunday to discuss the possibility of Dewey taking an $85,000 a year position in Potts Industries after graduation.

And the message on Pancho Arnez's voice mail (along with fourteen calls from the three coeds he was currently dating) from the mayor of San Antonio, who wondered if the handsome, soft-spoken lineman would be interested in a $70,000 a year position as head of CRAC—Committee for the Rehabilitation of Adolescent Cocaine Users.

Though defamed of late by the scandal-hungry press, big-time college football players are in general an enviable lot. Pampered and protected by the institutions of higher learning whose colors they carry into battle each week, most continue to receive in college the same perks and privileges that they did in high school. But who would have it otherwise? Are not these boys, after all, the flower of American manhood? And even if one maintained—defying both common sense and tradition—that there is no inherent virtue in athletic prowess, who could deny the heroic courage they display as they face injury and infamy each week in the arena?

No wonder that Boyd Farmer, President of Farmer Paper Products, was honored to accept Ricky Ritter's request for his daughter's hand over prime ribs at the Hunt Club Monday afternoon.

"I cain't think of anybody I'd rather call my son-in-law—and business associate," said the ex-Morgan linebacker to the lantern-jawed halfback, who he was certain would sire a brood of strong and handsome grandchildren on his beautiful and beloved daughter.

Let the almost-rans say what they will, big-time college athletes, provided they are lucky enough to stay healthy and enterprising enough to capitalize upon their opportunities, are truly among the most fortunate citizens of the greatest nation on the face of the earth.

• • •

All the advantages that come with being a successful big-time college football player were lost, however, on Reggie Muggins as he sat in Tom Hanagan's office at 9:15 Tuesday morning. Muggins had been arrested by Metro Police the evening before after punching out his fraternity brother Leroy Powell at Appleby's following the annual BAD/SAS variety show.

"Who the hell do you think you are?" snapped Tom. "You can't just go beating up people in public restaurants, no matter what they say to you!"

According to Reggie's version of the story, he and his fraternity brother had come to blows after Powell had made a crack about him being Coach Star's back-up boy. In actuality, it was more Powell's insistent flirtation with Teeny that had precipitated the violence.

"And if this were the only trouble you'd been in lately, maybe I could let it slide. But that little scene you made in your history class last week has everybody in the school talking."

After getting back his history test the previous Monday, Reggie had stood up in class, crumpled his exam in a ball and thrown it in the trash as he walked out the door.

"What are you trying to prove anyway?"

Needless to say, Tom wasn't really interested in hearing an answer to his question. And even if he had been, it's for sure Reggie wasn't about to share with him the feelings of humiliation, rejection, and anger which had been seething inside him like the waters of a steaming whirlpool bath for the last three weeks.

"And I mean it," said Tom, rising from his seat and motioning toward the door with a jerk of his head. "No more trouble!"

"Pshew, what a morning!" said Tom, pulling out his desk drawer and reaching for the Advil. After getting less than three hours sleep the night before, following a less than friendly meeting with the boosters and two hours spent downtown bailing Reggie out of jail, he and Jan had started to go at it as soon as the alarm rang.

"I've had it, Jan. Career or no career, you're the Mother of a family and I can't have you coming in after ten o'clock every night!"

"You've had it, hah!"

"That's right. It's time you got your head on straight. And this time your Uncle Clifton, who, by the way, you haven't called in two days, agrees with me. And so does Dr. Redman."

"You American men!" she hissed, slipping into a lacy black slip that Tom couldn't remember having seen before. *"You're all a bunch of silly little boys!"*

BUZZ BUZZ

"Yes, Savannah, bring it in and I'll sign it."

As Tom personalized a form letter of condolence to Birmingham Booster Riley Meadows, whose father had just died leaving him a large estate, he felt the warmth of Savannah's body beside him.

"There we go," he said, John Hancocking the letter with administrative flare, lifting up his head, and looking straight at Savannah's breasts.

"You know, Tom," she said, slipping the letter in an envelope, then slowly licking it, "some women don't know a good thing when they've got it."

"You think so?" he asked, searching her kittenish face.

"I know so. And some men don't know either."

Tom sat there and watched her jiggle out of the room and suddenly wondered why he was allowing himself to feel miserable. *This is ridiculous. Here I am, the hottest, well, one of the hottest athletics directors in America. I've got the game of the week coming up on NBC, beautiful babes drooling over me, and we lose one game and I start going to pieces. Get a grip, Tommy! Get a grip! You didn't get where you are being a worry wart. Relax. Two weeks from now after we get that Bowl sewed up, who knows, maybe I'll get a new gig, and if Jan doesn't start straightening up, maybe a new wife too—*

"No! That's ridiculous!" he said, suddenly shaken from his daydream by the ringing of the phone on the desk beside a photograph of Uncle Cliff, Jan, and the kids.

• • •

Chancellor Brewster could have been in a bad mood Wednesday morning. The latest *U.S.A. Today* poll showed his team down four points to number 22. Business School Dean Wally Summers had just told him that the Malaysian fish canning company in which he, Boomer and the Dean had invested had gone belly up. And there had been a rally of concerned citizens at the incinerator in Hargrove County protesting Commissioner Plunkett's decision to let J.P. Morgan University burn toxic waste there until the first of the year.

But the Chancellor, like his Athletics Director, knew that this was no time to let a few annoying negatives outweigh all the good. His football team was favored to win their Homecoming game by sixteen points before a national television audience. *The Chronicle of Higher Education* had called about doing a feature story on him. And his daughter Sweetie Pie was flying home for Homecoming.

RING RING

"Hello, Winnie," he said, picking up his personal line. "That's excellent. I was hoping General Ridley would decide to stay with us this weekend. Now don't forget to tell Lamont about the barbecue pit.... That's right.... And you spoke with the Mariachi band?.... I want them there by five o'clock as soon as we get back from the game.... What's that? ... No, I don't mind if Sweetie Pie brings a friend home with her.... A boy from Harvard? ... That's fine with me. Awright, dear, I've gotta go."

BUZZ BUZZ

"Yes, Anita. Send him right in."

"Have a seat, Jim," said Brewster to his speechwriter, Assistant Director of University Relations Jim Weatherbee. "How's that address of mine coming?"

"I think I got it," said the ex-New York ad-man and former Yale University administrator, beginning to read from a speech entitled "A Coat of Many Colors," which Brewster would be delivering at a curriculum diversification colloquium at Ball State University the following week.

> While there can be no doubt that it is the duty of the university in a pluralistic society to help foster the institutions of democratization through the implementation of a culturally diverse curriculum, this does not mean that we should abandon the traditional core curriculum on which the American liberal arts education is founded. The purpose of a multi-cultural curriculum is not to promulgate one set of cultural values over and against another; it is rather to present the student with an objective forum in which the writings of Salmon Rushdie can

be granted equal and unbiased consideration with those of William Shakespeare, and the political philosophy of Marcus Garvey given the same attention as that of John Locke.

"That's much better. And you put that stuff in about terrorism?"

"Yup, just like you told me. And by the way, Bill, congratulations on your OICUA appointment."

"Well, thank you, Jim. Thank you kindly."

After he'd escorted his speechwriter out, the Chancellor drifted over to his office window to watch the Morgan student body marching to class in the bright sunshine of a crisp October morning. Men and women, black and white, Asian and Latino, Jew and Moslem; athlete and egg-head; qualified and disabled alike, all of them pursuing their career goals, following their dreams. Yes, Chancellor Brewster knew, despite what some radical students and cranky professors like Thaddeus Wilson might say, he had reason to be proud. As he looked at the bust of Franklin Delano Roosevelt, which his mother had given him when he graduated from high school, he knew in his heart that he was doing his utmost to live up to the great statesman's example. And doing it while remaining true to the vision of the University's founder, J. P. Morgan, whose portrait hung behind his desk. *"You're doing a fine job, Brewster,"* smiled down J. P., who had long dreamed of the day when the South would be completely reabsorbed in military and industrial union with the North.

● ● ●

Thursday afternoon practice had been more vigorous than usual. And instead of "chilling out at that crib" that evening, Reggie Muggins was sitting on the bed in his dorm room watching a horror movie with Tootie.

"You see the way she stabbed that motherfucka' in the eye with that ice pick, shit!"

"Gimme som'a that popcorn before you eat it all, wouldja Tootie."

KNOCK KNOCK

"Who's there?" asked the quarterback. "You didn't tell nobody to come up here, did you, Tootie?"

"Not me, Reg."

"Who's there?" demanded Muggins, pressing the pause button on the remote.

"It's Atilla," said a voice from the other side of the door.

"I'm busy, 'Tilla."

"I gotta see you, Reggie. Open up, man."

"I wonder what the fuck he wants." Muggins motioned to Tootie to slide a mirror with several lines of coke on it under the bed, and he got up and opened the door.

"You don't mind if we come in, do you, Reg?" said the linebacker, pushing through the door with Zanzibar Jackson and DeVon White behind him.

"I guess not."

"Good." Atilla eased himself onto a chair across from the quarterback as DeVon White locked the door behind him and stood in front of it with his arms crossed over his chest.

"So what are you—"

"Shut up, Reggie," growled the linebacker. "I ain't here to listen to no mo' a' your booshit."

Silence.

"My boys and me come here to tell you it's time you got your shit together, Reggie. You startin' to create a bad vibe on this team."

"Whaa—"

"SIT DOWN, MOTHERFUCKA! I said it's time you get your attitude adjusted," ordered the bald-headed athlete, suddenly pulling the mirror from under the bed and dumping the coke on the floor. "This shit is fuckin' you up, brotha," he said, glowering malevolently at Reggie's sidekick. "And we ain't gonna let you ruin it for the rest of us. Ain't that right?"

"That's right," nodded Zanzibar and DeVon.

CHAPTER 17

Saturday, October 15
Homecoming

"I t's just plain inconsiderate of her," said Winnie Brewster, tightening the belt of her satin bathrobe around her fashionably waspish waist at 8:00 Saturday morning.

"Now now now, Winnie," said the Chancellor, sitting on the side of their king-size brass bed in his purple silk pajamas, slipping his feet into his slippers.

"Humph. That girl knows how impo'tant this weekend is to us—and to bring that boy home with her!"

"It'll be all right, Winnie. Trust me," he said, stretching out and reaching to turn the handles on the French doors that opened onto the second story balcony. "What a beau-tee-ful day for a football game. Just smell that air!"

"Good morning, Daddy!" rang out the voice of the Chancellor's daughter, who at that moment clip-clopped down the drive in the rear of the house in a velvet riding coat and jodhpurs, helmet and boots, astride Aristotle, a sleek chestnut gelding.

"Hello honey!" halloed Brewster.

"Buenos dias, Señor Brewster!"

"Oh, hello Miguel," said the Chancellor, trying not to let his irritation show when he noticed that the Harvard business school student whom Sweetie Pie had invited home was riding his favorite horse, Curriculum.

"I didn't think you'd mind if Miguel took out Curriculum."

"Er, no, Sweetie, that's just fine. And you're sure you can handle him, Miguel?"

"Oh, no problem." The handsome young Venezuelan laughed

and leaned over to pat Curriculum on the neck. "Hee's a leetle unsure of himself, but with the right training he could be an excellent mount."

"Ah—"

"You come down and veesit us at La Ceiba, and I'll show you some horses."

"There you go again, Miguel," said Sweetie Pie affectionately, leaning over and stroking his arm, "always tryin' to show off."

"I 'm not showing off," said the young caballero, his tie fluttering in the breeze. "Eet's true, my padre raises the finest horses in all of South America."

"Yes—well, you two enjoy your ride," said Brewster, "and I'll meetch'all on the verandah for brunch in just a little while."

"T'ank you, Meester Brewster. Come on, mi guerida, I race you down to the lake and back."

"You know, Winnie," said the Chancellor as he stepped back into the bedroom and closed the door behind him. "You're right, that was kinda inconsiderate of Sweetie Pie to bring that boy home without tellin' us what she was up to."

"Inconsiderate's not the word. It's downright embarrassin'. I mean, what are Clarissa and Betty gonna think?"

At Fulsom Field two hours later, Coach Star was being prepped by the NBC "Game of the Week" production team for the impromptu interview he would give at the beginning of the game.

"Right over here, Coach—How's that camera angle, Jerry? . . . Good . . . That's right, Tony, after you and the team run onto the field, you come over here and Bert will interview you—You sure you got that angle right, Jer? Okay, any other questions?" asked Mo Feinstein, assistant to the assistant producer, jotting notes on his clipboard. . . . "No? Good. Come on over here, Coach, Tom, and let me introduce you to Bert and Hank. And, I forgot your name, honey."

"Savannah McLane, Mr. Feinstein."

"Bert, Hank, this is Coach Star, Tom Hanagan, the A.D., and his assistant, Savannah McLane."

"Good to see you again, Tony," said Bert.

"Good to see you too, Bert."

"Boy, you're havin' a super year."

"Thanks."

"And it's a pleasure to meet you," said pro-football Hall of Fame's Hank Rowdy, looking frighteningly older without his make-up, as he leaned over Tom's outstretched hand to shake Savannah's warm little paw.

"Oh, thank you, Mr. Rowdy."

"Hank to you, honey."

"Awright, people, I guess if you don't have any more questions," said Mo looking at Tony.

"No, I think I got it," answered the Coach.

"And what did Mo say your name was, honey?" asked Bert Alpert.

"Yes, General, we are proud of what we've done here," said the Chancellor to General Miles Ridley as they stood on the deck of the Stadium Club forty minutes before game time, looking down on the Homecoming activities.

"You know, Bill, I can remember when J.P. Morgan was a quiet little university, in a sleepy little southern town."

"No more, Miles," said Chancellor Brewster, brimming over with hospitality, confident, after wining and dining Ridley at his home, that he had sold him on locating the Army's new bioterrorism research program at Morgan. "In fact, I think I can safely say that there's not another academic institution in the South, or in the entire country for that matter, better equipped to face the challenges—"

"Of the 21st century, yes, I'm sure you're right," said the General, taking a sip of his Bloody Mary, waving to a float full of giggling sorority girls dressed up like Daisy Mae being led into line behind a flat bed truck with "KICK BUTT" spelled out in purple and gold paper chrysanthemums.

"I've done everything in my power," continued Brewster, "to make sure this University has stayed on the cutting edge of every field of biomedical research: ultraviolet radon spectroscopy, polymer tissue engineering—"

"And one heck of a football team," said Ridley catching a glimpse of the Morgan players beginning to warm up on the field.

"Well thank you, Miles." Brewster beamed as the thud of drums began to echo from the Music Building parking lot.

"Ahh! the sound of drums!" said the General, who had served as a staff officer to Colin Powell during the invasion of Grenada. "It does an old soldier's heart good to hear 'em."

"Well, here's to old soldiers," said Brewster, as a police siren sounded beneath them and a campus security guard gave them the sign that their car was waiting.

"And to new research laboratories!"

As the Homecoming parade began to cruise around the stadium track, Coach Star made his way through the locker room, making sure his nervous but confident players were ready.

"Ready to go, Bobo?"

"Ready, Coach!"

"Asswad?"

"Let's kick some butt!"

"I guess it's time," said the Coach looking at his watch. "AWRIGHT GUYS! GATHER UP!"

Hello ladies and gentlemen, this is Bert Alpert and Hank Rowdy coming to you this afternoon from the beautiful city of Metro with the NBC "Game of the Week."

"Well, General, here's to the future," said Boomer Cox, standing at the window of the Chancellor's skybox raising his highball to toast their distinguished guest.

"Winnie, Betty, c'mon over here," said Brewster. "They're getting ready for the kick-off."

YEAAA MORGAN! KICK BUTT!

As the capacity crowd rose to its feet, the steel and concrete sta-

dium shivered to its foundations. Then POW! the kick-off went flying and the Homecoming classic was underway.

Nothin' doin' for the Cottonpickers on their first series, Hank.

*No, you're right, Bert. The Knights' defense looks really fired up
for this game today.*

*And here we go, first and 10, Morgan's ball on their own 32. Num-
ber 4, Jimmy Joe Wallace at quarterback takes the snap, drops back
in the pocket, plants himself, and hits Edwardo Holmes at the 47 for
a first down!*

"Now that's what I call getting off to a good start," crowed Brewster, slapping Boomer and the General on the back at the same time.
KICK BUTT! KICK BUTT!

That was a pretty play, Bert.

*Hank, you know a lot of people say this Wallace kid has one of the
best arms in the Mid-South.*

"Go Jimmy! Go Jimmy! Go! Go!" screamed the quarterback's
father, unable to contain himself as he stood between Felton Potts
and Harlan Gooch in the gallery.

"That's a good boy you got there, Jacky Joe, regular chip off the
old block."

As the crowd roared with great expectation, Wallace came to the
line, took the snap. . . . and Bingo! hit Holmes with a perfectly
thrown strike in the end zone for six points! TOUCHDOWN!
MORGAN KNIGHTS!

YAHOOOOOOOO!

"Well well well," clucked Brewster, already anticipating with
pleasure his victory march across mid-field at halftime to crown the
Homecoming Queen. "The boys seem to be on the ball today, don't
they?"

"Yeah they do, Billy Bob!"

Feeling as if a five hundred-pound gorilla had suddenly been lifted off his back, Coach Star heaved a sigh of relief as second string

place kicker Ward Grumbacher booted the point after. *Pshew. I don't know what I'm so uptight about.* Star rolled his head around on his shoulders and massaged the back of his neck. *Eddie's right, we could beat these guys with our walk-ons.*

But the Cottonpickers were not quite the pushovers Ed Tarmeenian had predicted. Though unable to move the ball offensively, their defense shook off the jitters, moved up their linebackers, and refused to let the Knights score again in the first quarter.

I tell you, Hank, this Cottonpicker defense has been putting on a courageous effort so far.

Yes, they have, Bert, but you've got to wonder how much longer they can keep it up. The Knights have had the ball for over fourteen minutes already this half.

KNOCK KNOCK KNOCK

"C'mon on in!" said the Chancellor, momentarily averting his eyes from the field where Ricky Ritter had just picked up another five yards.

"Hi Daddy, sorry we're late." Sweetie Pie led Miguel by the hand into the skybox. "Uncle Boomer, Aunt Betty, I'd like you to meet my boyfriend Miguel." The term "boyfriend" took the Chancellor aback for a moment. "And how are you, General?"

"Just fine, thank you." The General bowed graciously to the Chancellor's daughter and winked at Miguel.

"We'd 'a been here sooner, but I wanted to give Miguel a tour of the campus. Come on over here and take a look, Miguel. Isn't it a hoot?" Sweetie Pie stepped up to the window.

"First down, Billy Bob!" said Boomer, looking down at the field through his binoculars.

"Oh look! There's the queen's float!" said Sweetie Pie.

"Where?" asked Miguel.

"Right over there." She pointed to the track as the crowd once more exploded in a roar of applause when Tutomo Tongo ran a screen pass to the Cottonpicker 28.

"Awright! Awright!"

"What is it, Daddy?"

"We just got another first down, honey."

KICK BUTT! KICK BUTT!

"That's good," said Miguel.

"Yes it is," said Brewster, beginning to explain the game of football to the Venezuelan. "In football, Miguel, when you get a first down—"

"You don't need to explain, Mr. Brewster." Miguel smoothed back his shock of black hair, "I played for Princeton."

"Oh...."

As Jimmy Joe Wallace set the Knights down on the Cottonpicker 47, Coach Star unconsciously felt for his St. Christopher's medal.

Damn! Gotta get that thing fixed, he said, suddenly scooting down the line to cheer on Tongo, who shook off two tackles at the 25 and then cut across the grain at the 20,15, 10. *GO TUTOMO! TOUCHDOWN!*

"Atta boy!" screamed Star, tearing off his headphones and leaping into the air as the hometown crowd raised a cheer that shook the dust off the books in the classics department three blocks away.

Yeah, Rose is right, he thought. *This place is too small for me.*

Well, Bert, that was a sweet move by Tongo.

And a good call by Star, Hank. Let's take a look at it again on the replay. Wallace moves to his left, nice fake to Ritter....

"Well now," said the Chancellor, feeling so good he threw his arm over Miguel's shoulder, "I guess it's time for me to be headin' downstairs."

"Here, Billy Bob, let me straighten your tie," said Winnie, smiling up at the man her father said would never amount to a hill of beans.

"How do I look?"

"As handsome as ever, Daddy." Sweetie Pie gave her father a kiss on his cheek.

Chancellor Brewster exited his skybox and saw Senator Lil' Ed Horton coming out of the men's room.

"Senator Horton! What are you doin' here?"

"Shh—nobody's supposed to know I'm in town." Horton had left Washington the previous afternoon after helping ram through a bill authorizing another fifty billion dollars in aid to Iraq while slashing grade school lunch subsidies at home.

"And look who else is here," the Chancellor chortled as Tom Hanagan stepped out of the elevator. "How are you today, Tom?"

"Fantastic, Bill, how 'bout you?"

"Never been better. By the way, Tom, have you ever met—"

"Of course I have." Tom shook the Senator's firm soft hand.

"That's right, I forgot," apologized Brewster.

"You gentlemen must be feelin' pretty good, eh?"

Brewster winked at Tom. "You bet we are, Senator."

While the teams filed out of the stadium with Morgan leading 14-0, the Chancellor, Homecoming Committee Chairman Tyson Culpepper, and trustee BoDee Grimes, found their seats of honor on the riser at the end of the section C ramp to oversee the Homecoming festivities. Then Smokey Biddel crushed out his Lucky.

Lay-dees and gentlemen! Welcome to Morgan U-ni-versity Homecoming 2003. This afternoon the Morgan U-ni-versity Fighting Knights Band, under the di-rec-tion of Dr. Char-les Bodine, would like to lead you in paying tribute to the men and women of the American Armed Forces!

TWEET TWEEEET!

BOOM Tiddi BOM Tiddi BOOM BOM BOM!

As the percussion started to pound a military tattoo, the twirlers, batons balanced on their shoulders like guns, began marching across the field.

In every land, on every ocean, from one end of the world to the other, the American Armed Forces....

In the pressbox gallery, the Rev. Roy Nash—whose great great grandpappy Colonel Elijah Nash had helped lead the attack on Fort Pillow—lifted his glass to Tom Hanagan.

"We're proud of you, Tom, all of us."

"Yes sirree," said Willard T. Sanders, "it's been a long time since we had anything like this to celebrate around here."

"There's no doubt about it." drawled Milt Lee. "The best dang football in the country is played right here in the Mid-South."

"'Course, we don't wanna count our chickens before they're hatched," said Dudley Dunning, "but I figure. . . ."

After drawing themselves into the shape of an Apache helicopter and a Bradley fighting vehicle, the band finally turned itself into a tiara and trumpeted a fanfare, signaling that the moment had come to crown Her Majesty Queen Morgana.

And now, lay-dees and gentlemen, the mo-ment we all have been waiting for! reverberated Smokey's voice off the Women's Center walls, *the ca-rown-ing of the 2004 Homecoming Queen!*

As Chancellor Brewster started across the playing field to where the queen and her court stood with their proud fathers, a cheer went up from the crowd that took him back thirty-five years to the Homecoming game of his senior year. . . .

No such warm and fuzzy memories, however, filled the heart of Cottonpicker coach Bobby Bacon as he walked up and down the locker room, surveying the damage.

"Campbell's gone, dislocated kneecap. And I don't know about McNab," said Bacon's defensive coordinator, Jobe Tucker. "His whole arm feels numb."

"We can't afford to lose him. Did the Doc check him out?"

"Not yet," said head trainer Boo Westerly, taking off his red and black Cottonpicker cap to scratch his cropped head.

"Boo, we *gotta* pull this one out," said the prematurely gray coach, who couldn't stop thinking about losing his job . . . house . . . cars . . . and mind.

"Well, if somethin' was to happen to Wallace, we just might have a chance."

Silence.

"Think it's time to maybe play the bounty hunter?" The "bounty hunter" was the nickname for defensive end Mookie Fowler, former reform school standout and hatchetman for the Cottonpicker defense.

Westerly smiled. "Could be."

"All right," said Bacon, who the week before had given an address to a convention of Boy Scout leaders in Jacksonville entitled Fair Play. "I'll talk to him."

"And I crown ye Queen Morgana," said the Chancellor to Kathy Wang after delivering a three-minute oration on the virtues of female pulchritude, diversity, education, school spirit, and—you guessed it—Homeland Security.

YAHOO MORGAN!

As two Vietnam-era Jets which Tom had arranged as a surprise roared over the stadium, Chancellor Brewster felt faint with joy. This was the moment he had waited for since taking over at Morgan. And there were tears in his eyes when the band struck up *God Bless America* and formed itself into a gigantic American flag around which marched sixty great great granddaughters of the Confederacy with blinking batons.

In the Morgan locker room, Coach Star was also overcome with emotion. "Just keep your minds on what you're doin'!" he kept telling his players as his own mind kept wandering to Cosmopolis and the glorious future that awaited him there.

On the first play of the second half Wallace connected with Holmes for twenty-five yards. And on the second, with Tongo for another fifteen. The offense was clicking and the crowd was screaming in ecstasy. KICK BUTT! KICK BUTT! YEA MORGAN! Then, on first and 10 from the Cottonpicker 49, Jimmy Joe Wallace spun around to hand off to Ritter and UMPH! was speared in the back by "Hatchetman Fowler." Shaken like a rag doll, Jimmy Joe lay crumpled in a semi-conscious heap. OOOOOOO. A hush descended over the stadium, and Stitches Stevens and Doc Willis tore across the field where they found, to their relief, the quarterback conscious, though confused and temporarily unable to lift his arms.

"Jimmy Joe, count backwards from ten for me."

"I'm okay, Doc, really."

"You sure?" asked the physician, shining his flashlight in Jimmy's eyes.

"Yeah, I'm sure," said Jimmy Joe, now able to see clearly and move his hands."

"You sure you're sure?"

"Yeah." Jimmy Joe hoisted himself on his elbow and slowly raised himself.

"*HOORAY JIMMY JOE!*" rang out the crowd, relieved to see their champion standing, while the referee stamped off fifteen yards against the Cottonpickers.

Raising his hands and shaking his head as if he didn't understand why he'd just been warned about flagrant foul play, Bobby Bacon returned to the sidelines and huddled with his defense. "Okay, boys, we got 'em shook up now, let's sock it to 'em." And so they did. With no threat of the pass, the Cottonpicker linebackers moved onto the line and in three plays pushed Reggie Muggins back to the 34.

"If they can't play the game like gentlemen, they shouldn't be allowed to play," grumbled Chancellor Brewster.

"You're absolutely right," concurred Winnie and Betty as the Morgan field goal attempt went wide to the left of the goal posts.

"And you're certain your head feels okay, Jimmy?"

"Yeah, positive."

"No ringing in your ears?"

"Nope."

"You think he's okay, Doc?" asked Coach Star watching Cottonpicker quarterback Tito Bailey pick up another first down on a sweep.

"He looks okay to me, Coach. No tinnitus."

"Whadda you think, Stitches?"

"I dunno, Coach, that was a nasty shot he took. And sometimes.
. . ."

WHOAA! Star heard a roar, wheeled around and saw Tito Bailey falling across the Morgan 17.

"Yes, General, I think you will find that Metro is every bit as progressive and sophisticated as any other city in America," said Brewster.

Boomer nodded at the Chancellor's words.

"Why, our restaurants and shopping malls, not to mention secondary schools and hospitals, are second to none. And our ballet and symphony are—"

"Look at that boy go!" blurted the General, interrupting Brewster, pointing to the field where Cottonpicker quarterback Tito Bailey was streaking down the sideline to the 15, 10, 5, TOUCH-DOWN! PICKERS!

I tell ya, Bert, somethin' musta happened to this Cottonpicker team at half time.

Yeah, they look like a new team, Hank. And this Bailey kid can be dangerous when he gets rollin'.

"You sure you're okay?"

"Yes, I'm okay, Coach!"

"Awright, Jimmy Joe, go to it."

HOORAY, JIMMY JOE! KICK BUTT!

Jimmy Joe trotted back on the field, and the fans let out a holler that could be heard on the top floor of the engineering building, where Chinese graduate student Ling Ming was jotting notes to go with detailed photographs he had taken of the department's new laser focusing mechanism—information which he knew would save billions in developing weapons systems back home in Beijing.

LET'S GO JIMMY JOE! LET'S GO!

Although Jimmy Joe assured the Coach that he had recovered, it was soon evident that he hadn't. Tentative and impatient, he first overthrew an easy screen. Then on a third and 7 from his own 35, he rolled left, looked for Hayes, "heard footsteps," panicked, and tossed an interception to Calvin Briggs on his own 42.

"Oh, Jimmy Joe, boy! How could you do it?!" wailed his father, mortified in the presence of the boosters.

"And I just wanyou to know whadafantastic job you're doin'," slurred Bunny Culpepper, rubbing up against Tom Hanagan in the gallery. "Tysonanme—"

"Er, excuse me, Ms. Culpepper," said Tom, hearing a gasp and turning toward the field just in time to see Cottonpicker halfback Freedo Davis tearing across the 40, the 35, 30, 25. *This can't be happening*, thought Tom, watching Davis run, as if in slow motion, across the goal line. TOUCHDOWN, COTTONPICKERS!

Stunned by the Pickers' back to back scores, the Homecoming crowd became catatonic—and remained that way for the next fifteen minutes while the pigskin traveled from one end of the field to the other, with neither team able to break the 14 to 14 deadlock.

"That Wallace boy looks tired to me, Billy Bob."

"More like confused," the Chancellor said to Boomer after the General had left the box to go to the men's room.

"Maybe they oughta try Muggins."

"I don't know about that," said Brewster, suddenly hooting with delight as Cottonpicker punter Stan Collins shanked one out of bounds on the Knights 47. "Awright now, boys! Let's score one!"

Boy, what a break for the Knights, Hank. This is the best field position they've had all quarter. And here comes Wallace to the line. He takes the snap from Cluck ... hands off to Tongo. ... And he's in Cottonpicker territory. ... I tell ya, Hank, Wallace still looks shaky to me.

Yeah, you're right, Bert, and I'm not surprised. This Pickers defense has been zeroing in on him every play.

Here we go again. They've got Holmes in motion, Wallace drops back. ... and hits Hayes over the middle for a first down on the Picker 34!!

Resurrected from their torpor, the Morgan fans rose to their feet for a victory certain to be momentarily theirs. And then, on a first and 10, with 1:58 to go, Wallace swiveled to the left to pitch out to Ritter. . . . and KAPOW! the "Hatchetman" nailed him with another teeth-chattering tackle that sent the ball bouncing across the turf.

"Oh my God!" gasped Tom Hanagan, looking down at the kicking, clawing pile-up, five yards from where Wallace lay sprawled.

The Knights are signaling that they've got it, Bert.

We'll know in a minute, Hank, said the sportscaster, breathlessly watching as the officials pried loose the players from the writhing heap. *No! That's number 63, Cottonpicker safety Watt Stones with the ball, Hank. Yes! It's the Pickers' ball, first and 10 from their own 35.*

"I knew it!" stormed Clifton Calhoun, pounding his fist on the arm of the chair where he was sitting in the TV room of his suburban mansion. "I knew I should'a gone to the game." As he lowered himself in his La-Z-boy, his wristwatch started buzzing. "Beulah, it's time for my medicine!"

"I'z comin', Massa Clifton. I be right der. You want anythin' else wif your pills?"

"Yeah, a highball," joked Clifton, his eyes glued to the TV screen where they were removing a semi-conscious Jimmy Joe Wallace from the field. "Awright now, let's get it back!" Clifton let out a deep, rattling cough, and Tito Bailey hunkered down under center.

"Hut one hut two."

"Git him! Git him! Good boy, Bobo!"

Fifty-eight seconds to go, Bailey barked out the signals, took the quick snap and followed his lineman around the weak side where D'Amato had been sucked out of position on a blitz.

"Git 'im!" yelled Clifton, feeling a sudden twinge in his left shoulder. "You got that medicine, Beulah?"

"Here you is, Mas' Clifton."

"Come on now, boys! Stop 'em!" Clifton rocked forward as Bailey let it go, and— KAPOW! he got hit in the chest with a sledge-

THIRD QUARTER · 223

hammer just as Davis crossed the goal line for the game-winning
T.D.

"Oh ma God, Mas' Clifton! Mas' Clifton! Is you all right, Mas'
Clifton??!"

Tom saw Jan and bolted up from the couch in the waiting room of
the cardiac intensive care unit of Morgan Hospital. "Where in the
hell have you been? It's past 8:30."

"Is he going to—"

"We don't know," whispered Tom, opening his arms to embrace
his wife who walked past him to go hug Aunt Inez.

"Inez, are you okay?"

"Ooooo, oooo."

The waiting room elevator opened and out stepped Dr. Lucius
Thompson.

"How is he, Lucius?" gasped Inez, her hands clenched at her
breast.

"He's going to be all right, dear." Thompson took Inez's hands in
his.

"You're sure?"

"Yes, he's got the best team of cardiologists in the country in there
with him."

Inez burst into tears and collapsed in Jan's arms.

Tom looked at Lucius.

"Cliff has had a serious myocardial infarction."

"A—"

"Heart attack."

"But we have him stabilized."

"Thank God he's alive!" said Tom, embracing the two teary-eyed
women, inquiring of his wife in a whisper, "where the hell have you
been, Jan, I've been tryin' to reach you for three hours."

"Yes, thank God Beulah was there," said Brewster a half-hour later.
"And if there is anything you need, Inez, just call. All right, dear,
goodnight." Brewster hung up the phone in the second floor study

of his house and listened to the laughter and mariachi music from the deck of the pool below. He couldn't remember having ever felt so— he couldn't even think of the word he felt so wretched. In the time it takes to play two quarters of football, he had gone from the pinnacle of happiness to the pit of depression.

"There you are," said Winnie, poking her head through the door. "Are you all right, Bill?"

"No, not really," he sighed. "But I just spoke with Inez, and it looks like Clifton's gonna make it."

"Oh, thank God.... I think you better come on down now, honey, the General's ready to leave."

"I'll be down in a minute," said Brewster, looking onto the deck where the remaining party-goers, mostly young couples, the sight of whom made him feel very old, were drunkenly dancing in each others' arms. As he started to drag himself out of his chair, Sweetie Pie bounced in the room.

"Daddy!" she squealed, bubbling with a youthful effervescence that made him smile in spite of himself.

"Hel-lo honey, you havin' a good time?"

"Wonderful!" she blurted out, "I mean, as good as can be expected, considering."

"That's all right, baby." The Chancellor smiled and patted her hand. "You looking' for your momma?"

"No, Daddy. I was looking' for you," she said, putting on a serious face. "The way Momma's been actin' I'd be afraid to tell her."

"Tell her what, honey?"

"That Miguel and I are gonna get engaged, Daddy!"

"What did you say?!!"

"I said Miguel has asked me to marry him, Daddy! Oh, I'm so excited!"

"Ah, er, ah—"

"Oh, I just knew you'd understand!" Sweetie Pie threw her arms around her father. "I just hope Miguel's parents feel the same way too. You know we're not exactly from the same class."

"Well, you know, honey, that is something to consider."

"I know it is, Daddy. Miguel's told me it's not gonna be easy to get his parents' permission to marry a po' li'l American girl like me."

"WHAT?!!!"

CHAPTER 18

The Week of October 16

The coaches groaned at nearly every inch of footage they reviewed Sunday morning.

"For Chrissakes, Arnez! Stay put!" ... "You stupid asshole, White, get inside your man!" ... "He's over there, Bumhoffer, you dumb lump of shit!" "I swear, Tony," groaned Ed, "I've never seen these kids play so bad. And watch the next move by D'Amato—splat! Right on his ass."

Had they won, most of the team's mistakes would have gone unnoticed. But they hadn't, and to the bleary eyes of the hung-over staff, the players looked like Keystone Kops.

"I need a break," groaned Star. "Tell you what, guys, let's take ten and then we'll come back and watch the last quarter."

Grumbles of approval all round.

As he plodded to his office and sat down at his desk, on top of which lay the *Sunday Tribune* open to a photo of Cochise Cubbins sitting on the bench crying after the game, Tony was overcome by negative thoughts—dark, doubtful, disagreeable thoughts as unwelcome in the Brave New World of the Calhoun Complex as they would have been in Metro's downtown towers of commerce. Fortunately he didn't have to endure his own reflections long before Ed walked in the door.

"That was like watchin' a horror movie!"

"You're right, Eddie. I don't know what the hell we're gonna do if Wallace is really hurt."

"What does Stitches say?"

"He don't know for sure."

"How 'bout Willis?"

"He says he can't really see anything wrong from the tests, but—"

"Ah, he'll be all right. But those were some mean shots he took."

"He better be okay 'cause Muggins—"

"Is worthless, like you've always said."

"I can't figure it out, what's his problem?"

"Dope, Tony. Carver told me that Symeon Smith told him Muggins has been doin' a lot of cocaine."

"Jesus Christ."

"That's right, and that's why I keep tellin' you, buddy, we need to call Tomachek. I spoke with him last night. He said he's sure he can get us—"

"Not now, Eddie, please."

"Jesus Christ, Tony"—Ed heard Porky Watson calling him from down the hall. "I'M COMIN', WATSON!"—"It's time to make our move—now."

"Yeah, I know."

Alone again with his negative thoughts, Star was spared once more by the ring of the phone.

"Coach Star here."

"Just the man I wanted to talk to," came the warm and chilling voice of Hamilton Pigg. "Your wife said I could reach you at your office.... Yeah, I bet you have.... That was a tough one yestaday.... You just neva know, do you?" said the oil man, smiling as he watched his wife sit up on the deck of his yacht, tie her bikini top back on and walk over to join him. "But anyway, I was callin' to see if you'd sent that letta' of intent yet?... You're gonna send it today? ...I know, you been busy, but I tell you what, seein' as how you didn't get a chance to send it back to me yet, I'm gonna get my attorney to fax a new one to your boy Tubo this afta'noon.... Yes, I know you still have the old one, but.... Excuse me a second, Coach... Honey, would you tell Chichi to bring me a li'l Tabasco for my lobsta' salad?... Hello, Coach?... Like I was sayin', I'm gonna have my attorney send y'all a new letter.... Well, no, not exactly ... You know things have changed a little since I gave Tubo that first letter, and frankly the powers-that-be down here are havin' some second thoughts about a couple items" (like paying Tony the full $550,000 they had first offered him unless he won at least eight games). "So, like I said, I'm gonna send a new letter this afta'noon. . . . And you tell Tubo that I'd like your final decision as soon as possible. . . . Oh, let's say Friday, by twelve noon—*or the deal's off!* . . . *Silence* . . . "Well now, I'll let you get back to your x's and o's while the ole wife and I get ready for church. Have a good day, Coach." *CLICK.*

• • •

If Tom Hanagan seemed to keep steering the conversation on Monday to such deep and meaningful subjects as the transitoriness of life, the consolation of religion, and the need to share our feelings with our loved ones while we can, it was not, as Dudley Dunning suggested to the Chancellor later that afternoon because he was trying to avoid talking about Saturday's loss.

"Yes," said Tom, "I saw Cliff for a couple minutes this morning, Roscoe. And thanks to everyone's prayers, he's much better. . . . That's right, and the doctors are very optimistic. . . . Yes, it does kinda make you think, doesn't it? . . . The what? . . . No, I haven't thought much about the game, with Clifton bein' sick and everything."

BUZZ BUZZ

"Hello, Fulton. . . . How is he? . . . Well, I saw him this morning and thank God he's. . . . Oh, you mean Jimmy Joe (*gulp*). Well, Doc Willis is optimistic. . . . No, he couldn't find anything wrong. But we need to be careful. He took some mean shots Saturday. . . . Yes, I'm sure the Coach will have him back as soon as he can. . . . Cliff? He's doing well too," said Tom. "And according to the. . . . Oh, you gotta go? . . . Okay, I'll tell Clifton you called."

Despite what Dudley and others might have thought, Tom seriously meant it when he said he didn't know what he'd do without Uncle Cliff. The two of them had become close over the past two months, drawn together not only by the Knights' impressive string of victories but also their mutual concern for Jan.

I really am starting to worry that something is wrong with her,

thought Tom, hanging up after trying to reach Jan again at work. *First time we had a chance to sit down with each other for weeks was in the hospital, and she seemed like she was a million miles away....*
BUZZ BUZZ

"No, Savannah, I can't talk with Ms. Brooks right now!" *Silence*—I'm sorry, hon, I didn't mean to yell at you. Tell Ms. Brooks I'll call her tomorrow."

"Women!" he said, shaking his head.
BUZZ BUZZ

"Who?...Sure. Hey Blake, what's up?...No, I'm not lookin' forward to that booster meetin' tomorrow either, especially with Clifton sick and everything. In fact, while we're talkin' about it, I was wondering if you wouldn't mind if I slipped out of the meeting early...*Silence*...Blake?...You still there?"

• • •

Having exorcised their anger by subjecting the players to two hellish conditioning sessions on Sunday and Monday, Star and his coaching staff had returned to their normally supportive and solicitous selves by Tuesday afternoon.

"What the fuck are you doin', d'Amato?! When you see that guard start to pull, you follow him! You got it?!"

"You dumb motherfucker, Lewis?! I told you to break inside on that post pattern!"

As the trainers carried another member of the scout team—the fourth stringers who simulate the opponent's formations—off the field, it was clear from the way the humiliated players were hitting that they were looking for a chance to redeem themselves.

"They're popping each other like they mean it today," said Jet.

"They better be," said Star. "But I'm still not sure who to start at quarterback." Convinced by Stitches that, despite Dr. Willis' clean bill of health, Jimmy Joe Wallace should sit out at least one more game, the Coach was left with the unpleasant task of deciding whether to start Muggins or Gentry on Saturday. "Whad'da you think, Jet?"

"I dunno. Muggins looks okay today. But you never know with him. One day he's up, the next day he's down. On the other hand, Gentry ain't lookin' bad either—and he's at least consistent."

"Yeah, consistently mediocre," said the Coach. "But I think we better go with him anyway. And tell Muggins to come see me in my office after practice."

KNOCK KNOCK

"Yo, c'mon in." Star leaned back in his chair and watched as Muggins, affecting an air of defiant nonchalance, shuffled into the office. "Have a seat, Reg."

"Yeah, thanks. *I can see the Coach needs me now,* thought Muggins. *His boy got hurt and he wants me to save his ass.*

"You doin' okay?"

"Yeah."

"Good. You know we haven't had much of a chance to talk lately."

"Uh huh." *Maybe you been too busy talkin' to your boy Wallace.*

"And I guess that's why I've been feelin' like things aren't right between us."

No response.

"And you know, Reg, that upsets me. I like to feel my guys can talk to me when somethin's wrong. Like a father or a big brother."

"Right," said Reggie, who had never had a father at home he could talk to.

"You understand what I'm sayin'?"

"Yeah, I guess."

"I hope so, 'cause we need to communicate if we're gonna win ball games. Now I don't think there's any kind of black-white thing gettin' in our way, is there?"

"No, not really," said the quarterback, who, although he regarded the Coach's system as exploitative, didn't think that Tony was particularly prejudiced.

"So what's the problem then?"

"Problem?"

"You're not usin' drugs, are you?"

"Who told you I was usin' drugs?!"

"Nobody's said anything about you usin' drugs, Reggie. I'm just asking a question. Are you usin' drugs?"

"No!"

"Good. 'Cause sooner or later everybody who does gets caught."

"I told you I ain't usin' drugs, and that's the truth!"

"Okay, Reggie, I believe you. Anyway, the reason I needed to talk with you is because I'm thinkin' of startin' Gentry this Saturday."

Silence.

"'Course nothing is written in stone. But I just thought I'd tell it to you like it is. None of the staff thinks you've been playin' up to potential. And it's just not fair to the team to play somebody whose attitude isn't a hundred percent. You understand?"

Silence. Humiliating angry silence.

"Now, like I said, nothing's written in stone, and if I was to see that old desire and attitude, I'd be only too happy to have you in there leading this team." ... *Silence* ... "Well, I guess that's about it." Star shuffled some papers on his desk.

· · ·

On Thursday afternoon, an editorial appeared in the school newspaper, *The Knight Errant*, that sent shock waves rumbling from one end of campus to the other.

"What do you mean you don't know where he got the information?!!!" screamed Tom Hanagan over the phone at his sports information director. "He got it somewhere! ... Well, you damn well better find out!" ... *CLICK.*

RING RING

"Hey Blake ... Yeah, big trouble," said Tom as he looked at the headline of the newspaper on his desk:

ATHLETICS DEPARTMENT RAPES STUDENT
BODY FOR ONE MILLION MORE DOLLARS

232 · KICK BUTT

"You mean you haven't seen it yet? . . . Well, listen to this:

> On October 14th, the Athletic Advisory Committee,
> chaired by Dean Paul Fisher, approved a million dol-
> lar hike in the University's already over-inflated 23.4
> million dollar Athletics Department budget. Citing
> the increased cost of facility maintenance and debt
> service costs as the reason for the increase, Dean
> Fisher and his committee not only approved the
> increase but also drafted a resolution, sure to be
> approved at next week's meeting of the Board of
> Trust, stating that the Athletics Department's
> increased budget should be defrayed by a fifteen per-
> cent increase in our yearly student activities fee.
> Extortion is the only word for such underhanded
> activity. If Tom Hanagan and his gang of over-paid
> bureaucrats in Calhoun can't balance their budget,
> should we keep bailing them out? The Athletics
> Department at the University has lost on the average
> 1.84 million dollars every year for the last ten years.
> If any other department at this University lost that
> much annually. . . .

"Bla bla bla . . . Yeah, it goes on for two more pages. And they did up
a nice little list of facts on the editorial page:

> FACT: Of the 1034 NCAA, 290 NAIA, and 468 Junior
> College Athletics Programs in America, only ten to
> twenty are annually in the black.
> FACT: Forty percent of most athletics department
> budgets goes to paying the salaries of department
> employees.
> FACT: Graduation rate statistics. . . .

"The editor's name is Tim Randolph, the same troublemaker who
wrote that article last year criticizing remedial education courses. . . .

RING RING ... "Hold on a sec, would you? ... It's Brewster, I'll talk to you later.... Yes, Chancellor ... Yes I did.... You're angry? I could kill somebody.... I've been tryin' to find out how he ever got his hands on the information. (Statistics on athletics department finances, though not strictly speaking confidential, were at Morgan, as at most schools, by no means readily accessible.) I think campus security ought to look into it too. And that stuff about crime and violence at sporting events.... Of course it's ridiculous. You can't expect to bring 60,000 people onto a college campus and not have a few problems. I can assure you it was no one in this office.... Yes sir, I know you have your board meetings next week. And"—CLUNK. I swear I'm gonna tell Brewster where to stick it one of these days! I really am. He acts like I wrote that article." ... BEEP BEEP ... "Savannah, get Campus Security for me."

"Ah, I wouldn't worry about that stupid editorial, Tommy," said Coach Star when he and Tom were finally served their T-bones later that evening. "It's just some little faggot tryin' to get attention."

"Well he certainly succeeded."

"Not really. He didn't say nothin' that everybody doesn't know. People aren't stupid. Everybody knows what a racket college football is. And you know what? Nobody really gives a damn how much money we slip 'em, or how many drugs they take, or what percentage of them graduate from college. If they really cared, we'd have been out of business a long time ago. No, the only thing anybody really cares about is winning."

"I suppose."

"You know I'm right, Tommy. Of course you can't get caught red-handed.... Could you get us a little more butter, hon? ... I wouldn't worry about some stupid student newspaper article."

"You're right, Tony," said Tom, "I guess I'm just uptight about this coming weekend. You think we got this one in the bag?"

"This weekend? Yeah, I do." Star avoided his friend's eyes.

"We need to," said Tom, allowing himself for the first time all week not to exude confidence and positive vibrations.

"Yeah, I feel real good about this one," Star reiterated, devouring a huge chunk of steak.

"You must, 'cause I haven't seen you this laid back since July."

"Really?"

"Yeah."

"I guess I am feeling kinda laid back." Tony had started to feel more relaxed after he had signed and mailed off the revised letter of intent to Mike Tubo on the way to work that morning. "It's after the break that I'm worried about. We got some tough customers comin' up."

"And how's Wallace doin'?"

"He's okay. He'll be ready to go sooner than everyone thinks."

"Did you talk to Muggins yet?"

"Yeah, I did."

"And?"

"I dunno." Star carved himself another hunk of steak. "How's Clifton?"

"The doctor says it looks like he's gonna be okay."

"Whew. Jan must be relieved, huh?"

"I guess so."

"Whad'da you mean, you guess so?"

"I dunno, Tony, she's been acting so weird lately, I don't know what she's thinking."

"She's probably just upset."

"I don't know."

• • •

Since the days when Walter Camp first combed the backwoods of New England looking for semi-literate ploughboys to use in Yale's flying wedges, recruiting has been the name of the game. The best-paid, winningest coaches are always those who can recruit the best talent. No wonder, then, that on the Friday before Morgan played its weakest opponent, over sixty of the South's most sought-after prospects were on campus for two days of intensive pampering and promotion.

"That's right, Chancellor," said Tom Hanagan, "Luke and his parents had a tour around campus earlier this morning."

"Good," said the head administrator, smiling at Tennessee Prep football and basketball star Luke Meadows and his family. "And I hope you enjoyed yourselves."

"Yessir. You have a vera' beautiful campus," said Luke's mother. "It reminds me of Duke's."

"And Georgia's," added Luke's daddy, anxious to let Chancellor Brewster know what a highly sought after commodity their boy was.

"Yes, we do have some beautiful grounds here."

"And an excellent pre-law program," interjected Tom.

"One of the finest pre-law programs in the country," said Brewster, picking up Tom's cue. "Our pre-law students receive higher LSAT scores than any other private university in the South"—which was consoling to Mr. and Mrs. Meadows, since Luke's SAT scores were 200 points lower than the rest of his class. "In fact, many of our athletes go right on to law school here at Morgan. No, there's no doubt about it, this is the place for Luke to pursue both his academic and athletic careers. Did you have any questions you wanted to ask me, son?" Brewster smiled paternally at the 6-foot, 5-inch, 230-pound senior.

"Naw, I guess not," mumbled Luke, anxious to finish the interview, get rid of his parents, and find Morgan point guard Ronnie Ryan, whose job it was to show him a good time while he was in Metro.

"Well then, if you have any further questions, I'm sure Mr. Hanagan or Dean Fisher will be happy to answer them."

"Yeah, thanks," said Luke, visions of the exotic dancers Ronnie had promised to take him to see undulating through his adolescent mind.

"Yes, we would be proud to have a young man of your son's caliber at our University, Mr. and Mrs. Meadows," said the Chancellor, standing up from his throne chair by the fireplace. "Mighty proud indeed." Tom cleared his throat. "Oh yes, before I forget, Tom tells me you're in the plumbing business, Mr. Meadows." Mr. Meadows nodded. "You really need to meet Jim Ed Leech while you're in town. I'm sure you know who he is."

"Of course I do." Mr. Meadows bobbed his head up and down at the mention of the Mid-South's most prosperous wholesale plumbing goods supplier.

"He's one of our biggest supporters here at Morgan, always ready to do whatever he can for the program. Well, it's been a pleasure, Mrs. Meadows, Mr. Meadows, Luke. I'll see y'all tomorrow."

• • •

Saturday arrived none too soon. For six long days, Chancellor Brewster, Tom Hanagan, the coaches, team, boosters, alums, and a million Purple Knights fans had been smarting from their nationally televised loss to the Cottonpickers. The players needed redemption, the fans wanted revenge.

Despite several injured starters and Red Carlisle's prophecies of doom, Coach Star was confident of victory over the 0 and 6 Southwest Missouri State Porcupines. He and his staff had worked round the clock to get the team ready for the game. And as he watched his players enthusiastically knocking shoulders, butting heads, and growling obscenities on the sidelines across the field from the Porcupines, he felt confident that if Gentry could refrain from turning over the ball, his team would go into their second break poised for post-season play—and he into the next round of contract negotiations with Pigg in a position of power. *You need this one, Tony*, Mike Tubo had told him on Wednesday. *Otherwise, Pigg's not gonna give in on any points.*

"AWRIGHT, GUYS, NOW LISTEN UP!" roared Star as the referee signaled that Morgan had won the toss, "This is the most important football game of your lives. . . ."

The crowd in the stadium gallery were on edge. Tom made the rounds as quickly as he could, and then excused himself to go see his Aunt Inez on the 50.

"You don't need to sit down here with us, Tom," said Inez. "You go back upstairs." Coach Star's secretary, Peaches Perdue, had accompanied her old bridge partner to the game.

"No, no, Inez, I insist," said Tom.

"Well, awright," she sniffed.

"And you're sure there's nothing I can get for you?" he asked.

"No, I don't think so." Inez looked at Peaches.

Peaches shook her head. "No thank you." And suddenly she remembered what it was she wanted to tell Tom. "Before I forget, somebody named Bobby Brooks called us yesterday looking for you."

"Bobby Brooks?"

"Yes. She said she'd been trying to reach you all week at your office and hadn't had any luck."

"It's been a hectic week."

More like dreadful, he thought as he watched the kamikaze squadrons take to the field for the kick-off. *Back and forth to the hospital to see Clifton, fighting with Jan, dodging phone calls.* Yes, it *had* been a bad week — much worse, in fact, than Tom suspected. For if he'd known why his friend Tony never had time to talk about his contract; what Dudley Dunning was discussing with Kansas City Chief's coach, Mel Beerbauer on Wednesday; or where Jan was calling from Thursday night; he would have been even more out of sorts than he was. *They've been on my back all week: Brewster, Dunning, the whole pack of them. They're like a bunch of spoiled children. You treat 'em to a coupl'a ice cream cones and they expect a banana split every night. If we don't win this one, they won't be fit to live with. And I can tell Tony's upset. No matter what he says. Poor son of a bitch, he's probably worried about his contract.*

Seventy rows above the disc-rupturing ruckus on the floor of Fulsom Field, Chancellor Brewster was, like his Athletics Director, worried. But, unlike Tom, he knew better than to let it show. "Yeah, we win this one," he said, watching from the sky box window as

Ricky Ritter ran a reverse down to the Missouri State 34, "every Bowl committee in the country will be after us."

"I s'pose so," said trustee BoDee Grimes, sipping his Gentleman Jack.

"You gotta think positive, BoDee," said Brewster. "Why, if we hadn't kept our chins up, we'd never be where we are today!"

Seemingly unruffled by the presence of the Board of Trust opposition leader in his skybox, Brewster was a picture of conviviality. "C'mon now, everybody, let's have a toast to ole Morgan." Even though he knew that BoDee had come to the trustees meeting from Dallas gunning for him, armed with the latest financial figures—hospital revenue off 17 percent, contributions to the 2005 Endowment Campaign down 20 percent, tuition costs up 7 percent—he knew better than to let this ruthless self-made billionaire see him sweat. One sign of weakness and BoDee would lead the wolves in for the kill. "Looks like you need that drink of yours freshened up a bit, Tyson."

"Don't mind if I do, "said BoDee's head co-conspirator.

"Hold on, everybody!" shouted Boomer as Anthony Gentry suddenly hit Lewis in the flat. 5, 4, 3, 2, 1, TOUCHDOWN!"

"Like I said," crowed Brewster, filling Tyson Culpepper's high ball glass, "don't make any plans for New Year's Day! Cee-gar, BoDee?"

Yes, BoDee was a formidable adversary, but the Chancellor was determined, as he told his wife while he dressed for the game, not to let anybody run him off *till he was gol' darn good and ready to move on*. Nor was it just pride that steeled him. He felt a moral obligation to keep BoDee Grimes from gaining control of the University. An outspoken opponent of affirmative action, minority studies programs, and funding for gay and lesbian social organizations, the lean and cantankerous fifty-three year old BoDee had even gone so far as to stipulate that not one cent of the three million dollar gift he had given to his Alma Mater the year before be spent supporting the "One World One People" International Studies consortium or the "Medgar Evers" lecture series, both of which had earned Morgan the highest grades in national academic circles.

THIRD QUARTER • 239

"FUMBLE! It's a fumble!" roared Brewster, after the Porcupines deep man coughed up the ball on his own 16. "We got it! We got it!"

No, the Chancellor was not about to let BoDee turn back the clock. He and his University Relations team had spent thousands of hours and millions of dollars putting Morgan in the top twenty-five academic ratings. And just because his sources of funding had temporarily dried up with the downturn in the economy, it didn't mean he was going to hand the school over to a bunch of wealthy philistines.

"Awright, boys, put that ball in there!" . . . TOUCHDOWN! *KICK BUTT! KICK BUTT!*

"Well now, BoDee, 14 to zip. And we haven't even started the second quarter. There's just nothin' like a *good* football game, is there?"

Good was not the word, however, that any but the most fanatical Morgan partisan would have used to describe the game. Eighteen turnovers, 245 yards worth of penalties, miscues, and missed tackles—the Knights-Porcupines game was a gridiron comedy of errors that ended as it had begun on a bobbled play which Morgan turned into three more points in their 42 to 6 rout of Missouri.

As the Chancellor and his guests watched the students swarm onto the field and begin pulling down the goal posts, he smiled.

"Looks like it's gonna be a hot time in the old town tonight, eh BoDee?" And indeed he was right—hotter than he'd ever dreamed.

KiPhi sorority sister DeeDee Grimes had started partying at the SAE House immediately after the game. And by 10:00, the effects of the Ecstasy and beer she'd been drinking all afternoon had begun to wear off. Too early to call it a night, BoDee's beloved daughter decided to go back to her dorm room and get some more drugs.

"Y'all stay here and dance," she said to her suitemates. "I'll be all right on my own."

But unfortunately, when DeeDee got out of her purple Corvette in the parking lot behind Natchez House—the garden apartment dorms where the children of the well-to-do enjoyed the amenities of suburban condo life while they attended college—she wasn't alone.

Rodney Hampton, out on early release from the Metro Juvenile Detention Center, and his main man, Angelo Brown, also recently released from jail after serving two years of an eight year sentence for robbing and brutally beating a seventy year old black woman in the Projects, were on the prowl.

"Check dat out," whispered Rodney as he and Angelo watched DeeDee woozily weave her way from the parking lot toward the dormitory.

"Yeah, jus' like I tol' you, man," said Angelo. Angelo had recently heard that the west end of campus—considered a dangerous neighborhood for crime after a mugger had nearly stabbed to death a foreign student following a basketball game—was again safe for business.

"Let's go," said Rodney, slipping with his friend from the shadow of the catalpa trees that lined the street behind Natchez House.

DeeDee stumbled up the sidewalk to the door of her dorm and began to fumble with her keys. Angelo and Rodney crept up behind a dumpster and were just about to pounce, when a student on a bicycle turned the corner at the end of the walk.

"Fuck!" cursed Angelo, watching as the student cruised past them. Then a light went on up on the second floor of DeeDee's dorm.

"Shit!" growled Rodney, preparing to depart when he noticed that DeeDee had left her keys in the door.

"You see what I see, Angelo?"

"Yeah, man, whad'da you wanna do?"

"I dunno."

"Lez wait and see if she comes back out."

"I got a better idea. C'mon!" Rodney walked to the entrance of DeeDee's apartment and gently rapped on the door two times.

"Man, whatchoo doin'?" whispered Angelo, nervously looking up and down the walk behind him. Rodney knocked several more times, then slowly turned the knob and cracked open the door.

"Hello, is anybody home?"

No answer.

"Hello," he repeated a little louder. "Is anyone in?"

Hearing no reply a second time, Rodney slipped into the darkened apartment, followed by Angelo, gun in hand. No sound coming from the floor above, Rodney tiptoed to the foot of the stairs, and once more called out. Again there was no reply. Surmising that DeeDee had passed out, Rodney left Angelo to guard the front door and pussyfooted up the stairs, where he found her on a bed in the back room. Looking at the billionaire's daughter lying there, her golden hair spilling out over a purple satin pillow, her skirt hiked up revealing the unshaven down of her thighs, Rodney thought of rape.

"C'mon, man, hurry up," came Angelo's voice from downstairs.

But, alas, this was neither the time nor the place. *Some other evening, perhaps*, whispered Rodney to himself. Then he leaned over DeeDee and gently began to open the purse that was slung over her chest ... gently ... gently. Suddenly DeeDee opened her eyes and let out a blood curdling "RAAAPE!" that sent Angelo flying through the front door, across the dormitory lawn and into the safety of the shadow of a hedge that ran along the parking lot.

"RAPE! HELP! RAPE!"

Down the stairs and out the front door, Rodney would have also escaped had not campus patrolman Charlie Doolin just at that moment arrived at the dorm to resuscitate a comatose partyer. Hearing DeeDee's cries, he saw someone streak past him and was instantly in pursuit. Down the walkway, past the picnic tables, through the volleyball pit, Rodney was about to lose Doolin when "MOTHA-FUCK!!" he tripped over a toy truck in front of the married student apartments and flew headfirst onto the pavement.

"Stop! Right there! Halt!"

As Rodney rose to his feet, Sgt. Doolin, fearing that he might be suspended if he pulled his revolver, clubbed Rodney over the head with his flashlight. *UGH!* Down went the stunned juvenile delinquent. The sergeant reached for his phone and up sprang Rodney. No stranger to the strength of the drugged and drunk, Doolin again let Rodney have it with his flashlight. And this time, Rodney, hands and face covered with blood, did not get back up. As the sergeant stood panting over the dazed youth, two other campus policemen, who had been ticketing illegally parked student cars, ran up with guns in hand.

"Don't move! Put your hands behind your head, boy." Patrolman Grundy Gates straddled the bleeding ex-convict and kicked his legs apart so he could search him for weapons.

"Good work, sarge," said the other patrolman, his chest heaving from his 200-yard dash.

"Thanks, Wilbur," said Doolin, leaning back against a no-parking sign as the night air was suddenly pierced by the sound of a voice shrieking "POLICE BRUTALITY! POLICY BRUTALITY!"

"I saw the whole thing," yelled Cedric McKinney, a second year law student, running up to the policemen.

"I saw it too," wailed Dr. Sarah Green, an overweight middle-aged economics teacher who had just returned from a six-month sabbatical in Cuba. "You brutally beat that young man."

"POLICE BRUTALITY! POLICY BRUTALITY!" shouted Cedric McKinney to a crowd of gawking students who had begun to gather on the sidewalk.

"You betta get outta here, boy!" growled patrolman Gates, "and take your friend with you."

"Are you threatening us?!" threatened Dr. Green.

CHAPTER 19

Later that night

ou done good, Billy Bob, said the Chancellor to himself yawning contentedly as he turned off ESPN. *Real good,* he repeated a moment later slipping off his bathrobe and slippers and climbing into bed beside his wife. *No way after that ball game today the Board won't go along with the new learning disability center. I can see ole BoDee's face right now.* The Chancellor chuckled as his head hit the pillow, and in less than five minutes he was enjoying a deliciously lubricious dream in which he, dressed in nothing but a football helmet and shoulder pads, was about to ravish a beautiful young black woman who bore a striking resemblance to Dr. Noweeta Hayes.

Then, at 12:20, the phone on his night table rang. "Yesss?" he said. "Who? . . . What?!! Say that again, Dudley. . . . BoDee's daughter raped?! . . . Oh my God! . . . You're at the emergency room? . . . Of course. I'll be right there."

Forty minutes later the Chancellor found Dudley and Clarissa Dunning standing outside a small examination room in the emergency pavilion of the University hospital. The Dunnings, unbeknownst to him, had been entertaining BoDee Grimes at their home when the police called about his daughter.

"So how is she?"

"Dunno," said Dudley. "BoDee and the doctor are in there with her right now. Po' kid was babblin' like she was outta her mind."

"When did you get here?"

"About 11:30 I guess. Campus security called us at the house."

"Did they catch the—"

"Yes, campus security ran him down about two blocks from the dorm. Twenty-one-year old nig—black, out on parole. The usual story."

"This is dreadful, simply dreadful."

Calling Dr. Luker, Dr. Luker, you're wanted in the ER.

"How long has BoDee been in there with her?"

"'Bout half an hour now. They had to give her a sedative to calm her down."

"I don't know what this world is coming to," muttered the Chancellor, shaking his head. "Things like this never used to happen here."

"You're right! They didn't!" snarled BoDee, stepping out of the examination room. "And it's incompetent idiots like yourself who are responsible for them happening now! What kind of place are you running here anyway?" roared the Southern Baptist billionaire, livid with rage after being informed that sperm had been found in his daughter's vagina.

"I'm sorry, BoDee, I really am," stammered Brewster, reaching out and trying to calm the enraged parent.

"You're goddam right you're sorry, the sorriest excuse for a Chancellor—"

"Ah, Mr. Grimes,"—Dr. Luker poked his head through the door— "could you come back in here a moment?"

"C'mon Billy Bob, let's go sit out in the waiting room," said Dudley, taking him by the arm.

It was not until two hours later, after Chancellor Brewster and the Dunnings had left the hospital, that DeeDee was sufficiently in control of herself to tell her father that he didn't need to worry about her getting pregnant, because she was taking birth control pills prescribed by Dr. Elmo Smart at Student Health.

"What?!! I swear to God I'll have that sonofabitch fired!" bellowed BoDee in righteous indignation—and relief.

What DeeDee did not tell her daddy or the doctors was that the sperm in her vagina actually belonged to quarterback Anthony Gentry. Whether she withheld this information out of fear of her father's wrath or from confusion as to exactly what had happened is uncertain. What is certain, however, is that her failure to tell the whole truth led to a scandal that disrupted not only the Morgan student body, the faculty and the administration, but most importantly, the football team.

FOURTH QUARTER

CONVERSION

All people care about is bread and games.

JUVENAL
Satire 10

CHAPTER 20

The Week of October 23

Tom Hanagan opened the Sunday newspaper to the local section and couldn't believe his eyes. *"MORGAN COED ASSAULTED IN DORM ROOM. At 10:30 P.M. on Saturday evening, Morgan coed Bodeena Grimes was assaulted in her Natchez House Dormitory.* Outraged that someone had assaulted the daughter of one of his acquaintances and shocked that the University had allowed the story to go to print—BoDee had demanded it—Tom wondered what Brewster would do next. *Damn,* he thought as he reached for the phone, *I'm glad I'm not in his shoes.*

• • •

Indeed there were those who said the alleged rape of BoDee's daughter two days before the Board of Trust's fall meeting was a crisis that Brewster could not weather. But great challenges inspire great performances. And Chancellor William R. Brewster had never been in finer form than Monday morning when he opened up the Board of Trust meeting with a lengthy prayer for healing and harmony; a promise that the perpetrator of Saturday night's horrific deed would be prosecuted to the full extent of the law; and a proposal that the Board of Trust immediately set up a committee to formulate *"the most expeditious means of expanding the present campus security network so that there should never in the future be cause for anyone associated with Morgan University to suffer the emotional agony and moral outrage to which we have all been subjected this weekend."*
CLAP CLAP YES YES
In the wake of the Chancellor's masterful display of crisis man-

agement—and the lavish football theme luncheon he threw for Board members at noon—the charges of financial mismanagement leveled against him by the emotionally spent BoDee later that afternoon sounded insignificant and cranky. And by the time the Board members broke for dinner, after approving the Chancellor's request to build a new learning disability center, all that anyone was talking about was the need for a more technologically sophisticated campus security network—and what a butt-kicking the Knights had given the Porcupines on Saturday.

• • •

But the smile of self-satisfaction on the Chancellor's face as he buttered his toast the following morning vanished when he read on page three of *The Tribune* that ACLU attorney Irwin Girsh, Rodney Hampton's new legal counsel, was asking for a federal inquiry into his client's beating and arrest.

"I thought you said you had that story squelched!" exploded Brewster after reaching University counsel Ames Thackston at home.

"Really, Bill, I don't know what could'a—oh Lawd!" said the pajama-clad attorney, suddenly remembering that his brother-in-law, Lewis Lyons, the Local News editor at *The Tribune*, was on vacation in Hot Springs for the week. "I'll get on it immediately."

But the damage had been done. At the very moment the Chancellor hung up after speaking with Thackston, *Tribune* publisher Clarence Drumbacher, just back from a convention of the American Newspaper Association in Atlantic City, sat down on the commode in his Magnolia Hills home and saw the Hampton-Girsh item. With his nose for a good story, Drumbacher instantly knew he had something.

Yeah, this sounds ree-al int'restin', said the publisher, laying down the paper and wiping his rear, *ree-al int'restin'.*

When Drumbacher's afternoon paper, *The Chronicle*, hit the stands later that day, the DeeDee Grimes story had moved to the lower left-hand corner of the front page:

RAPE SUSPECT HELD BY METRO AUTHORITIES

"Yeah, I like it," said Drumbacher over the phone to *Chronicle* head editor Art Jamison, while he fed a piece of roast pork to his basset hound Jefferson. "That's right, Arty, if we don't tell 'em too much too fast, we can ride this one out for days.... Carlisle? ... Yeah, we're gonna get together first thing tomorrow."

• • •

On Wednesday morning, the DeeDee Grimes rape story, which was about to become known as the Rodney Hampton brutality incident, jumped to the top of the front page:

RAPE SUSPECT CHARGES POLICE BRUTALITY

"You bet your boodie," said Drumbacher to *Tribune* senior editor Charlie Rucker, offering him a Quixote cigar from the humidor on his desk, "now we got ourselves some real news!"

By dinnertime, everyone in Metro was talking about DeeDee and Rodney—everyone but Jan Hanagan and Stefan Bazitski. They had more important things to discuss as they sat in Stefan's efficiency apartment, two blocks from where Rodney Hampton had been beaten.

"What are you thinkink, Jan?"

"Oh—nothing," she said, her frosted blond head thrown back in the threadbare armchair where she sat watching Stefan prepare tea.

"Just one moment and samovar will be ready." Stefan smiled. He had talked Jan into coming over to his place after they had dined together at the Bangkok Palace. "Finally you get to taste real Russian tea."

"I can't wait," she said, looking amusedly up at the poster of Rudolph Nureyev that was scotch-taped to the ceiling over his bed. "I love the poster, Stefan."

"Yes, someone to look up to." Stefan laughed and walked from behind the kitchen counter with two cups of tea. "Here you go."

"Thank you."

"And then what you do"—he sat on the dilapidated couch next to her chair—"is take sugar cube, put it in your mouth like so, and then drink your tea."

"Huh."

"But if you want, you can put sugar right in."

"No, that sounds like fun." Jan took a sugar cube out of the cereal bowl on the coffee table in front of them. "Mmm good." She laughed and swished the warm tea over the cube in her mouth. "You learn something new every day."

"Yes, somethink new every day," said the dancer, suddenly turning very serious, reaching for her hand. "Jan—"

"Please, Stefan, what happened yesterday," she said, looking into his blue eyes, "should never have happened." On Tuesday, Stefan and Jan had motorcycled out to Katchakootchie Falls. And after consuming a loaf of French bread and Brie with a bottle of chardonnay, they had fallen into each other's arms and made love beneath the Indian summer sun.

"No Jan, what happened was somethink you wanted to happen."

"That's not true, Stefan," lied Jan, who had found in Stefan's arms a passionate release that had been missing in her relationship with her husband for years.

"Jan!" he said, dropping to his knees in front of her chair, taking her by the shoulders.

"Oh Stefan!" she replied, tears welling up in her eyes. Suddenly she was in his arms, clinging to his neck as he lifted her up and carried her to his bed. "Oh please, Stefan," she murmured, not sure whether it was revenge or desperation or love that had brought her to his apartment.

"Please what?" he asked as he laid her on the bed and began to kiss her.

"Oh please," she begged, her mind awash in shame and desire, "please don't stop."

• • •

On Thursday afternoon, the *RODNEY HAMPTON BEATING* incident took a new and unexpected turn.

"At the top of the news this evening," began Channel 2 newscaster Rod Neal, "we have just learned that the two eye witnesses to the Rodney Hampton beating, Dr. Sarah Green, Professor of Anthropology at Morgan University, and Mr. Cedric McKinney, a second year student in the Morgan University School of Law, have both offered to testify at a grand jury hearing on behalf of Mr. Rodney T. Hampton. And this just in! In a late breaking development from the Public Safety Building, Channel 2 reporter Rebecca Blasko has just learned from Sandy Crutch, spokesperson for the Metropolitan Police Department, that in light of preliminary medical investigations, Mayor Phil Ransom has ordered Rodney Hampton released from custody."

"Wow! Ole Billy Bob's not gonna like hearing that," said Tom Hanagan as he sat in his office watching the news, waiting for a call from Blake. "Man, what a mess!" ... *RING RING* ... "Yeah Blake! I just heard about it.... You're right. Ransom will do anything to get re-elected.... So what's up? ... Two hundred grand? ... You're kidding?! That's fantastic! I tell you what, why don't I just meet you and Sinks at the club. ... I knew he'd cough it up if we won one more! ... What's that? ... Yes, Cliff's doin' fine—I guess," said Tom, who had started to worry about his uncle after he'd walked into the hospital room the evening before and found Clifton sitting in bed— with the World Series game turned off—reading a book entitled *The Other You: Adventures in Self-Discovery*. "He's just starting to go nuts being cooped up in that hospital. But he'll soon be out.... Okay, buddy. Good work. See you in a half hour."

• • •

Shortly after 8:30 Friday morning, Rodney Hampton, with a bandage on his nose and his momma and attorney by his side, appeared on the front steps of the Morgan Administration Building.

YEAAA! HOORAY! rang out the voice of the 500 people who had started gathering with their picket signs at six o'clock that morning. *WE WANT JUSTICE! WE WANT JUSTICE!* they chanted as de facto demonstration leader Symeon Smith hobbled up to the microphone in his cast and raised his arms for quiet. *POLICE BRUTALITY!* screamed sociology professor Latisha Jones, the bill of her satin Malcolm X ball cap turned fashionably to the side. *DOWN WITH THE FASCIST PIGS!* yelled poli sci professor Mona Steinfield, recycling the rhetoric of her salad days at Barnard.

"Thank you all," echoed the voice of the fullback. "Thank you for comin' out here this mornin' to show your solidarity and support. ..."

The Chancellor looked down from his third story window at the crowd gathered in front of Morgan Hall and scowled. Too busy peddling office machinery and computers in the late 60s and early 70s to have attended a demonstration, this was Brewster's first taste of organized protest, and he didn't like it. "I'm an open minded man," he said to provost Sam Edwards, who stood beside him looking down as Symeon Smith raised both fists in a gesture of defiance, "but I tell you, Sambo, there's no reason for this. I've always been sensitive to the concerns of minorities on this campus."

BUZZ BUZZ

"Mr. Cox is on the line, sir."

"Yes I'll take it, Anita." Brewster's bushy brows knit together as he observed the University chaplain being introduced by Symeon Smith. "Yeah, Boomer, we've got a heap of trouble out here today. The TV trucks are down there right now. I was gonna have the police run 'em off, but I figured—Right. ... I guess about five hundred of 'em. Whad'da you think, Sam? ... Yeah, about five hundred. There's a lot'a white ones too, students, staff, and a bunch of faculty. ... Don't you worry about that, we've got the Dean's secretary takin' names. Well, I'll be damned!" said the Chancellor, bursting into obscenity when he saw Dr. Nathan Cosby, Assistant Professor of Sociology and Director of the Booker T. Washington Cultural Center, standing upon the administration building steps. "I can't believe it! That sonofabitch Cosby is here too. Why, if we hadn't brought him down here and given him that damn doctorate degree. . . . Exactly! And with what we pay him!. . . Yes, I've thought about suspending Sgt. Doolin. . . . I know, and if BoDee's goddam little tramp of a daughter. . . . Yes, the rest of the members think I should fire Doolin too. . . . Of course Ransom is responsible for all this, he and that bastard Drumbacher. . . . No, he hasn't called me back for the last three days. . . . Okay, Boomer, I'll talk to you later."

At 3:30 that afternoon *The Chronicle* hit the streets with a headline that read:

MORGAN STUDENTS PROTEST POLICE BRUTALITY

And at 3:55, two University security guards unlocked the front doors of Morgan Hall, and the Chancellor, amidst a chorus of cat calls and hissing, appeared on the front steps and announced his intention to suspend Sgt. Doolin from the force until a full inquiry could be made into the Rodney Hampton case. Expecting at the very least a hearty round of applause for his magnanimous gesture, Brewster was shocked and outraged to hear Morton Karp, a third year law student, cry out, with the unanimous approval of the crowd, "We aren't leaving here until you suspend Chief Staples too."

Speechless with anger and barely able to control his urge to throttle the bearded and bespectacled student who had just defied his authority, the Chancellor angrily turned heel and amidst boos and laughter stormed back into Morgan Hall. Furious at his humiliation and fuming with the knowledge that any further concessions would appear to be weakness in the eyes of the Board of Trust, the President-elect of the National Association of Private College and University Administrators retreated through the arched stone doorway of his office to contemplate his next course of action.

"So where the hell is everybody?!!" said Ed Tarmeenian after he and the other assistant coaches arrived on the practice field later that afternoon and noticed that all but two of his black players were absent.

"I think they're at that demonstration," said Porky Watson.

"Demonstration?!"

"The Rodney Hampton demonstration."

"Gimme that fucking phone.... Tony ... Yeah, it's me. Listen, we got trouble.... That's right.... And half the team's over there.... Awright, I'll take Carver and Woods with me."

Though the appearance of Coaches Tarmeenian, Carver and Woods in the crowd at Morgan Hall was enough to persuade several of the African-American players to scurry back to the gym—"If you ain't out on that field in fifteen minutes," said Coach Carver, "you're through! You understand?!"—it was more the rain that began to fall on the demonstrators at around 4:15 that replenished the ranks on the muddy fields behind Calhoun.

"I don't know what the hell's goin' on. But if anyone of you misses practice because you're jerking off at some protest," ranted Wesley Woods "you're outta here!"

Spared by an act of God from what could have been a violent confrontation had the campus security forces tried to clear the steps of the administration building, the Chancellor sat in his office shortly after 5:00 munching on a cold pork barbecue sandwich that Anita had smuggled in the rear door of the building earlier that afternoon.

"Somebody's gonna pay for this," grumbled Brewster as he watched footage from the demonstration on the 5:00 News. *And according to Morgan fullback and student protest leader, Symeon Smith, the demonstration will continue until the students, faculty and staff of Morgan University are satisfied that those responsible for the beating of Rodney Hampton—*

BUZZ BUZZ

"Yes, Anita," he said, wiping his mouth as Rodney Hampton stepped up to the microphone and urged everybody to "be like cool."

"Your wife is on the line."

"'Hello, Winnie ... Yes ... Of course I am!! ... No, not many now, it started raining about forty-five minutes ago. ... I just got off the

phone with Sam. . . . A few of the hospital workers too. . . . That's
right, but he called in the police and had them arrested immediately.
. . . No, we can't allow this to spread. . . . I don't know when I'll be
home. I've got Cosby comin' to see me—look! there I am! On
Channel 2," he said, turning up the volume as he appeared on the
screen. . . . "I do look in control, don't I. . . . Yes, very angry," he said
as he watched Morton Karp defy him. . . . "What did Dudley say?! . . .
Well, you tell Clarissa that if her husband knows so damn much
about running a university, he—" *BUZZ BUZZ.* "Hold on a second.
. . . Gotta go, Winnie. . . . What's that? . . . How do I know if we'll be
going to the Halloween party tomorrow night?! . . . Awright, bye
bye."

BUZZ BUZZ

"No, Anita, I can't talk with BoDee Grimes right now. Did
Drumbacher call yet? . . . Hmm. . . . Cosby's on his way over? . . .
Awright, thanks."

At 5:45, the Chancellor called the dean of the graduate school to
let him know how much he admired the courage of the faculty members who had stood up and let their opinions be known at the
demonstration. . . . *Yes, each and every one of them, Harvey, though
I'm not sure their courage is gonna help me get the Board to approve
that new pension and medical package I've been fightin' for.* And ten
minutes later, Dr. Nathan Cosby arrived for his emergency meeting.

BUZZ BUZZ

"He's here," said Anita into her intercom, smiling at Dr. Cosby,
who was looking rather pale as he sat on the waiting room couch in
a starched white shirt and tie he had put on after removing the dashiki he had worn at the demonstration.

"Tell him I'll be a minute," said Brewster in an unpleasant tone of
voice that didn't escape Dr. Cosby's notice as it came over the intercom. "By the way, Anita, did Ms. Hayes call back yet?"

"No, sir."

"All right. Anita, if you want to go now, that'll be fine. I can let
Dr. Cosby in myself."

"All right, thank you, sir."

As the well-fed, middle-aged sociology professor watched Anita tidy up her desk and then slip on her raincoat and walk out the door, he became increasingly filled with fear—a gut wrenching, throat clenching fear of losing his job. *Whadam I gonna do if he fires me? Whadam I gonna tell Opal?* fretted the former black militant whose conspicuously consumptive wife had, on the 95,000 dollars per year the Chancellor paid him, grown accustomed to the "good life" in white suburbia: a split-level house, two new cars, two teenage children enrolled in Metro's most exclusive private school. *Oh please, Lawd, don't let him fire me.* Dr. Cosby knew jobs like his were hard to find, even for a white man.

Then Dr. Cosby heard the sound of the doorknob turning, and all at once he was looking up at Chancellor Brewster.

"Sorry to keep you waiting, Nathan." Cosby shot up out of his seat and Brewster squeezed out a half smile and extended his hand. "It's been a long day. Come in."

Maybe he's not gonna fire me after all, thought Cosby as the Chancellor directed him to one of the throne chairs in front of the stone fireplace.

"Well now," said Brewster, much to Nathan's surprise assuming an almost easy air of cordiality, "you must be pretty tired after all the activity on the front steps here."

"Ah—yes sir."

"We don't have this sort of thing happen around here very often."

"No, sir."

"And that's good." Brewster's smile disappeared and his eyebrows knit together.

Oh oh, here it comes.

"Just between you and me, Nathan, I'm not sure that public demonstrations ever really accomplish much in the end."

Silence.

"Of course I realize what a difficult assignment you have at the University. That's the reason I hired you in the first place—because I thought you were capable of handling the job."

"Yes, sir," stammered the sweaty-faced administrator, during whose eight years as spokesperson for the black community at Morgan there had not been a single public demonstration.

"And as you know, I have been generally pleased with the job you have done. But—"

Oh please, please don't fire me!

"As one friend to another, I have to tell you, I'm not altogether convinced your involvement in today's demonstration was in the best interest of the African-American community on campus."

Silence.

"You know better than anyone how committed I've been to the cause of diversity and equal rights at this University."

"Oh yes, sir." *Maybe he's not gonna fire me.*

"And I don't think there's anyone who can deny my record on this count."

"No, sir."

"But in regard to this Rodney Hampton affair, I'm not sure it's wise for us to let things continue on as they did today." Dr. Cosby shifted in his chair. "Of course I realize that you and the other members of our faculty must listen to the dictates of their conscience."

Actually Nathan's conscience had very little to do with his appearance at the rally. Had that "little voice inside" been the only one he had to listen to, Nathan Cosby could very easily have stayed in his plush office working on his new book, *The Racial Imperative,* flirting with his young administrative assistant.

"And personally," continued the Chancellor, "I have always had the utmost respect for those who listened to their conscience"—

He's gonna keep me! Halleluja! He's gonna keep me—

"Particularly when it meant they had to *suffer* for it."

Ooooooo

Brewster leaned back in his chair and stared at the man he had emancipated from the drudgery of a 28,000 dollar a year job at Tennessee State University.

"Is that all?" asked Dr. Cosby.

"Yes, Nathan—*for now.*"

A half hour later, after taking a drive in his new BMW convertible to think things over and pick up a broiled chicken breast and some fries at Wendy's, Nathan Cosby reached for the phone in his office at the cultural center.

"Hello, Sister Garvey, this is Brother Cosby.... Salam alaikum to you too.... Yes it was quite a day," he said, looking up at the Zulu shield and spears on his wall. "You know that's right.... Of course, we did.... Of course, we are.... Yes, this administration's gotta start wakin' up.... Absolutely.... Right on, sista, I couldn't agree more, although I gotta tell ya, I'm not sure how much good it's gonna do for us to go out there tomorrow."

• • •

The huge protest rally planned for Saturday morning never materialized. Whether the crowds were kept away by the continuing cold drizzle, the awesome line-up of football games on TV, or the carefully reconsidered position of several campus leaders is hard to say. By noon, the Channel 2 News truck left to cover a sewer explosion downtown, and the sixty or so people who had shown up—mostly Symeon Smith's fraternity brothers and some shaggy graduate students—had started to pack up and head home.

"What happened to everybody?"

"Man, I don't know," said Symeon, picking up a pile of leaflets.

"There ain't nobody here, not even brother Cosby."

"Yeah, you're right," said the fullback, who had been looking forward to his debut on national television.

"Yo, Symeon! Symeon!"

"Yeah," answered the dejected fullback, turning around and seeing Prof. Lou Sazlow and his wife Barbara.

"Oh, hello professor."

"Symeon, I want you to know that Barbara and I support you and your cause completely."

"Yes we do," chimed in Barbara, giving Symeon a big hug.

"It's time that the law enforcement agents in this country realize

FOURTH QUARTER · 259

that they can't go around terrorizing innocent men, women, and children."

"Yeah, you're right, professor."

"This isn't Nazi Germany we're living in," said the balding professor, his gray beard wagging in the breeze.

"No it ain't, professor," said Symeon, folding up one of the chairs he had brought over from the BAD frat house.

"Well, anyway, we just wanted to tell you how we feel."

"Yeah, thanks."

RING RING RING

"Chancellor Brewster's office," said Anita, merrily picking up the phone. "Oh hello sir, no they're all going home now." She looked out the window. . . . "Maybe sixty at the most. . . . Yes, they hung around for about an hour and a half. . . . No, there were hardly any teachers."

"Was Cosby there?" asked the Chancellor giving the A-OK sign to Boomer and Lamar. . . . Yeah, I kinda figured that cooler heads would prevail. . . . That's right. Okay honey, thanks for everything, you have a good rest of the weekend." *CLUNK*.

"Well, gentlemen," said Brewster, smiling broadly as he picked up his pool cue, "it doesn't look like I'll hafta' to call in the National Guard after all. . . . Now, let me see if I can sink this eight ball in that side pocket, then we can all go watch the LSU-Alabama game while Geneva whips up some of her corn cakes and shrimp étouffée."

CHAPTER 21
The Week of October 30

The fire of protest which Chancellor Brewster thought he had stomped out Saturday morning burst back into flames on the practice field behind Calhoun on Sunday afternoon.

"So where the hell is everybody?!!" raged Coach Star, rain dripping off the brim of his *Kick Butt* cap.

"I told you we should'a never gave 'em yesterday off," growled Ed.

"CARVER!"

"Yeah, Coach."

"I thought you said you had this situation under control."

"We did. Me and Wes talked to the players for an hour yesterday afternoon," said the linebacker coach, wiping his face with a towel. "We had everyone chilled out, and then that Carlisle story came out in the paper this morning and got everybody riled up again."

"I'm gonna kill that sonofabitch! I swear I am!" fumed Star, who along with every other sports fan in Jefferson County had read Carlisle's column in the Sunday *Chronicle,* accusing Morgan University and its Athletics Department of racism and minority exploitation.

RING RING

"Hanagan residence," huffed Tom. He had been downstairs getting hot dogs out of the refrigerator for the kids' lunch. "What?!! I thought you said.... The Carlisle article, huh.... Yeah, I read it this morning.... That sonofabitch, somebody oughta kick his ass.... You're right, Tony, we gotta do something, and fast.... I'M COMING, ERIN! ... Listen, let me see if I can find somebody to watch the kids.... No, she's at work. I'll come right over."

• • •

At 2:30 Monday afternoon, Tom Hanagan, in an attempt to defuse the bomb that was threatening to blow the roof off the Calhoun Complex, met with the African-American members of the football team in a closed session.

"And I give you my word," he said, "that I have spoken to the Chancellor about your grievances and he has assured me that he is doing everything in his power to make sure that all the guilty parties in this affair will be brought to justice. Yes, Asswad?"

"Does that include Police Chief Staples?" asked the defensive back.

"As far as I know, yes it does. Ah, Dr. Cosby, I believe you and the Chancellor talked about this very issue on Friday, didn't you?"

"Er . . . ah, yes, we did," said Cosby. "And I told the Chancellor that the African-American members of this community need to know that not only Sgt. Doolin—"

"Who has been suspended," interrupted Tom Hanagan.

"Yes, who has now been suspended, but anyone else who is guilty needs to be held accountable for the violation of Rodney Hampton's civil rights."

"Yes, Mustafa?"

"How can we be sho' this is gonna happen?"

"I give you my word, not only as the athletics director of this school, but also as a fellow athlete and a life-long supporter of the rights of minorities."

"Yeah, yeah, we know how much you love black folks," said the split-end defiantly, rousing snickers around the room. "But what we want to see from you before we go back to work is the suspension of Captain Staples."

"And that's exactly what I want as well." Tom wiped his sweaty forehead with his hanky. "But you've got to realize it may take days to accomplish our objective. And in the meantime—"

"You want us to get back out there, right?" said Symeon Smith, his leg propped up on a chair.

"Yeah, that's right, Symeon. Now you guys all know," said Tom, drawing a deep breath, "that my real concern in all this, the real reason that I'm talkin' with you like this, without any of the coaches around, is that I don't want to see any of you jeopardize your futures. I'm serious," he said, raising up his hands to quiet the players. "It's true. As much as I admire the courage that all of you have demonstrated in standing up and making your opinions known—that's what this country of ours is all about after all—and as much as I think your actions may be completely justified,"—he looked out at the players slouching in their seats looking derisively back at him—"the Coach has told me that anyone who doesn't show up for practice this afternoon will be kicked off the team."

Boo hiss.

"I know," shouted Tom, "I know how you feel, but you gotta remember that when you decided to matriculate at the University, you also made a commitment to this athletics program." (*Hiss hiss*). And our situation here is no different from what you would find at any other college or, for that matter on any professional team in this country." (*There is a sudden quiet in the room*). "That's right, gentlemen. The reason that I have come here today to urge you to honor the commitment you have made to this University, your families, yourselves, and to the Coach and me, is because I care about you. And I don't want to see anyone in this room jeopardize their academic or athletic future for any reason—no matter how justifiable it may be. All of us here are morally outraged at the brutal way in which a minority member of this community has been treated. BUT, if we are going to change this school and nation so incidents like this can't happen in the future, we must make the most of ourselves, so we can make a difference. To brand ourselves as radicals and malcontents, so that no university *or* professional athletic organization would wish to associate with us, would be to do a disservice both to ourselves and to the cause of freedom."

In defense of duty and blatant self-interest, Tom had been eloquent, and at 3:00 all but Mustafa Lewis, Leon Banks, and Ntumo Arnold were out on the practice field.

"You done good, Tommy," said the Coach over his mobile phone as he stood atop his tower on the side of the field watching his black players halfheartedly going though their warm-up exercises with the rest of the team.... "Yeah, they'll be okay. I'll see you later. Thanks."

RING RING

"Coach Star here.... Yeah, Porky, did you take care of it?"

"I'm doin' it right now, Coach," said the graduate assistant as he removed Mustafa Lewis's name from his former locker.

"And you cleaned out those other two assholes' lockers too?"

"Yup."

"Everything?"

"You bet."

"That's good. I want every single trace of 'em gone. And don't forget their names on the wall of the weight room."

"All right."

"So whad'da you think, Eddie?" said Star, zipping up his jacket against the cold wind blowing from the north.

"Thank God Hanagan is as full of shit as I've always said."

• • •

"Abe, is that you? ... I'm sorry I'm callin' so late," said Milt Lee, sitting in the knotty pine-paneled office of his suburban home on Tuesday evening. "What a day! Do you know how hard it is to evict someone from an apartment you own? Sometimes I wonder whether this real estate business is worth it. One thing's for sure, if they ever really do away with welfare, I'm gettin' out.... What's that.... So you've heard about this Rodney Hampton stuff? ... What a mess— innocent?! Are you kidding me? C'mon, Abe, we've been around too long to fall for that crap. He's probably the same sonofabitch that robbed my wife up at the school this spring—and it's getting worse here every day.... Our suit? ... Well, I think the University has decided to settle with us out of court.... Who knows, maybe even a hundred grand.... Hold on a sec, let me check the other line."

"Abe? I'm back.... Just Tuesday and I feel like I've been workin' all week. Anyways, about my order, I think maybe half as much this time.... I dunno, I got a bad feeling.... Well, for one thing the black players are giving the Coach trouble, and for another, the Chancellor is still refusing to get the Coaches' new contracts worked out.... It does sound fishy but that's what Ed tells me.... No, something ain't right.... Basketball?.... Now, that's an idea. We play our first game on the 12th.... Yeah, lemme look into it.... Awright, I'll call you Friday."

• • •

Lamont leaned out the window of the Chancellor's car Wednesday morning and pressed in the code number he'd been given over the house intercom. The massive iron gates of "Glory Land" slowly swung open, and he drove up the estate's meticulously manicured magnolia-lined drive.

"Now this is what I call a real spread," said the Chancellor. Brewster had been privileged to visit Manly Dunnings' estate once before—when he was interviewed by Dudley's father for the chancellor's job—but that afternoon he'd been so excited that he was scarcely able to appreciate Glory Land's baronial grounds and architecture.

"Yeah, dis is sumpin', idn't it?" said Lamont as he rounded a curve and saw the Dunning mansion looming before him. Set atop the highest hill in Jefferson County on four hundred priceless acres, Glory Land had been built with part of the fortune Manley's grandfather had made from supplying Union troops with shoes and horses during their occupation of Metro. Only twenty minutes from downtown by car, a special trolley line—erected at public expense in the 1890s—had once come right to the gate of the estate.

Lamont wheeled around a row of boxwoods and started up the horseshoe-shaped drive to the front porch.

"Quite a place," said the Chancellor, gaping at the mansion, at one end of which stood a courtyard and stables, and at the other a marble fountain and verandah which overlooked rolling meadows and hills to the west. In front of the house where Lamont stopped was a grassy oval with a flagpole flanked by a pair of Parrott guns whose bronze barrels were being polished by an elderly black man who nodded at the Chancellor's car.

As Lamont jumped from the limo and opened the Chancellor's door, they were joined by another elderly black gentleman in butler's coat and bow tie who requested that the Chancellor follow him up the front steps of the white-columned house.

"Come right dis way, sir," said the servant, ushering Brewster into the foyer and taking his coat. "Mista Dunnin's 'spectin' you."

Though Brewster was by no means a stranger to wealth, he couldn't help but be impressed. The interior of Glory Land was a spitting image of Wentworth, the famous Georgian Manor in Bath, England, presently owned by soccer star Pug Harrison. Crammed full of antiques by generations of Mrs. Dunnings—who had apparently suffered from *horror vacui*—everywhere you looked there were signs of wealth—and more wealth. Here was a 13th century Norman tapestry, there a 16th century Ming vase, a Louis XIV clock, a Joshua Reynolds oil portrait, and a 19th century Biedermeyer couch.

Now this is real class. Sure wish Winnie were here, thought Brewster as the butler escorted him through the foyer past the ballroom and library into a dimly lit TV room. Manly Dunning was sitting in a tattered old club chair watching *The Flying Leathernecks* while he peeked at a golf match in one corner of his giant screen and the stock reports in the other.

"Ahem," said the butler, clearing his throat.

"Just one second," said Manly, raising his finger and watching as Ernie Ells sank an eighteen footer. "Wooooo, yes! . . . What is it, Maurice?" asked Manly, still not turning around.

"The Chancellor's here to see you, sir."

"Oh, I forgot all about him." Manly pulled himself out of his chair with a groan and invited Brewster into the room. "C'mon in, Chanc'llor."

"Thank you, sir. It's a pleasure to see you again."

"Yeah, good to see you too." Manly hiked up his pink and blue plaid golfer slacks, then walked over and gave Billy Bob's hand a shake with his seventy-nine year old, still firm, golfer's grip. "Maurice, pull up a chair for the Chanc'llor. And go open those blinds."

"Yassir."

"There now, Chanc'llor, have a seat," said Manly. Unlike his son Dudley, whom he affectionately called the "runt," Manly was a tall man, wizened by his years, but still energetic in his gestures. "And Maurice," he said, pointing to four different colored phones on the coffee table beside his chair from which he ran the Dunning empire, "tell Lucille to hold my calls."

"Yassir."

"And while I'm thinkin' of it, Chanc'llor—"

"Bill, please, Mr. Dunning," interrupted the Chancellor, embarrassed at how absurd his title sounded in the presence of the man who had given final approval to his getting the job.

"All righty, Bill." Manly smiled at Brewster with ingratiating familiarity, "how 'bout a little drink?"

"Oh, no thank you, sir."

"Ah come on now, Bill. Maurice, bring us two Glory Land teas."

"Yassir."

"Well now, Bill," said Manly, "I 'preciate you comin' to see me at the drop of a hat like this."

"No problem." The Chancellor smiled and smoothed out his tie.

"'Cause I really feel like we need to have ourselves a little talk, considerin' everything that's been goin' on lately."

"Everything that's been going on?" said the Chancellor quizzically.

"You know, down there at the school and all."

"Oh." The Chancellor still wasn't sure what Manly was talking about.

"As you know, I don't get down to the campus much anymore— what with the nine holes I had put in here a few years back. In fact, I doubt I've been in that sky box 'a mine more than five times over the last few years, and that was for the State games—Cigar, Bill?"

Manly pushed a box of real Cuban cigars toward the Chancellor.

"Ah, no thanks, Mr. Dunning, it's a little early for me."

"Humm, well then, reach in there and grab yourself one for later."

"Thank you."

"But that doesn't mean I'm not still the biggest dang fan of Morgan football that you'll ever meet. I might not go around talkin' about it as much as ole Clifton, or Harlan, but I love my Alma Mater. And I guess that's part of the reason"—Manly paused to light his cigar—"I was (*puff puff*) so supportive of you becomin' Chancellor of our University."

"Maybe I will have that cigar after all." The Chancellor pulled the cigar out of his coat pocket and prepared it for lighting.

"Yes, I knew that you were the man for the job here, Bill, and I'm sure Dudley has told you how I fought for your appointment."

"Yes (*puff puff*) he has."

"And I'm still convinced that I was right."

"Well, thank you, Mr. Dunning."

"Why, the way this school's grown over the past ten years, it's just amazin'. We've become one of the foremost academic institutions in America. C'mon in, Maurice. Well, here's to the future, Bill." Manly clinked his glass against the Chancellor's, "and to that Bowl game we're gonna be in at the end of this year."

Brewster smiled, took a large swig from his glass and nearly choked on the bourbon in his iced tea.

"Yeah, good ole Glory Land tea." Manly smacked his lips. "You were quite a ball player yourself, weren't you, Bill, varsity football and baseball, if my memory serves me right."

"Well yes, but Texas Tech wasn't much of—"

"There's no need to apologize. We can't all play with the big boys." He gestured to the gleaming trophy case that sat across the room. "No, it's not who you play for, it's how well you play the game that counts (*puff puff*). You know I think I learned som'a the most important lessons of my life playin' football, and I'm sure you did too, Bill."

"Yes, that's—"

"Like in that 1942 season," interrupted Manly.

"The year you were an All-American?"

"Well now, I can see you know your Morgan football history. Yeah, well, that was a strange year all right. At the beginning of the season we were picked by every sports writer in the South to finish at the bottom—kinda like what happened to us this year—and truth is we should'a. We'd lost most of our best players to the service, and there was no way that anybody thought we could win a game, much less tie for the championship. But you know, Bill, we had an assistant coach, ole Bubba Walker—he was killed later at Iwo Jima—who believed that anything was possible if you believed hard enough. And I can still recall how he sat us all down just before the first game and read us all those nasty things the sports writers were sayin' about us. I swear he got us so fired up we could'a licked both Hitler and Hirohito that afternoon. Ole Bubba was right, there was nothing we couldn't do if we believed with all our heart that we could do it."

"That's absolutely true," said the Chancellor, moved by the rhetoric and the bourbon.

"Yeah, that was a mighty big lesson (*glug glug*). But you know what? I learned an even mo' important lesson on the last day of the season. As you probably know, the Mid-South championship was up for grabs that year (*puff puff*). We were undefeated and so was State. Now, I guess most people kinda thought we had a little edge on 'em cause I'd been gettin' better' 'n better with each game. I was already the number one rusher in the Mid South, and I was closin' in on Tommy Snerdly. You want that drink of yours freshened up, Bill?"

"I'm all right, thank you, Mr. Dunning."

"Anyways, to make a long story short, on the second play of the game, as the crowd rose to its feet a'roarin' and a'hollerin', I started dashin' around the left end behind my fullback when suddenly I tripped over his heel, came down on my foot the wrong way and broke my ankle. Well, you could'a heard a pin drop in that stadium as they carried me out. And I guess there wasn't a soul in the place who thought we had a chance to win that game, cause my back-up man, ole Dugger Fulsom, Doc's younger brother, hadn't played more than four quarters all season. 'We're done for,' that's what everybody thought. But you know, Bill (*puff puff*) they were all wrong, 'cause that lil' Dugger Fulsom came into that game and not only ran for a hundred and seventy five yards, he made three interceptions to boot, one of 'em at the end of the fourth quarter that set up the game winnin' touchdown."

"That's a great story."

"Yup. That was a big game, all right. And it taught me the most important thing I ever learned."

"What was that?"

"Well sir, as I lay there in that locker room, listenin' to the end of the game with tears of joy in my eyes, I came to realize that no matter how important we think we are, there's always somebody out there who can do the job just as good as we can. . . . or maybe"— Manly looked Brewster squarely in the eyes—"even better."

Silence. Prolonged, pregnant silence.

"Now, how did I get carried away on that?" said Manly, shaking his head and chuckling. "Guess I'm just gettin' to be a scatterbrained ole man like my wife keeps tellin' me."

"And so how long were you there, Billy Bob?"

"I dunno, Winnie, I guess about an hour," said Chancellor Brewster, washing down two extra-strength Excedrins with a glass of orange juice later that evening. "I hope I'm not gettin' a cold. My throat sure feels raw."

"Oh, you'll be all right, Billy Bob, it's just the change in the weather. Did he mention this horrible Rodney Hampton business?"

"Yes, he did."

"And—"

"He told me he thought I'd handled the situation about as well as could be expected." The Chancellor massaged the back of his neck with his hand. "But —"

"But what?"

"But he wasn't sure that all the Board members felt the same way he did."

"That's ridiculous. No one could've handled the situation as well as you did."

"I know, and he said as much himself. But some of the members are very upset."

"That BoDee Grimes! A lotta nerve he has criticizing you."

"I know, honey, I know."

"And did Manly talk about anything else?"

"Not much else. We talked about football a little."

"Football?! You men and your football. I can't understand why Manly Dunning would waste your important time talkin' about football."

"Ugh, I think my glands are swollen."

"You just need to have your dinner, you'll be all right."

"I hope so."

"Geneva made some of those honey glazed pork chops you like."

"I'm not very hungry."

"Football! Imagine talkin' about football in that beautiful house filled with all those gorgeous antiques! Did he show you any of the Chippendales that Verna bought at Sotheby's last year?"

"No, dear, just a Sherman tank he picked up when they were in Arizona."

• • •

"You bet we're gonna beat 'em!" yelled Tom Hanagan to the crowd in the booth across from Tony and him at the Time Out Bar.

"Yeah, hon, I'll have the usual. How 'bout you, Tom?"

"Fine. And you can bring those onion rings with my beer."

"Numero uno!" said the Coach, flashing two thumbs up toward the bar.

"You seem like you're in a pretty good mood, Tony."

"Hey, why not?"

"You see *USA Today* gave us ten points?"

Star nodded. "The way I figure it, Tommy, we're about one game away from Bowl city."

"Everybody in good shape?"

"Pretty much."

"How 'bout Wallace?"

Star frowned. "Not sure yet."

"That's not good."

"No it ain't. But we don't need Wallace to beat the Hogs."

"And you finally got the black kids under control?"

"No problem," lied Tony, who had threatened to fire Wesley Woods that afternoon if he didn't get the African-American players to improve their attitude.

"Man, I was scared—Thanks, honey—Ooo watch it, Tony, the mozzarella sticks are hot! That situation was gettin' outta hand."

"Yeah, that sonofabitch Carlisle got everybody riled up."

"No kidding (*chomp chomp*). So, did you get a chance to go over that contract I gave you yet?"

"Hey, there's my good buddy Al," said the Coach, waving a chicken wing at the owner of the Cadillac dealership who supplied cars for his wife and him. "Yeah I did, but I think we should wait and see what happens."

"Wait and see?! What the hell you talkin' about, Tony? You keep stringin' me out and Brewster's gonna—"

"Hey!" Star looked severely at his old high school teammate. "This is a business, Tommy. No matter how good a' friends we are."

"I'm not arguing with that, Tony, but—"

"But what? Relax, pal." Star laughed. "Let's just win this one Saturday and then we can worry about the contract, right?"

"Sure, but I gotta tell you, even if you beat 'em by fifty points, Brewster isn't gonna—"

"Give me one more cent. I know and I ain't worried about that right now. I got only one thing on my mind," said Star, as the waitress served them their salad, "and that's winnin' this game. And what you should be worryin' about, Tommy, is which Bowl we're gonna go to."

"I'm sorry, Tone."

"Hey, what's to be sorry for? Eat your dinner and enjoy. Bring us a coupla' more brews, wouldja, hon?"

• • •

"Wake up, Tony! Wake up!" said Ed Tarmeenian, leaning across the aisle and shaking his friend. "Wake up!"

"Wha, what—what?" mumbled Tony, opening his eyes and coming to from a nightmare in which his football players were moving in slow motion while a gigantic boar charged in and out of their ranks tearing them to pieces with his tusks. "Man, I don't know what I was dreaming." Star blinked and looked at his wristwatch. "We cross Ole Man River yet?"

"A few minutes ago."

"Good." Tony let up the blind on the cabin window and looked out at the patchwork quilt of soybean fields and cotton seven thousand feet below.

"It's been a long two weeks," commiserated Ed.

"Tell me about it. Hey, hon," said the Coach to the stewardess, "would you mind gettin' me a cupacoffee?"

"Anyways, I was talkin' to Jet while you was snoozing. He says you're planning on startin' Holmes at end."

"Yeah, I wasn't sure I liked the two tight ends idea after all."

"Huh."

"Sounds like you agree with Jet."

"I dunno, Tony. I kinda liked movin' Cubbins into Lewis's spot and using the two tight ends. You really think Holmes is fast enough to beat Rutherford?"

"I know what you're thinkin', Eddie, but after going over the films again last night, I think the less we do to confuse Gentry the better. I don't think he ever really felt comfortable with the new setup."

"You thought anymore about usin' Wallace?"

"Yeah I have."

"He's been lookin' pretty good to me."

"Yeah, he did yesterday for sure. But I gotta agree with Stitches about him not bein' a hundred percent yet."

"Maybe so, but. . . ."

"Yeah, I know, sometimes you gotta take a chance. But we got three more games to go after this one."

• • •

By 2:00 Saturday afternoon, Marion C. Pickens Stadium was crammed with 78,000 fans hoping to see the Porkers ruin the Knights' chances for a Bowl and pay homage to their retiring athletics director, Jim Mack Brewer.

And now, ladies and gentlemen, blared Hogs stadium announcer Bailey Murphy, *let's give a big SOOOOOWEEEEE to the man who's made our Porkers a force to be reckoned with in the world of intercollegiate athletics, Mr. Jim . . . Mack . . . Brewer!*

SOOOOO WEEEEE!!!! OINK OINK OINK!

As the Bristling Hogs marching band struck up the A.S.U. fight song, and the Porkerettes waved their orange and black standards, an open top limousine drove onto the stadium track. In the back seat sat Jim Mack Brewer and A.S.U. president Dr. Faulkner T. Fentress and their two lovely wives.

"I sure hate to see you leave us, Jim Mack," said Dr. Fentress, smiling at the crowd and waving his hand.

"And, believe me, I hate to go," said the beloved Jim Mack sitting next to him in his orange blazer, waving his arms over his head.

"And you're sure you're doin' the right thing?"

"Yeah, I think so, Faulkner," said the fifty-five year old former Hog All-American, who had recently tendered his resignation. In September, Jim Mack had learned from a friend in the state legislature that a secret committee had been set up to investigate misappropriation of funds in the athletics departments of the state's universities. "After twenty years coachin' and fifteen years as athletics director, I think it's time for some new blood."

"I guess you're right," said Faulkner Fentress as the band began to play a rendition of *Jimmy Mack When Are You Comin' Back*.

"*Hatchoo*! I feel terrible," grumbled the Chancellor, taking a seat beside his wife in the stands behind the Morgan bench.

"You'll be all right. You wanna take another one of those cold capsules?"

"I just took one a half-hour ago," he said, massaging his tender temples. "If only we didn't have to go to that party at Fentress's tonight. And I know he's gonna insist on me going hunting with him tomorrow morning."

"Now don't be such a baby, Bill, you know you always look forward to goin' boar hunting when we come down here. All you got is just a little ole cold, honey."

"Hey, Billy Bob!" said Boomer Cox, leaning across in front of Winnie. "You want some peanuts? How 'bout you, Betty?"

The Chancellor and Boomer had brought their wives with them, as they did each time they traveled to Gruntsville. Betty Cox's momma's people, the Pucketts, were related to the Fentresses.

"Where'd Dudley go?" asked the Chancellor, buttoning up his topcoat as a cloud momentarily obscured the sun.

"I think he went up to the skyboxes to talk to a business associate," said Boomer.

AND LET'S HEAR IT ONCE MORE FOR JIM! MACK! BREWER!

SOOO WEEEE PIG PIG PIG!

"Now, that boy is a good 'un," said Boomer, throwing a handful of peanuts into his mouth.

"Yeah, they don't make 'em like Jim Mack anymore," said Brewster, his voice suddenly drowned out by the roar of the crowd as the teams came back on the field for the beginning of the game.

"By the way, Billy," asked Boomer as they stood up and clapped for the Knights, "did Hanagan ever get that contract back from Star?"

"You know I'm not sure, with everything that's—*hatchoo*—been goin' on this week. Why do you ask?"

"I was just wondering," said Boomer, putting his fingers to the corners of his mouth and letting out a piercing whistle in the direction of the bench where the Knights were all nervously awaiting the toss of the coin. "You remember ole Harley Drummond down in Cosmopolis?"

"Yes."

"Well, he heard from a fishin' buddy of his that if Tom Hanagan didn't watch out, ole Howdy Morrison might just steal his coach away from him. Here you go, Winnie, here's your Coke. . . . And Betty, your nachos."

"Oh, he did, did he?" said the Chancellor, looking down at the end of the bench where Tom Hanagan was talking with Stitches Stevens. "I'll have to have a little talk with him later on—*hatchoo*."

From the opening play of the game—a fair catch that Cochise Cubbins momentarily bobbled on the 17-yard line—it was obvious to the Morgan fans that it was going to be a long afternoon. The boycott the African-American players had staged at the beginning of the week had left the whole squad demoralized and disorganized. The split-second timing on which a good offense relies wasn't there; and play after play the Hogs' defensive tackle Dareem Brown and defensive end Orleans DuPrez penetrated the Knights' front five, dragging Gentry, Ritter and Harris down before they got to the line of scrimmage.

GO HOGS! OINK OINK OINK!

But thanks to Ed's "hit men," the game remained a stand-off with neither team being able to hold on to the ball for more than two or three series of downs.

But as the clock neared the end of the first quarter, Anthony Gentry, on a play action pass, rolled to his right, reared back, and BINGO! was picked off by Hogs' cornerback Tremayne Jarvis. As Jarvis sped down the sideline past Dewey Dobbins . . . Ricky Ritter . . . Coach Carver, and a gang of excited photographers, Tom Hanagan realized that the one who had really gotten screwed when Rodney Hampton broke into DeeDee Grimes' apartment was himself.

TOUCHDOWN! PORKERS!

"What the hell were you doin'?!!" yelled Coach Star as the point-after defense team lumbered onto the field. "Gentry! I thought I told you to eat that ball if you didn't have anyone open!"

Silence.

"What did we practice all week for?!" he ranted, stomping his feet on the ground, suddenly realizing that he was making a scene in front of seventy-eight thousand people. "Muggins! . . . MUG-GINS!"

"Yeah, Coach," said the quarterback, grabbing his helmet from under the bench and lazily shuffling up to Star's side.

"You ready?"

"Yeah, sure."

The Morgan offense, after taking over at the 20, lost four yards in two plays.

"Jesus Christ!" howled Star, tearing off his phones as Muggins ran into his own blockers on a third and 14. "What are we doin' today?!"

"Are you okay, Tony?" asked Ed, who had never seen his friend over-react like this before.

"No, I'm not okay! Did you see that play?!"

"Yeah I did. But relax, Tony, it'll be all right."

But ten minutes later nothing had changed. Each time Morgan got the ball, they gave it away.

"They look outta synch," said Boomer Cox, shaking his head after Muggins intentionally threw away a third and 15 pass.

"That's an understatement," groaned Brewster, massaging his aching temples.

"Sometimes having that extra week off can hurt you," said Boomer. "I remember how that happened to us in '62. We were undefeated goin' into that first break, then we came back two weeks later and lost four in a row."

GO PORKERS! OINK OINK!

By the middle of the second quarter things had also started to go wrong on defense.

"Goddam it! What the hell were you doin,' Bowers?!!"

"I thought—"

"You thought what?!" roared Coach Star.

"Man, what's wrong with him today, Eddie?" whispered Jet out of the corner of his mouth.

"I don't know, Jet. I've never seen him like this before."

"Maybe he's still upset about that protest stuff."

"I don't know," said Ed, "but if he don't cool off, he's gonna blow the kids' minds."

• • •

"I gotta go get something to drink," said Brewster, rising from his seat in disgust after the Hogs kicked a field goal from the 35. "Anybody need anything?"

"No thank you, honey, you just go ahead," said Winnie as he pushed past her.

"He's really not feelin' well, is he?" said Boomer.

"No, he isn't. He's been feelin' poorly for about three days now, since he got home from that meetin' with Dudley's father."

"Yeah, ole Manly's enough to give anybody a case of the willies."

"He's not a very nice man, is he, Boomer?"

"Well I don't know as I'd say that exactly."

"I could tell he really upset Bill the other night. He looked white as a ghost when he got home. Imagine that Manly Dunning tellin' Bill that he couldn't be having any more trouble with the coloreds at the school."

"Billy Bob didn't tell me about that."

"Yes, and then he told Bill that when they started raisin' a ruckus at the school it was bad for the whole community. I swear, that Manly Dunning has such a small town mentality."

"Humm."

"And then tellin' Bill that he better make sure the trustees have something to brag about at New Year's. Can you imagine telling the

Chancellor of Morgan University that the most important thing he can do is make sure his football team plays in some Bowl game?"

"Ahhh—"

"And after feelin' sick all Thursday night," whispered Winnie as she saw her husband returning, "Billy Bob insisted on goin' into the office on Friday afternoon to meet with Noweeta."

"Oh really?" Boomer smiled.

"I tried to tell him he should rest, but he just wouldn't listen— You decide not to get anything to drink, suga'?"

"Lines were too long," said Brewster, lowering himself onto the aluminum bench next to his wife.

"You know it really is too bad we gotta go to that party at Faulkner's tonight." Winnie patted her husband's hand.

Ten minutes later, with no further scoring by either squad, the half ended, with the Porkers leading 10 to 0.

"Now I'm not gonna scream and holler at you," screamed Coach Star at his players as they stood around in the locker room ready to go back out for the second half. "You all know how much is riding on this game. We win it and we're the first Morgan football team in twenty years to go to a Bowl. We lose—I'm not even gonna think about it. Because I know that when you hit that field there's gonna be one thing on your mind and only one thing. And that is WIN-NIN' THIS GAME! You understand me?!"

"Yeah!"

"I said, do you understand me?!"

"YESSS!"

"I can't hear you!"

"YEAH, KICK BUTT! LET'S GO GET THOSE PIGS!"

Inspired by the Coach's hectoring and by a tipped punt they took over at the 43, the Morgan offense five minutes later was threatening on the Porker 16. Then on third and 4, after faking a pitch to Harris, Gentry kept the ball and threaded his way into the end zone for six!

KICK BUTT! KICK BUTT!

"Awright, Gentry!" yelled Boomer, picking his wife Betty up off her feet in a bear hug.

Sparked by the touchdown and extra point, the Morgan fans began to warm up.

KICK BUTT! KICK BUTT!

And four plays later, after Butt Bowers stripped the ball from Adonis Turner, the Knights offense had the pigskin back on their own 46.

"Okay, guys! Let's get some points!" barked Coach Star, nervously pacing up and down the sideline like a dog behind an invisible fence.

And on the next play, the offense did exactly as he ordered, when Gentry hit Tongo with a slant pass at the 7, 5, 3, TOUCHDOWN!

Feeling his sinuses suddenly open up for the first time all day, Brewster was on his feet pumping his fists in unison with Teeny McAdoo as the point after put Morgan on top 14 to 10.

"You got anything left in that flask of yours, Boomer?"

"You betcha, Billy Bob."

• • •

"Here we go again," sighed Faulkner Fentress, walking over to the sky box bar to fill his glass.

"Don't give up yet, Fess," said Jim Mack. "We're only down by four."

"Can I get you another drink, Jimmy?"

"Naw, I'm awright for now."

"Tell me the truth," said Fentress, rejoining his Athletics Director at the window. "Whad'da you think about this here Coach Star?"

"Well," said Jim Mack, sipping his whiskey and looking down at the field where Star was excitedly gesticulating to his defensive players after Einreich had just sacked Turner, "he ain't bad."

"Lotta folks say that with the right organization he could be really dangerous."

"Maybe."

"I've been hearin' rumors lately that he might be gettin' ready to jump ship."

"Where to?"

"I've heard Cosmopolis."

"Humm, well, there's no doubt about Star havin' the *want to* part," said Jimmy Mack, watching Star talking with Ron Carver on the headphones. "Way he left ole Art Mink with his dick hanging out when he went to Morgan, it's for sure he ain't gonna let loyalty get in his way. But I'm just not sure he's got what it takes to run a really big-time program."

Unable to move against a rising Purple tide, the Porkers were again forced to punt four plays later.

"I think we got 'em on the run, Billy!"

"Hand me some of those peanuts, would'ja, Boomer?"

Then Gentry took the snap, dropped back in the pocket . . . and found Holmes at the Porker 9.

HOORAY! KICK BUTT! KICK BUTT!

"Now this here's what I call a football game." Brewster was grinning from ear to ear.

"We got 'em now." Boomer slapped his old high school teammate on the back. "Where the hell is Dudley?"

KICK BUTT! KICK BUTT!

First and goal, Coach Star sent Gentry back on the field with a slap on the buttocks in which DeeDee Grimes had buried her fingernails three weeks before. Then he came to the line, rattled off the signals . . . and KAPOW! got hammered by Orleans DuPrez and coughed up the ball.

OOOOOOOOOO

The officials pried the last of the players loose from the pile-up on the 9, and the Porker fans roared with delight. Not only had Morgan lost the ball, but from the looks of Gentry, who lay writhing in pain on the 18, they had also lost their quarterback.

"What did I tell you, Fess. Orleans to the rescue."

"You were right, Jimmy Mack. That Orleans is a good boy, idn't he? Jus' like his Daddy was."

"Yeah, ole Napoleon was a work horse too."

"I hope we can keep Orleans aroun' here next year."

"I wouldn't count on it, Fess. He's a honest to God hardship case."

"I thought you said you coached his Daddy."

"I did."

"And?"

"After he put in his time, he went back to work on ole Kaleb Bigsby's farm like his Daddy did before him."

"You mean to tell me that workin' on Kaleb's cotton farm was the best job he could get with a college degree?"

"A what? You been readin' too many of those Hog club booster brochures, Festus. Only place most of these boys go after their eligibility runs out, less of course they're good enough to play pro, is right back where they came from. Hey lookee there now, our ball, first and 10."

"WHAT THE HELL WERE YOU DOIN', GENTRY?!" screamed Coach Star.

Silence.

"Gentry, I'm talkin' to you! What the fuck were you doin' on that play?!!"

Silence.

"How's that ankle, Stitches?" said Star, turning away from Gentry in disgust.

"I'm afraid he's done for the day." Stitches spit a long gob of tobacco juice on the ground.

Having literally torn the momentum from the Knights' hands, the Hogs were nevertheless unable to hold on to it themselves. Three plays later they were forced to punt to the Knights, who, four minutes after that, punted it back to the Porkers. And so the gridlocked game went on until late in the fourth quarter when it seemed that time had finally run out for the Hogs.

As Tom Hanagan watched Adonis Turner set the Pig offense down on their own 33, fourth and 4, with 2:35 left to go, he was palpitating with anxiety. One play was now all that stood between his team and a Bowl. Then Turner took the snap, dropped back to pass, and found hit tight end Martel Hendrix for a first down at the Morgan 35.

"Shit!" Tom sank to his seat. And rose up fifteen seconds later as Turner dropped back to pass . . . got chased out of the pocket . . . broke to the sideline and let one go for Stamps at the 3! Complete!

HOORAY PORKERS!

"This isn't really happening," said Tom, the concrete quaking beneath his feet.

"It can't be true," said the Chancellor.

But three time-consuming plays later, Turner snuck it in for six to put the Pigs on top 17 to 14.

SOOOOOOWEEEEEEEE! PIGS! PIGS! PIGS!

Still, a minute and a quarter is a lot of time—even if your quarterback has been doing coke all week. And fifty-eight seconds later, after Ritter broke loose for 20 and then for another eighteen, the Knights stood on the Porker 34.

KICK BUTT! KICK BUTT!

Fourth and 2, with seventeen seconds left, Coach Star called his last time out, and, deaf to the roar of the fans, stood there trying to decide whether to go for the first down or send in his kicker and go for the tie. In desperation he went for the first down.

"What the hell's goin' on!" exploded the Chancellor, who would have been equally perturbed if Star had decided to kick.

I hope he knows what he's doin', muttered Tom to himself.

Then the clock began to tick, Muggins took the snap, started toward the right side, cut back to the left, looked for Harris . . . looked for Dobbins . . . and got flattened by Orleans DuPrez behind the line of scrimmage.

HOOOOORAAAAY HAWGS! OINK! OINK! OINK!
SOOOWEEE PIG!

CHAPTER 22
Sunday, November 6

The taste of defeat still bitter in his mouth, his congested head throbbing from the liquor that Faulkner Fentress had forced on him the evening before, Chancellor Brewster bumped down a washed-out dirt road on Jim Mack Brewer's hunting lease at 7:15 Sunday morning, huntin' hawgs.

"You havin' a good time?" yelled Faulkner Fentress, trying to make himself heard over the roar of the jeep and the barking of the dogs running through the brush ahead.

"Yeah, just fine, Faulkner, just fine," said the Chancellor, holding on to his seat with one hand and wiping a glob of mud that had just flown up into his face with the other.

"Look out for that branch, Billy Bob," yelled Dr. Fentress, as the jeep hit a deep rut in the dirt road and suddenly swerved violently to the left. "Wow, that was close...."

ARF ARF ARF, HOWLLLL ... ARF ARF ARF.

"They can smell 'em now, cain't they, Bubba."

"Sho' can, Doctor," said the toothless jeep driver, turning around and almost colliding with a tree limb.

"I'm sure glad that rain fin'ly let up!" yelled Dr. Fentress to his fellow head administrator.

"Yeah, me too, Faulkner," said Brewster, alternately fevered and freezing beneath his camouflage hunting suit.

"Hey! There's one now!" yelled Jim Mack, jumping out of the mud-splattered jeep in front of them.

ARF ARF ARF HOWL.

"Go git 'im, boys," hooted Bubba to the dogs as he drove the jeep through a thicket into a small clearing through which ran a muddy stream.

"C'mon, Billy Bob!" yelled Faulkner, pulling out his .357 Magnum. "Maybe you'll have a little more luck today than you had yesterday, har har har."

As the Chancellor leapt out of the jeep, he grabbed the roll bar to steady himself. "God, I feel awful," he muttered.

"C'mon, Billy Bob! And keep an eye out behind. Sometimes these hogs'll sneak up on ya."

"I'm comin', Faulkner." Brewster stumbled his way through the brambles.

ARF ARF ARF HOWLLLLL ... As the baying reached a frenzied pitch, a boar burst through a canebrake and charged at them, ripping the air with his tusks.

"There he is, there he is!" whooped Jim Mack, looking with delight as a large tan and white hound named Elmo charged the pig and clamped down on its left ear.

OINK OINK SQEEEAL.

"Holt on! Elmo! Holt on!"

SQUEEAL OINK!

"Watch out, Faulkner!" yelled Jim Mack—the boar lunged left and rolled over in a whirl of kicking feet and slashing tusks trying to shake the dog.

GROWLLL SNAPP SQUEEAL HOWL.

No sooner was the pig back on its feet than Elmo's brindled brother, Remus, chomped down on the hog's other ear.

SQUEEEALLL.

Frantically kicking its hind feet and shaking its head, the grunting hog, beset by a third dog, suddenly wheeled right, and gored Remus's flank from brisket to loin.

GRRRRRRR OOOOOOOOOO!

Remus clung tenaciously to the pig's neck, while blood and steaming blueish-white entrails gushed from his belly.

SQUEEEAL ARF ARF ARF!

"Time to end this brawl," said Jim Mack, disappointed that they would have to kill the pig so soon. "The honor's yours, Billy Bob."

Brewster, who was normally a good shot, raised his pistol and fired, but the bullet went wide of the lurching pig.

"You just aren't havin' any luck this weekend, are you?" Faulkner laughed while Jim Mack took aim at the boar, squeezed the trigger of his .45, and blew off the top of its head.

"Good shot, Jimmy! Good shot!"

The hog crumpled to the ground, Remus rolled over beside his twitching quarry, and began a long drawn-out whine. Unable to rouse the dog as it lay on the bloody red clay in front of him, Bubba knelt beside Remus and looked at his wounds. Then, with a tear in his eye, he stood up, cocked his pistol, and put a bullet through his pet's brain. As the blood-spattered hunters stood around looking at the carnage, congratulating each other on a successful hunt, Chancellor Brewster excused himself, stumbled to the bushes, and vomited up his breakfast.

"Guess them ole Morgan boys ain't used to the sight of blood," joshed Faulkner Fentress.

"No, I guess not," said Jim Mack, slipping his pistol back in its holster.

• • •

"I don't give a damn what Jet thinks," said Coach Star, bolting up from behind his desk.

"Hey, relax, Tony," said Ed.

"What are you talkin' about, relax!" exploded Star. "I got enough problems without my staff playin' Sunday morning quarterback with me."

"You got it all wrong," said Ed. "Jet wasn't complaining, all he said was he thought you should'a conferred with us on that last series, like you always do."

"Fuck Jackson! I'm the head coach here, and I don't owe him any goddam explanations for what I do. You understand?"

"Sure."

"I mean it. I won't have him or anyone else second guessing me, not as long as I'm runnin' the show."

"I don't think—"

"I don't care what anybody else thinks. What I say goes, that's the way it's got to be, and if Jet or anybody else doesn't like it, there's the door!"

"Jesus Christ, Tony, what's wrong with you?"

"I'll tell you what's wrong. A month ago we were the hottest team in college football, and this week I'm not sure we're even gonna wind up with a winning season."

"I dunno." Ed shrugged.

"Yeah, but I do."

"If it hadn't been for that sonofabitch Carlisle getting our black kids riled up, we would 'a beat those bastards yesterday."

"I can't argue with that."

"And this week we gotta play the Warriors, and they tore Tech apart yesterday."

Ed nodded. "But with Wallace and DeGama back—"

"We still aren't sure about either of 'em, Ed."

"Now Tony, don't take this wrong, but if it'd been me, I would'a played Wallace this week."

"Oh really? If it'd been you, huh? Well, Ed, maybe that's the reason that I'm head coach and you ain't."

Silence.

"I'm sorry, Eddie," said Star, suddenly realizing he had gone too far. "You're the only one here who really understands."

"You're right. And I'll tell you something else, you and me are gonna go talk to Hanagan this week about those contracts. This is getting ridiculous. I know it's got you upset just like the rest of us. What kinda bullshit is this?"

"You're right, Eddie."

"I know I am. If we don't go talk—"

"Don't worry, we will." Star walked across the room and threw his arm around Ed's shoulder, "but for today let's try to stay focused on the Warriors."

"Okay, Tone, but—"

"I promise we'll take care of business this week. Did Turk get that footage ready to go yet?"

"Yeah, and Porky oughta be back with those pizzas any minute."

"I'll be right in," said Star.

"Okay, buddy."

As Tony sat in his office thinking about his near and distant future—neither one of which looked particularly rosy on this cold, gray November morning—the thought occurred to him, as it never had before, that maybe the game was getting to be too much for him.

CHAPTER 23

The Week of November 6

When Tom Hanagan walked into his office Monday morning, Savannah and Bill Conner were leaning up against the file cabinet groping each other.

"Ahem."

"Oh! Tom!" said Savannah, pushing Bill away in embarrassment.

"Mr. Hanagan," said Bill, looking at his boss with a foolish and cocky grin on his handsome face.

"I guess there isn't enough work to do around here." Tom walked straight into his office. "Savannah, when you have a minute, I'd like to talk with you."

"Yes, sir," she said, slapping Bill away as he tried to sneak another kiss. "Git outta here, Billy."

Tom hadn't slept well. When Jan had arrived home at 11:00 the two of them had gone at it. *What do you mean, where was I? I was at work where I always am!* And in the morning they had started in again when Tom suggested that if she cared about O'Hara she would have taken him for a trim weeks ago. *"Maybe you and that goddam dog of yours would be happier living alone!"*

Barraged by telephone calls, faxes, and e-mails from disgruntled fans, boosters and alums all across the United States (one supporter had even emailed from Shanghai), Tom was exhausted by the time Blake Stevens walked into his office at 11:30.

"What a morning!" groaned Blake as he collapsed in the chair in front of Tom's desk.

"Tell me about it!" Tom leaned back in his chair and loosened his tie.

"Any word on those Bowl bids?" asked Blake.

"I talked to Dietrich at the Fruit Bowl and they're still interested. And the Beaver Bowl guys wanna see what happens this week. But the Hoola and the Citrus are gone."

"Have you told anybody yet?"

"No."

"Me neither. You gonna let the boosters know what's goin' on tonight?"

"Tonight? I dunno. There's gonna be a lot of gloomy faces in that hotel room."

"Yeah, everybody's bitchin' about the way Tony coached that game."

"Well, maybe 5 and 3 isn't bad," said Dr. Lucius Thompson, puffing a cigarette that evening in the lobby outside the Dixie ballroom, "but we've all been countin' on a little more than a winning season."

"I know," said Tom.

"And I'm not the only one who's disappointed," said the surgeon, heading back into the ballroom where they were getting ready to serve the Boosters their Chicken Camelot.

Disappointed with what, asshole? thought Tom. *That Morgan isn't in the basement this year? You give people an inch—*

"Oh hello, Inez," said Tom as he saw his aunt approach the door.

"'Lo, Tom."

"Cliff told me he's comin' home tomorrow. You must be—"

"Disappointed. Everybody is very disappointed about that loss Saturday. It never should'a happened."

"I know, Inez. And I—"

"Oh, there you are, Estelle," she said, abruptly walking off to talk with Estelle and Harlan Gooch.

By 10:15, everyone had left the Camelot Club meeting and gone home to watch the rest of the Rams-Titans game, except Bill Conner and Savannah McLane, who sat in the piano bar in the hotel lobby holding hands watching the leaves fall from the Japanese maple on the patio.

"It's getting cold out there," said Bill.

"I don't like the cold." Savannah shivered.

"Yeah, I know what you mean." Bill stroked her hand. "And it doesn't look like we're gonna get that holiday in Miami after all."

"That's not true," said Savannah. "I'm goin' to Florida in February for a week."

"That's not what I mean, honey. I'm talkin' about that Bowl game we were all planning on going to."

"Oh yeah," said Savannah dispiritedly, lowering her head to suck on the straw of her Orange Blossom.

"So, ole Tombo read you the riot act, huh?"

"Well, sort of. He said he didn't want any office romances goin' on."

"Not that he wasn't carryin' on himself."

"Bill!"

"Just joking, baby, just joking. I like Tom, you know that. He's been like a father to me. But I'm worried."

"About what, Bill?" she asked, tilting her kittenish little head to the side gazing languidly into his eyes.

"About everything."

"Everything?"

"The department, honey."

"Why?"

"Well, you know I've been playing golf with Sam Edwards on the weekends—which reminds me, I've got to call Dudley Dunning about playing next week."

"Mr. Dunning called you?!"

"Yeah. Didn't I tell ya?"

"Bill, I'm impressed. You know everybody."

"You have to. Anyway, from the little bits of information I've been picking up," began Bill, relating ten minutes of hearsay and gossip to which Savannah gave only halfhearted attention as she gazed at his jutting jaw, dreamy blue eyes, and sparkling white teeth.

"Can you take me home now?" she purred, finishing off her drink and beginning to feel sleepy.

"Oh sure, honey," he said, breaking off his analysis of Calhoun politics to flag the waiter.

• • •

Noweeta Hayes left work early on Tuesday afternoon. After going home to feed her two cocker spaniels, she drove to the Airport Marriott, where she took out a room for the night on the 18th floor. Once inside her suite she popped Dean Martin's Greatest Hits into the CD player, slipped out of her gray business suit, and drew herself a warm, strawberry-scented bath. *Everybody loves somebody sometime....*

An hour later, after powdering herself and polishing her nails, the sinuous sprinter re-emerged from the steamy bathroom and slowly dressed in front of the mirror. "He's gonna love these," she reflected, glancing back over her shoulder to see how the leopard panties and brassiere she had special-ordered from Fredericks looked from behind. Rummaging through her overnight bag, she then pulled out a black velvet choker and tied it around her neck. "Perfect," she said, smiling into the mirror, tingling at the thought of him tearing it off her. It had been nearly three weeks since they had been together, and there had been desperation in his voice when he'd called and told her in a hoarse whisper that if "Junior" didn't get "a taste of her brown suga' before long, he was gonna bust." She liked it when he talked to her like that. She knew she shouldn't, but she did. And although she found her relationship with him demeaning at times, the only real satisfaction she had ever found was with white, middle-aged, preferably southern men like him.

If Noweeta had lived in any other country but America she might have enjoyed her sexual proclivity without ever being troubled about its correctness. But she felt guilty that she liked white men. In consequence, she had sought help from several different analysts, all of whom agreed that her "problem" stemmed from her stepfather, Hans Slafonhandler, a Dutch medical student who had married

Noweeta's unwed mother, an attractive mulatto nurse from Puerto Rico, during his residency at Johns Hopkins. From age thirteen until sixteen, when Hans abandoned Noweeta's mother and moved back to Amsterdam, she and Papa Hans had carried on an illicit relationship behind her mother's back. According to her therapists, this had left her emotionally crippled and incapable of finding fulfillment with males of her own ethnic background. Although she had tried, at the suggestion of her counselors, to develop lasting relationships with men of color, it was inevitably to men such as the one for whom she now waited that she turned.

KNOCK KNOCK

"Who is it?" she said playfully, opening the door a crack.

"Who do you think it is?" he said, barging in the room.

"Oh baby." She threw her arms around his neck and kissed him as he pulled off his topcoat. "Thank goodness you're finally here."

"Glad to see me, huh?"

"Yesss," she murmured, helping him out of his pinstripe suit coat.

"I'm glad to see you too. You got my drink ready?" He loosened his tie and plopped down on the edge of the bed.

"Comin' up, suga'." She said bent over to get the highball glasses from the refrigerator and felt his hands on her buttocks.

"Ummm, now that's—" (*Hatchoo!*)

"Gesundheit, baby." She handed him a glass of bourbon on the rocks and sat down next to him on the bed.

Glug glug glug. "Yeah, I feel better already," he said, licking his lips after he'd tossed off his first glass. "These last two weeks have been murder."

"For me too," she said, kissing him on the neck, running her hands over his chest as he leaned back on his elbows.

"I swear if anything else goes wrong—" (*Hatchoo!*)

"You okay, honey?"

"I will be soon." He pulled himself back up and smiled when he noticed the black choker around her neck. "Weren't you wearin' that at the Halloween party the other night?"

"Uh hum."

"And I told you I liked it, didn't I?" He reached out and ran his finger down her nose and over her glossy lips. "Yeah, you were the regular belle of the ball," he laughed, feeling "Junior" growing hard as she took his finger in her mouth and sucked on it. He stood up and started to unbutton his shirt.

"Here, let me do that, baby," she said kissing his neck as she undid his buttons with one hand and unzipped his fly with the other. "I can tell Junior is glad to see me."

"Whoa, whoa now, hold on there," he said, pushing her away while he refilled his glass. "You could at least let me have another drink."

"I'll try, honey."

"Besides," he said, stepping back, laying down the George Dickel bottle, "I haven't had a chance to get a good look at you yet. . . . Yeah, that's right." He smiled as she started revolving on her heels in front of him. "Now take off that thing you got on, and let me get a good look at what you're wearin' underneath."

"Like this?" She let her black filmy camisole fall over her high heels onto the floor.

"Yeah, just like Sheena, queen of the jungle." He chuckled and walked over to her, stripping off her leopard skin brassiere.

Two hours later he lay stretched out naked on his belly, his head over the edge of the bed smoking a cigar while Noweeta sat astride his buttocks massaging his back.

"That feel good, honey?" she asked, kissing him on top of his head.

"Yeah, perfect. God knows I needed this after last Saturday. That game was a total disaster."

"I know."

"By the way, baby, where'd you put my coat?"

"I hung it up in the closet."

"Get it for me, wouldja? There's something in the pocket I need. Yeah, here it is," he said, pulling out a satin-covered jewelry box.

"For me?!" exclaimed Noweeta. Her birthday was on Thursday.

"Go ahead, open it up."

"Really?!"

"Go ahead now," he said, sitting up in bed.

"Oh honey! They're gorgeous!" she gasped, removing a string of pearls from the box, and then getting up on her knees to model them in the mirror.

"You like 'em?"

"Oh I love them!" she said, turning around and dragging him down on top of her in bed. "You know something, honey?"

"What?" he said, leaning over and kissing her.

"You don't do anything halfway, do you?"

"No, I guess I not," chuckled Boomer. "With me it's whole hog or nothin', yuk yuk yuk."

• • •

"Awright! Attaway to hustle! Whad'da'ya you think, Jet?"

"I don't know what Stitches is worried about. Wallace looks fine to me."

"Me too," said Star. "Let's run that Blue series down once more."

What Coach Star said was true. Jimmy Joe Wallace—in fact, all of the players—looked better than they had in a month. Gentry's ankle seemed fine, and even Reggie Muggins, who had cut back on the coke after one of the assistant trainers told him that there would be a random drug test that week, looked sharp.

"Awright, Muggins! Good move! . . . You check out DeGama?" said Star, clapping his hands together.

"Yeah I did," said Jet, who had earlier watched the kicker put ten in a row over from the 45. "He'll be good to go."

"That's good, cause we're going to need 'im. This Injun defense is tough from inside the 20."

• • •

By 3:00 Thursday afternoon, Tom was done in. A contingent of drunken boosters from Jacksonville had insisted on his meeting them at a topless club downtown where they kept him until three. Ordinarily, Tom would have found the experience at least amusing, but the night before had been another sleepless one. From two until he got up at 6:30 he had tossed and turned on the guest room bed, thinking about the hostile phone conversation he'd had with the Chancellor: *And, Tom, another thing I learned playing football—there's nobody on the team who can't be replaced. Nobody!*

BUZZ BUZZ

Tom picked up the phone. "Yes? . . . No—tell Ms. Brooks I'm not"—Then Tom recalled the scowl on Jan's face when he walked in the kitchen that morning—"On second thought, Savannah, maybe I will talk to her. Hey Bobby. I'm sorry I haven't got back. . . .Yeah, super busy. . . . Next week?" He thought a moment. "Tell you what, I'll call you Monday."

At a loss what to do about dinner—after Tony had canceled out on him so he and Rose could meet with a Century 21 agent—Tom decided he'd go surprise Jan at the store and see if she wanted to get a bite before he had to be back at the gym for the pre-season tip-off basketball game. *Maybe the two of us can sit down and have a real conversation for a change.*

Unfortunately, by the time he arrived at the store, Jan had already left to eat—though her assistant Valerie couldn't remember where.

Frustrated in this as he had been in everything else that day, Tom decided to grab an order to go at the International Food Emporium on the mall mezzanine. But with just forty-three shopping days left until Christmas, the Emporium was jammed with teenage mall rats and sweat-suited matrons feeding themselves and their runny-nosed broods Chinese, Mexican, Italian, and Indian junk food before heading back to spend the rest of their spouse's next paycheck.

"Damn it!" growled Tom, who by now was in serious need of a drink. Then he remembered there was a Ruby Tuesday's across from the computer game arcade.

"We have about a half hour wait, sir," said the harried Morgan honors student who was working as a hostess.

"That'll be all right." Tom looked at his watch. "I'll just go to the bar."

"All right, Mr. Hanagan, we'll call you as soon as we're ready."

Tom sat down, ordered a double vodka martini, and began to check out the crowd in the restaurant. *No, it can't be!* But it was. In a booth at the end of the bar Jan was animatedly chatting away with a handsome young blonde man, who reached out and grabbed her hand just as she noticed Tom.

"Tom!—ah, er, what a nice surprise," she stammered, drawing her hand away from Stefan, her cheeks turning the color of the autumn leaves in the silk scarf draped over her shoulder.

Tom didn't say a word.

"Well, don't just stand there. Sit down and join us. Tom, this is Stefan Bazitski, my aerobics instructor."

Stefan rose and extended his hand. "Pleezed to meet you sir."

"Yes, this is my lucky day," said Jan, still trying to regain her composure. "First I run into my aerobics instructor, and then I meet up with my husband.... tee hee hee."

"Yes, very lucky day," repeated Stefan nervously.

"And here comes our waitress," she chirped. "Tom, why don't you sit down and order something."

"I don't think I feel hungry." Tom stood there, staring at Bazitski.

"No, we aren't quite ready to order yet." Jan smiled at the waitress. "Please, Tom," she said taking him by the arm, "sit down!"

Tom pulled his arm away, his eyes still glued on Bazitski.

"Good Lord," she said testily, once more herself, "is there something wrong with you?"

"I'm not sure," he said a moment later, looking at her.

"Not sure of what?" she asked, without a hint of deceit showing on her particularly radiant face.

"I don't know," he said. "But I think I should be getting back to the school."

"Well, I suppose if you must."

When Tom got back to his car and turned on the ignition, local sportscaster Bo Hanks was talking about him.

"Yeah, there's a whole lot'a basketball fans here in Metro who think Tom Hanagan made a big mistake when he fired Coach Evans. What do you think, Andre?"

"Scratch Evans is very good coach," said Andre Watsiznamich, the twenty-three year old, seven foot four inch, 295 pound center for the Rumanian team, whom Bo was interviewing before the Morgan game. "I play against him last year when I was at Carolina."

But Tom didn't hear a word that Bo or Andre was saying. All he could think about was: *the look on her face when she saw me sitting in the restaurant . . . and the way she pulled her hand away from that greasy bastard. I should'a punched his teeth down his throat right there and then*, he said to himself, jamming on the brakes to a screeching halt at a red light.

"And so how do you like playing for the Rumanian team, Andre?"

"I like very much, Bo," said Andre, who was in the process of negotiating a deal with the San Antonio Spurs. "Playing for my country is great honor."

I should'a known, said Tom. *I should'a known. Hell! I have known! Coming in late every night for weeks. And the way she goes off every time I suggest to her that she should be home with our children.*

"To me, Bo, der are some t'ings even more important than money."

"Yeah, I know what you mean," said Bo, trying to figure out what Andre could possibly be talking about.

I can't believe it. I just can't believe it, said Tom, who, given his own track record, wasn't particularly disposed to giving his wife the benefit of the doubt. *I can't believe she'd do this to me and the kids. I just can't.*

But by the time he had returned to his office and poured himself several stiff ones, his better sense had begun to prevail. *No, she wouldn't, not Jan. What am I thinking of. I must be losing my mind. I see my wife dining with some foreign goon and all of a sudden I'm convinced she's having an affair. That's ridiculous.* He shook his head. *Jan would never do that to me* (glug glug) *or the kids. What she said makes sense. She ran into him at the mall and invited him to eat with her. Nothing strange about that. But then why was he holding her hand? No, that's not true, he wasn't holding her hand, he just reached for her hand. I've done it myself.* Tom suddenly became worried again. *But Jan's not that kind of girl. Chill out, Tommy* (glug glug). *Take a few deep breaths.... Yeah, that's better. God, I musta come off like a real jerk in the restaurant. I'll hear about it tonight, that's for sure.* Tom laughed as he thought about Jan yelling at him for acting like a jealous idiot in front of her aerobics instructor.

But as strong a case as Tom's Good Angel made for his wife's innocence, his Bad Angel was the more practiced pleader. And it wasn't long before the voice of doubt, which the vodka had temporarily drowned, began to buzz again in the depth of his heart. All but indiscernible at first, the whisper of suspicion soon turned into a murmur of insinuation that changed into a scream of condemnation, so loud that the roar in the Morgan gym as Andre Watsiznamich sunk the winning shot at the buzzer was barely audible above the din inside his head. *If I get my hands on that sonofabitch, I'll break his neck,* raged Tom, not even bothering to excuse himself when he nearly bowled over Dudley Dunning on his way out of the gym.

"I refuse to have anyone, most of all you, Tom Hanagan, accuse me of carrying on a ridiculous illicit relationship with my aerobics instructor!"

"Calm down, Jan, calm down," said Tom later that evening, "or you'll wake up the children."

"Let them wake up!" she screamed. "I've never been so embarrassed in my entire life! This isn't Saudi Arabia we're living in. Women are allowed to talk to men whom they happen to meet in public restaurants!"

"I'm sorry, Jan, if I—"

"Acted like an idiotic jealous husband!"

"Yes."

"Well please, don't let it happen again." Jan burst into tears and slammed the bedroom door in his face.

"Is Mommy all right?" asked Erin, popping her frowzy head out of her bedroom door.

"Yes, honey, everything's fine, just go back to sleep."

• • •

The cold weather predicted by the Weather Channel failed to materialize on Friday. Instead, Metro found itself basking in the congenial warmth of an Indian summer day. Soft, sweet, brief and breathless, there is no time more splendid in the southland than that season in early November. The warm sun hangs like a ripe persimmon above golden fields, and the crickets fiddle their harvest home to the happy sons and daughters of Dixie, who, returning from their labors at the end of a long day, were flabbergasted to hear on the evening news that Coach Star had been carrying on secret negotiations with the University of Cosmopolis about their head coaching position!

"WHAT?!" roared the Chancellor, almost falling out of the La-Z-Boy in his den.

"Oh God!" gasped Tom, turning up the sound on his car radio.

"Motherfuck!" growled Coach Star, standing in the middle of his office with a towel around his waist, watching the TV.

RING RING

"I don't know anything about it," said Tom to the Chancellor, as he pulled through the entrance of Fox Chapel Estates.

RING RING

"They don't know what they're talkin' about, Tommy," said Star, reaching for his Palm Pilot to find Mike Tubo's number.

RING RING

"I don't how it could'a happened," said Mike Tubo, who had leaked the story about Coach Star—to protect his 20 percent for doing the deal—after he had heard that Steve Tomachek had been talking to the New York Giants about a job for Ed Tarmeenian and a friend of his. "Honest, Tony, I don't know what went wrong," reiterated Tubo, turning his Jaguar down Wilshire Boulevard headed for the UCLA campus. "It must'a been Pigg. He's the only one who could'a done it."

"And I give you my word of honor that it's all a lie," said Coach Star to the disheartened and distrustful members of the team whom he had called to a special meeting in Calhoun Hall later that evening. "You guys gotta trust me. I haven't talked to anybody about goin' anywhere. I believe in this program and I believe in you." He looked around at the players, many of whom were contemptuously smiling back at him as if to say, *Sure, Coach, we believe you.* "And that's all I'm gonna say."

KNOCK KNOCK

Yeah, who is it?" Star was sitting in his office after the team meeting, trying to figure out what he was going to tell Ed and Jet.

"It's Ed."

"It's open, buddy. C'mon in. . . . Man, that was not fun." Star rose from his seat as Ed Tarmeenian walked in the room. "I think those stupid kids really believe those lies."

Silence.

"I can't believe it. Can you imagine anybody making up stuff like that about me?"

Silence.

"Have you ever heard of anything so ridiculous?" Star shook his head.

"No, I ain't," said Ed, staring at him across the room.

"I mean, it's got to where you can't trust—don't tell me you believe it too?"

Silence.

"Gimme a break!" said Star, throwing his arms up. "Does everybody around here believe those lies?"

Silence.

"Wouldn't I of told you if I was doin' some kinda deal?"

"I dunno, Tony."

"Ed, you're my friend, the only real friend I've got here. Believe me."

"So what did he say, Eddie?" asked Jet as Ed walked out of the Star's office.

"I dunno."

"Is it on the level?" asked Pete Cossacky as Ed lumbered past the tape room.

"I dunno."

"What's the scoop, man?" asked Ron Carver as Ed walked into his office and slammed the door. . . . *BANG! THUMP! THUMP! CRASH!*

"No, there's nothin' busted that I can see," said Stitches Stevens twenty minutes later, binding an ice pack around Ed's black and blue hand. "But the next time you punch something, why don't you go use one of them dummies we got downstairs and not the wall in your office."

CHAPTER 24

Saturday, November 12

When the teams trotted onto Fulsom Field for pre-game warm-up Saturday afternoon, there were more rumors flying than footballs.

"You know the man's lyin'," said Buster Hooper, who had flown into Metro that morning after selling 400 acres of "prime residential real estate" adjacent to the site of a future sewage treatment plant.

"He's as guilty as sin," said Roy Nash, breaking off a conversation he was having with Wendell Sinks about a new quarterback Wendell was anonymously footing the bills for at Living Waters Prep School.

"The way I look at it," said Dudley to Boomer and the Chancellor, "this will just make our job easier if we don't win today."

"Good point, Dud," said Boomer, winking at Noweeta Hayes as they stepped off the pressbox elevator.

"And it really doesn't matter whether Star's tellin' the truth or not—which of course he isn't—'cause now," said Dudley, grinning as he made a squeezing motion with his hand, "we got him by the balls."

"Yeah we do." Boomer smiled.

"Yeah," said Brewster, also smiling, though not exactly sure why, since he knew that any fist closing on the Coach's gonads would surely mean the tightening of the pressure on his own.

In the Knights locker room, where the team was about to take to the field, controversy was also raging—though not so much about Star's future plans as the game ahead. For the present, the coaching staff had set aside their concerns about the future. What they were fretting about was whether or not to play Jimmy Joe Wallace.

"The boy ain't ready," insisted Stitches Stevens. "That head 'a his ain't healed yet." And, surprisingly, Ed Tarmeenian, who never tired of telling players that broken bones get stronger once they mend, agreed.

"I know it ain't none of my business, Tony, but I don't think the kid's ready either. After he got popped a coupl'a times Wednesday, he looked disoriented to me."

On the other hand, Jet Jackson—who had, since the *Sports Illustrated* spread, also been secretly negotiating with several schools— "felt like to where Jimmy Joe is ready as he's gonna get. His fingers might still be a little numb, but hell, we've all had that. And besides,"—he laughed—"if we don't let him play pretty soon, his father's gonna come over here and shoot us all."

Star scratched his head—with an index finger that had never worked right after being broken a second time before it had fully healed—and considered the opinions of his assistants. "Let's go with Muggins."

"Muggins?" said the coaches, who had anticipated him starting Gentry.

"Yeah, Muggins," said Star, knowing that if his assistants were surprised, Lou Motley, the Warriors head coach, would be too. "We'll do like we did in Cambridge. Bang away at the right side, soften 'em up on the line, and when they start getting tired, bring in Wallace."

"Sounds okay to me," said Jet.

"Yeah, me too," agreed Ed, unable to look the Coach in the face.

"I'm glad you agree, Eddie. Hey, what happened to your hand?"

As the 43,000 suspicious fans at Fulsom Field gave Morgan a less than ecstatic welcome, Boomer Cox offered a toast to the Chancellor. "Billy Bob, here's to you and Winnie, and"—he thought a moment—"to the future!"

"Thanks, Boomer," said the Chancellor, laying down the game program. He had just been gazing at an ad for a Caribbean vacation getaway which featured a photo of a distinguished looking gray-haired gentleman like himself and a curvaceous young bikini-clad native girl, who bore no resemblance to Winnie. "And here's to Betty and you, and"—Brewster wanted to say 'Victory' or 'Bowl'—"to good friends!"

"Yeah, to good friends!" Boomer gave his wife a big hug and kiss. "Hey, is that Muggins in there?"

"I believe it is," said Brewster as Reggie Muggins broke to the near side and got dumped for a six-yard loss.

"I thought Hanagan told you Wallace was all right?"

From the first snap, Tom Hanagan could see that the Injuns were considerably more motivated than the Knights. Both their defense and offense, which had just come back on the field for the second time, appeared ready and determined. The Morgan players, on the other hand, seemed dispirited and sluggish. The Indians were gaining several yards on each carry. And then on second and 2, quarterback Dan Waffler dropped back to his own 49, saw Abdullah Mac-Intosh in the end zone and hit him for six points.

TOUCHDOWN!

Five minutes and forty-three seconds into the game, the Indians had taken their first scalp.

BOOM, BOOM BOOM BOOM, BOOM BOOM BOOM BOOM

As the Indians' war drums reverberated off the south end of the stadium, Tom, who had forgotten about Jan in his anxiety over the game, began to think about her again. It worried him that she had been so willing to accompany him and Inez to the game. *She's bein' too nice....*

Taken aback by the Warrior TD, Coach Star looked down the bench at Jimmy Joe Wallace, then at Stitches, who pretended to be looking the other way. And he called Anthony Gentry to the sideline.

"Whatever you do, Anthony, don't throw it away!"

"Okay, Coach."

"You understand?"

"Yeah, Coach, I understand."

But on third and 8, as he was being jackknifed between Willie Waters and Marty Mantuski, Gentry tossed it into the arms of cornerback Tyrone Turley, who scampered twenty-three yards for another TD.

Unable to control himself, Coach Star ripped off his headphones and tore into Anthony Gentry in an arm-waving fit of anger and profanity so violent that it raised a boo of disapproval from the disgusted crowd.

"Wallace!"

"Yeah, Coach."

"Are you warmed up yet?"

"Ready, Coach."

"Awright, you're up next," he said, not looking at Stitches Stevens.

"Yes, this is Dudley Dunning calling from Fulsom Field for Coach Beerbauer. . . . Hello, Max," said the industrialist to the Kansas City Chiefs' offensive coordinator. . . . "Yes, congratulations on the big win last Sunday! . . . What's that? . . . No, I'm afraid it's not lookin' very good for us here. That's why I'm callin'. . . . Yes, definitely, we need to get together again and talk . . . As soon as possible. . . . Uh huh. I suppose you're gonna be all tied up over the Thanksgiving holiday. . . . Oh really? Well, in that case, I was wonderin' if you and I could get together and talk a little turkey, yuk yuk yuk. . . . How's Friday afternoon? . . . Good. I'll call you Tuesday night."

"I just can't believe it." Brewster stared blankly down at the field. "Honest to God, Boomer, I can't believe it."

"Hey, it's not over yet, Billy Bob, here comes Wallace on the field."

"What do I have to do?"

"Cheer up, honey," said Winnie, rubbing his back.

"I've tried everything."

"Really, Bill, it's only a game."

"Only a game?!" The Chancellor looked with annoyance at his wife and then pitied her for her ignorance.

"Hey lookee there, Billy Bob! Our ball, first and 10 on our own 43! Come on, Wallace! Come on! You can do it. He's got Holmes open in the flat. FIRST DOWN!!"

LET'S GO, JIMMY JOE! LET'S GO!

"I'm tellin' you, Tony, that boy ain't ready yet."

"Red eagle four," said Star to Edwardo Holmes, ignoring Stitches Stevens and sending the wide receiver back into the game.

"I mean it!" said the trainer, stepping over the lines of Star's phones following him down the field.

"Awright! Good play!" yelled Star as Tutumo Tongo sprinted around end for seven yards.

"That boy's gonna get hurt."

LET'S GO, JIMMY JOE! LET'S GO!

"He ain't ready to play."

"Look, Stevens," said Star, finally wheeling around, "you go sit down on the bench over there and keep your mouth shut, you understand!"

"Yeah, I think I do." Stitches spit a gob of tobacco on the ground and walked away.

"Let's go! Let's go!" yelled Star as Pete Cossacky informed him from the booth that Tyrone Turley was leaving a big hole open down the middle. Star signaled in a bomb to Wallace.

Hut one, hut two.

And just as ordered, Jimmy Joe dropped back in the pocket, set himself, and hit Harris with a perfectly thrown sixty-yard strike.

YEA KNIGHTS! GO MORGAN! KICK BUTT!

As the Morgan cheerleaders led the crowd in a rousing round of KICK BUTT, Manly Dunning, standing on the tee of the seventh hole at Magnolia Hills with Mayor Phil Ransom, Tyson Culpepper, and BoDee Grimes, ordered his caddy to turn up the portable radio.

And here we go, Butch. Wallace at the line, sends Tongo in motion

*to the near side. . . . He's dropping back. . . . In trouble at the 15. . . .
He's gonna keep it. . . . He's got room . . . 8 . . . 5 . . . 1. TOUCHDOWN!
JIMMY JOE WALLACE!*

"Humm," said Manly, exchanging significant glances with BoDee
and Tyson Culpepper as he pumped the golf ball cleaner up and down
and the half came to an end. "Phil, I believe the honor is yours."

Down 7 to 14 at halftime, Coach Star, Stitches Stevens and Jet Jackson gathered for a powwow down the hall from the locker room.

"I'm the Coach around here, and don't you forget it," said Star,
trying to hold his voice down.

"All I'm tellin' you is — "

"I don't give a damn what you're tryin' to tell me, Stevens. I'm
calling the shots, and if you don't like it, there's the door."

"Well, if that's the way you feel," said Stitches.

"Yeah, that's the way I feel," snarled Star. "If Willis says Wallace
is okay, he's okay."

"I agree," said Jet. "The boy's head is gonna ache some, the way
those Injuns are hittin' today, it's only nat'ral."

"And you're sure he's all right, Doc?" Star asked the physician
several minutes later after he finished injecting painkiller in Dewey
Dobbins' shoulder.

"Accordin' to all the tests," said Willis, "there's absolutely nothing wrong with him."

*And we're very privileged to have on the halftime show this after-
noon,* said Butch Sanders, *Mr. Tom Hanagan, the Director of Athletics and Jerry McDonald, coach of the Morgan women's soccer team,
which is having a whale of a year.*

Yeah, thanks, Butch.

*Now, I suppose there's a lot of people out there who don't know
that the Lady Knights' soccer squad is the top-seeded team —*

"Shut that thing off, will you, John-Boy?" said Manly Dunning to
his caddy.

• • •

"Thank God that's over," said Chancellor Brewster as he and Winnie stepped back into the sky box after spending halftime in the gallery.

"Now that wasn't that bad, honey." Winnie gave a sign to the bartender to pour them two fresh ones. "I think you're just still worn out from that cold you had last week."

"Maybe, but those boosters were like to drive me crazy today."

"I keep tellin' you, you're takin' this football business too seriously. You're the Chancellor of a university, not a professional football franchise."

Silence.

"I mean, what do people expect from you? You've got more important things to worry about than whether the Morgan football team goes to some Bowl or not."

"Yes, I suppose."

"'Course you do. Landsakes, Billy Bob, the future of this nation is in the hands of you and other men like yourself. Isn't that right, Boomer?"

"Idn't what right, Winnie?" asked the contractor, who was looking at the half-time scores from around the Conference on the television.

"I was just telling Bill that the future of this country is in the hands of men like him and yourself."

Boomer thought about it while he lit up his cigar. "Yes, I guess you're right."

"You guess?! Why, if you and Bill and all the rest of the good, honest, upstanding citizens like yourselves started worryin' a little bit more about what kinda world your grandchildren were gonna live in and less about these silly games a' yours...."

When the reinjected and rejuvenated Warriors—many of whom in their Mohawk haircuts, earrings, and painted cheekbones looked like the Cherokee and Choctaw braves who had once hunted squirrels and scalps in the environs of Fulsom Field—came out on the field for the second half, they were howling for Purple blood. Nor were they disappointed when Butt Bowers hobbled to his feet after the kick-off pile-up with a large bleeding gash on his shin.

WOO WOO WARRIORS!

Capitalizing on Bowers' untimely exit from the field, Coach Motley ordered Danny Waffler to air it down the middle, which he did to perfection on two quick twenty-yard gainers to Jesse Sanford and Abdullah MacIntosh.

WOO WOOO WOOOO WARRIORS!

But once in Morgan territory, Ed's iron men dug in and yielded only twelve yards in the next seven plays. Unfortunately for the Knights, that was twelve yards too close to the goal as Injun place kicker Charlie Baresfoot (who actually *was* part Native American) proved when he split the uprights and put the Warriors on top 17 to 7.

BOOM, BOOM BOOM BOOM!

Down by 10, and desperate not to let the game slip away, Coach Star placed his career and Jimmy Joe's health in the balance—and sent Wallace back in after a twenty-three yard kick-off return by Harris.

"Awright now, let's score some points!"

And five minutes later, using a series of short pass plays which caught the Injun linebackers off guard, the Knights were on the Warrior 30.

KICK BUTT! KICK BUTT!

"I think we're gonna score one, Billy Bob!"

LET'S GO, JIMMY JOE, LET'S GO!

But in the shadow of the goal posts, the Warrior defense stiffened, and three plays later the Knights found themselves on the 21, fourth and one very long yard to go. Calling time out to consult with Jet and Pete upstairs, Star decided to go for it.

YEAAAA! HOORAY! GO MORGAN!

"Well?" said Brewster, turning to Boomer.

"Well?" said Boomer, looking back at his friend.

Hut one.

Ron Cluck and the offensive line surged forward with Jimmy Joe following right behind.... As the crowd held its breath, the officials peeled the players off the pile and Star saw they had come up short.

BOOOO! HISSSSSS! BOOOO!

But just how short he didn't find out until two minutes later when Doc Willis came over to him and whispered that Wallace was hurt.

"No!"

"Too dizzy to stand up."

"What's the problem?"

"Beats me," said Willis, looking back over his shoulder toward the bench where two of the trainers had just helped Wallace lie down on the grass. "He musta got hurt on that last pile-up."

"Jesus Christ!" cursed Star as Abdullah MacIntosh raced past him down the sideline for twenty yards.

WOO WOO WOO WARRIORS!

"Lemme go talk to him. Hey Jimmy Joe ... O ... O ...," said Star, his voice echoing inside the quarterback's head. "Are you all right?"

ITE ... ITE ... ITE?

"I dunno ... O ... O ... O ..." mumbled Wallace.

"Damn! ... AM ... AM ... AM ...!" growled Star, suddenly wheeling around as the Warriors picked up another fifteen.

"What are we gonna do, Doc?"

"Give 'im a minute, I think he'll come 'round." Doc Willis bent over the quarterback and shined a flashlight in Jimmy Joe's eyes.

But five minutes later, after Charlie Baresfoot kicked another Warrior field goal, Jimmy Joe Wallace was lifted onto a gurney.

"That's ma baby they're takin' away. That's ma baby!" wailed Tammie Wallace hysterically.

"Well," sighed Boomer, handing his pale and expressionless friend a half-full tumbler of Gentleman Jack.

Brewster took the glass without a word and emptied it.

This can't be true, said Tom Hanagan to himself as he watched

Injun linebacker Dweeb Huskers do a war-dance around the body of Anthony Gentry whom he had just sacked for a three yard loss.

But it was. And though the crowd did not start to file out of Fulsom Field until the middle of the next quarter—after the Warriors scored three more unanswered touchdowns—they all knew that when the ambulance carrying Jimmy Joe Wallace had disappeared into the tunnel, so did Cinderella's chance of ever finding Prince Charming.

CHAPTER 25

The Week of November 13

Breep . . . *We've got a 10–52 . . . crackle . . . in progress at the Pizza Hut on the corner of Jefferson and Morgan. A Hispanic male . . . breep . . . in a Pittsburgh Steelers jacket. . . . crackle.*

"So what happened, Finney?" asked Sergeant Tommy Sutton. The lights of the five patrol cars that had answered Finney O'Donnell's call danced on the wet pavement.

"Well, as soon as he come in," said the proprietor of the Pussykat Club, motioning toward the man in the back of the sergeant's car, "I could tell he was drunk on account 'a how he kept bumpin' into things. Then he decides to get himself a seat up front. And before I know it, he jumps up on the stage and starts dancin' with Cleopatra."

"Cleopatra?"

"Yeah, she's that new colored girl I was tellin' you about."

"Oh yeah. And what time was that, Fin?"

"Bout 12:30, ain't that right, Spud?"

"Yeah, that's right, boss." Spud, the club's bouncer, leaned on the door of the police car holding a bar towel full of ice on his eye.

"And?"

"Well, as soon as this here feller sees Spud comin', he starts to hollerin' how nobody can't trust nobody anymore. And before you know it, he puts his head down, charges right for Spud, and knocks him clean off the stairs. And that's when I thought I better call you."

"Lemme out'a here! Lemme out'a here!"

"Hey boy," said the burly sergeant looking in the rearview mirror at Ed Tarmeenian, "I tol' you before you betta' shut your mouth if you know what's good for you."

"Yeah, I kinda feel sorry for him," said Finney. "I guess his girlfriend or wife musta done him wrong."

"Oh yeah?"

"I figure, the way he kept blubberin' 'bout how you can't trust nobody."

"And you've never seen this guy before?" Ed normally went to the Body Shoppe.

"I don't think so."

Breep . . . We've got a 10–56 . . . crackle . . . at University and Morgan.

"Busy night, eh Sarge?"

"Yeah, it always is after football games, especially when we lose."

"Yeah, that was pretty disappointin' today, wadn't it?"

"Tell me about it. And I took my boys to the game too."

"Now you be careful, Tommy," said Finney, slamming the door.

"I will. . . . And now, Mr. Tar-a-meen-i-an," said the sergeant, slowly mispronouncing the coach's name as he looked at Ed's driver's license. Then he suddenly realized who was in the back of his car. "Coach Tarmeenian, I'll be damned!" And for a moment the sergeant thought about tearing up the report and calling Ed a cab. Then he remembered leaving Fulsom Field the afternoon before with ten minutes left to go, and he pulled down State Street headed for the Public Safety Building.

• • •

There is absolutely no truth to the rumor, Butch, said Coach Star Sunday evening. *I give you my word.*

"He doesn't lie any better than he coaches football, does he?" said the Chancellor as he sat at home watching the Tony Star Show, talking on the phone with Boomer Cox. "He's just diggin' his own grave, like Dudley said. Look at him. Why his lip is even twitchin'" — Actually it was the Coach's inability to reach Mike Tubo that had set his lip a-twitch — "Imagine him thinking he could hornswoggle us like that. . . . What? . . . Do I think Hanagan will fire him? . . . If he wants to keep his goddam job he will. . . . No, I haven't talked with Clifton, but. . . . Here comes Star back on. Listen to him. He thinks we can beat the Tigers this week. Who's he tryin' to fool?"

• • •

For the first time in a week Tom had not lain awake thinking about Jan. Sunday night it was his upcoming meeting with Brewster that kept him from sleep. But exhausted as he was, it was with a firm and resolute step that he marched up the stairs of Morgan Hall for his nine o'clock meeting. Tom had vowed that he was not going to be bullied. *I'm through taking crap from him. At 5 and 4, I've got nothing to apologize for. And if he doesn't like it, there's plenty of other schools out there who could use someone with my talent.*

But once inside the overheated lobby of the administration building, where the receptionist greeted him with the kind of look you give someone who has just been informed they have an incurable disease, Tom's resolve began to weaken to such a degree that when he emerged from the stuffy elevator on the fourth floor, along with several secretaries who had gone dumb the moment he climbed aboard, he could feel the sweat beginning to drip from his armpits. Nor did it help to boost his morale when Anita, who normally had a smile and good word for him, looked up from the letter she was proofing and without a word pointed toward the Chancellor's half-open door.

When Tom stepped inside, the Chancellor was standing with his back to him watching the last of the leaves fall from the sugar maple outside his window. Deciding it was probably best not to interrupt, Tom waited in the doorway until the Chancellor, without turning around, motioned for him to take a seat in front of his desk. A moment later, Brewster, still looking out his window, asked Tom if he knew why he'd called him to his office.

"I suppose."

"Good," he said, wheeling around with the ugliest look on his face that Tom had ever seen, "'cause I figure anyone I'm payin' a quarter of a million dollars a year oughta be smart enough to figure out why I wanna see them. Don't you think so?"

Tom nodded.

Brewster laughed malevolently. "I figured you'd agree." He sat down behind his massive oak desk. "But then you and I have always agreed on things pretty much, haven't we?"

"Pretty much."

"I guess that's because all great minds things alike, eh?"

"Could be," said Tom, loosening up a bit.

"In fact," said Brewster, "we think so much alike, I bet I can tell you what you were thinking when you walked in here a few minutes ago."

A silent shrug.

"See if this doesn't sound right." Brewster threw back his head as if he were trying to imagine what had been going through Tom's mind. "I bet you were thinking that you'd taken about enough guff from ole Billy Bob. *Hell, I've got a winning record, I don't know what he's complainin' about.*"

Tom shook his head no.

"C'mon now, admit it."

Tom shook his head again.

"Of course you were. And I bet you were thinking there were a lot of other schools around that could use somebody as talented as you."

"No, not really," Tom began to say.

"Well, YOU GODDAM WELL BETTER HOPE THERE ARE!" Brewster slammed his fist on his desk. "'Cause if this season keeps headin' south like it has, you're gonna have to find some other place to plug in your computer, you understand?!!"

"Yes, but—"

"BUT WHAT?!"

"BUT . . . I DON'T APPRECIATE BEING SCREAMED AT!" said Tom before he knew what he was saying.

"You what?" said Brewster, flabbergasted that Tom had dared to raise his voice to him.

"I said I don't appreciate being yelled at." Tom felt as if his heart was going to burst through his shirt.

"Oh you don't, do you?" Brewster lowered his voice to a menacing growl. "Then you probably don't want to hear what the members of the Athletics Committee have been telling me to do either."

Silence.

"No, I'm sure you don't. BUT I'M GONNA TELL YOU ANYWAY!!"

When Tom emerged from the Brewster's office fifteen minutes later, there was a grim smile on his lips. In a fit of pride and anger—which he already regretted—he had stood up to his boss and attempted to communicate man-to-man. Good material for a movie or a song, but in the real world, always a bad idea.

• • •

Clifton Calhoun was pruning dead blossoms off the giant gold marigolds that grew on either side of his driveway when Tom pulled in the following day at noon.

"How's the patient feelin' today?"

"Betta than I've felt in years, Tom."

"You know you're startin' to look like Robert E. Lee, Cliff."

Clifton smiled and stroked the growth of white stubble on his face. "You like it?"

"It looks great." Tom walked beside his uncle up the gravel driveway toward "Old Times," the Calhouns' white-columned, red brick ante-bellum house. Clifton stopped at the top of the porch stairs and pointed to the Katakoochie River in the misty distance.

"What is it, Cliff?"

"Why it's the river, boy."

"Yeah, the river," said Tom, not sure what Clifton was getting at.

"Just look at her."

Inside the house Clifton led Tom through a creaky-floored sitting room into a parlor decorated with colonial heirlooms. "It's such a warm day I thought we might take lunch out on the verandah."

"Sounds good to me," said Tom, walking past a portrait of Inez's great grandfather dressed in his gray and butternut uniform.

"Is you ready fo' lunch yet, Mista Clifton?"

"In a few minutes, Beula." Clifton threw open French doors that led onto a magnolia-shaded patio.

As Clifton filled his nostrils with the fragrant autumn air, Tom gazed out over a gigantic greensward that sloped down to stables and several wood cabins which had served as servants quarters until the mid-sixties.

"What a beautiful day!" said Clifton. "And you know, Tom"— Clifton motioned to his backyard—"until about a month ago I did-n't appreciate any of this."

Tom studied Clifton's face and remembered what Inez had said about him acting peculiar lately. *I'm afraid he might'a suffered some kinda brain damage when he had his attack.*

Clifton unbuttoned his cardigan and sat down in a wrought iron lawn chair. "Inez and I have been so caught up in all thoses goings-on at the school that I never took the time to smell the roses."

Tom nodded.

"But thanks to that attack of mine I'm finally seein' things more clearly."

Tom wondered.

"Seriously, when I think about all the time I've spent frettin' and fumin' about football and basketball and baseball games, goin' to luncheons and banquets tryin' to raise money for a bunch of"— Clifton couldn't think of the word—"who don't even know how to spell Morgan University."

"Now c'mon, Cliff, not all the boys are as bad as that."

"No, there's a few of 'em—darn few—who are actually int'rested in getting an education. But we know that most of 'em are only in school for one reason." Tom couldn't argue. " I guess I ought'a know." Clifton shook his head. "I made it possible for a lot of 'em to be there. Slipping 'em money, gettin' 'em summer jobs and cars. And all for what?"

Tom shrugged.

"Then all the sudden there I was a month ago starin' death in the face. It changes a man, Tom. It really does. Changed me anyway. It made me get my priorities straight and realize life isn't just a game." Cliff peered off in the distance. "For forty years all I did was eat, drink, and sleep sports. When I wasn't at the game or the club, I was watching it on TV. I never could understand why our daughter Missy hated that dang squawk box so much till I was on my back in the hospital last month. There I was, not sure whether I was gonna see another sunrise. And what do they do? They hand me a remote control so I can watch the baseball play-offs. Lord Almighty. What was it Missy used to say to Inez and me about the television?" Clifton scratched his head. "Bread and games, yeah, that was it."

"Bread and games?"

"Yeah, that's what one of those ole' Roman boys said life was like in Rome. Seems things got to where all anybody cared about was stuffing their bellies and watching games in the Coliseum—Beulah I think we're ready now!"

"So," said Clifton several minutes later, settting down his sweet tea, "I imagine things must be pretty hectic lately."

Tom wiped his mouth and began to speak—

"Well, if I were you, I wouldn't let it bother me too much."

Tom gave his uncle a confused look. "What do you mean, Cliff?"

"Just what I said, what I've been sayin' to you since you got here today. Life is too precious to waste your time frettin' about things you've got no control over."

"You've got a point, Cliff, but—"

"But nothin'. Hell, Tom, you'd probably be better off"—Clifton didn't finish his sentence.

"Better off what?"

"Just better off."

"Have you heard something, Cliff?"

"No, not exactly."

"What do you mean, 'not exactly.'"

"Just what I said. The only person I've talked with lately is Lucius."

"And?" asked Tom.

"He said there's a couple people on the Board who've been talking about needing some changes."

"Was Dunning one of them?"

Clifton shrugged.

"How 'bout Brewster? What's he sayin'?"

"Honest, Tom, I don't know. You want another piece of sweet potato pie?"

"Jesus Christ . . . No thanks, Cliff."

"But like I said, Tom, I wouldn't worry. More than likely everything is gonna work out just fine." Tom searched his uncle's eyes. "So anyway, how's my niece doing?"

• • •

Reggie Muggins never missed Professor Fisher's Contemporary Human Sexuality Seminar on Wednesday mornings. The class genuinely interested him and he loved entertaining his fellow students with his raunchy accounts of coming of age in the ghetto. But today the seat next to Teeny McAdoo was empty. Reggie and Tootie had left campus early that morning to score some of the uncut rock that had arrived at Bow Wow's the night before. As they pulled in sight of the Bow Wow's "crib"—a two-story townhouse in the JFK Housing Project—Reggie picked up his cell phone to let "his man" know he had arrived.

"Yeah brotha', we here," said Bow Wow, throwing two large wads of bills and a .45 automatic into a gym bag and sliding it under the couch.

Ten minutes later, Reggie and Tootie were seated on Bow Wow's black leatherette couch in front of a giant screen TV, examining a chunk of pink-hued Bolivian flake the size of a tennis ball.

"Dis is the baddest blow I had in a long time, man."

"*Snorrrrt* . . . Yeah, it's some smoove shit," said Tootie.

"I knew you'd like it. My new man got hissef a lot better line of products." Bow Wow chuckled and chopped up another line of the pharmaceutical-smelling coke with a gold-plated safety razor.

"Bow Wow, baby," came a voice from the bedroom upstairs where the dealer's girlfriend Juanita was watching the soaps, "you got people comin' to see you?"

"Wha?!"

"I sayd is somebody comin' to see you?"

Bow Wow ran to the front window and peeped through a crack in the blinds. Then he emitted a "mothafuck," reached under the couch, grabbed the money and the .45 and ran to the rear of the house. As Bow Wow reached the back door, his cousin Ronnie, who had been in the back bedroom making crack, appeared in the kitchen with a sawed-off shotgun.

"Who is it, Bow Wow?"

"It's Jelly Bean and he's got Flakey and T-Man with 'im." Jelly Bean was Bow Wow's former supplier and leader of the local chapter of the Bad Bloods gang.

"Shit! I told you we was lookin' for trouble." Ronnie ran into the living room with Bow Wow and someone began to pound on the front door.

"What we gonna do, Reggie?" Tootie stood in the kitchen, trembling from head to toe.

"We gonna get the hell outta Dodge is what we gonna do," said the quarterback, his chest heaving with panic as he fumbled with the back door locks.

"Hurry up, Reggie, hurry up!"

"I got it!" Muggins flung the door open, looked right and left, then tore down the steps toward the alley. But as he hurdled the bushes that lined the back yard, he heard a gunshot and then Tootie cry out, "I'm hit, man, I'm hit! Help me!" Muggins paused, but only long enough to hear a second shot before he lit out as fast as his legs would carry him.

When Tom got in Roy Nash's Town Car to go have lunch at Hooters, he heard on the radio that there had been a shoot-out at the JFK Housing Project earlier that morning which had left Ms. Juanita Hayes of 2904 Jefferson Pike Drive and Mr. Charles Turner of 6407

Tyner Place in critical condition. According to a neighbor, the incident had taken place after Mr. Turner and his fiancé got into an argument with two unidentified men about parking in Mr. Turner's spot.

"That's a likely story," said Nash, waiting to pull out of the parking lot until he had watched the micro-skirted Savannah strut out of Calhoun and climb into her car. "What these kids need are more places they can hang out and play basketball."

"You're right, Roy," said Tom, wondering how Savannah could possibly have forgotten to cancel the luncheon engagement he'd made with Roy two weeks before.

"Kids don't get into trouble when they get enough religion and athletics." Roy pulled out of the parking lot. "You know, Tom, if we could build a gymnasium on every corner of every ghetto in America, I guarantee we could lick this crime problem."

"You're probably right, Roy," agreed Tom as Roy began to give him his strategy for Saturday's upcoming game.

At 1:30 that afternoon, Reggie Muggins heard his dorm room telephone ring. Scared to answer, but frightened not to, he finally picked up the receiver and heard, to his relief—and terror—Tootie's voice on the other end of the line.

"You a sonofabitch Reggie, you know that."

"What you talkin' about?"

"You know what I'm talkin' about, Reggie."

"You okay, Tootie?"

"No thanks to you."

"You're not in jail, are you?"

"No, I ain't."

"Thank God. You know I tried to come back for you—"

"Cut the booshit, Reggie, I'm in no mood to be fucked with. I need to get my leg fixed. I think it's broke."

"Where you now?"

"The apartment, and I need you to bring me the car and enough bread so I can get my ass back to Memphis."

"How bad is it, man?"

"Bad enough. Now git over here before I call an ambulance."

"No! Don't do that, Tootie. Whatever you do, don't do that!"

"Then hurry up."

"Awright, brotha, I'll be right there."

Tootie hung up the phone, reached up and loosened the bandage he had tied around his throbbing skull. Miraculously, the bullet with which Flakey thought he had "offed" Tootie had only grazed his head.

• • •

When the Coach returned from lunch the following day, Teeny McAdoo was sitting outside his office waiting for him.

"Can I see you just a minute, Coach?" said the worried-looking cheerleader.

"Sure hon." Coach Star followed her into his office. "What's up?"

"Reggie wanted me to tell you he's not gonna be at practice again today."

"What?!"

"He's too sick to come."

"You tell him," said Star, his temper flaring, "if he's too damn sick to make practice he needs to see Doc Willis."

"He's too sick to see Doc Willis."

"Too sick to see Willis? What's wrong with him anyway?"

Silence.

"Teeny, what's wrong with him? It doesn't have anything to do with drugs, does it? cause if it does—"

"Please, Coach," said the cheerleader, bursting into tears. "Reggie needs help."

Twenty minutes later, Star and Teeny walked through the door of Muggins' off-campus apartment.

"Teeny?" came a sick and desperate-sounding voice in the next room. "Is that you?"

"Yes it's me, baby," said the cheerleader pointing to the bedroom door.

Coach Star stepped in the room and saw his quarterback curled up in a ball on the floor.

"Jesus Christ!"

Tom was sitting in the waiting room of Star's office when the Coach arrived after practice later that afternoon.

"Didn't Peaches call you about tonight?" asked Star.

"Yeah, she told me dinner was off, but I still need to see you a minute before you go."

"Sure."

"Kids are really sick, huh?"

"Yeah, and I think Rose has got it now too," lied Star, gesturing for Tom to have a seat as he sat down behind his desk. "Whew! What a day! So anyways, what's on your mind?"

"Well, for one thing," said Tom, planting his elbows on the arms of his chair—

"Yeah?"

"I'd like to know, and this isn't between the athletics director and the head football coach, this is between friends—if you've really been talking to Cosmopolis."

Star rocked forward in his chair. "Ab-so-lutely not."

"You're sure about that?"

"Positive. I got no reason to lie to you, Tommy. You're my friend. I love you like my own brother."

"I see," said Tom, who had been dreading this moment of truth since last Friday. "You know, Brewster doesn't believe you."

"Fuck Brewster. I don't give a damn what he—"

"And neither do I."

Silence.

"You hear me, Tony?" said Tom, his heart starting to pound. "I think you're lyin' to me."

"Take it easy, Tommy, take it easy."

"Fuck you, Tony! You hear me!" Tom jumped up out of his seat. "You're lyin' and you know you are!"

"Awright, awright," said Star. "So I did talk to Cosmopolis, but it was only once and that was after they kept buggin' me to call 'em back."

"You expect me to believe that?"

"It's the truth, Tommy. Honest to God. I was plannin' to tell you myself, but Tubo told me not to."

"Tubo? What does he have to do with this?"

"He's the one that put 'em on to me. I guess he heard we were having trouble getting Brewster to sign the contract."

"What are you talking about? It's you that's been sitting on that paper."

"Yeah, but that was after—"

"After what?! You know, Tony, I could'a lost my job, in fact, I still might, with you jacking Brewster around like this."

"Whad'da you want me to do? I got a wife and kids, just like you, Tom. You know as well as I do that we can't trust Brewster. Why, he'd screw both of us in a New York minute. That's the kind of sonofabitch he is. He doesn't care about anybody but himself."

"You're right, he doesn't. And let me tell you something, if you don't win these next two games for him and make sure we get into a Bowl, you're gonna find out just how little he does care."

"Are you threatening me, Tommy?" said Star, now also on his feet.

"I'm not threatening you. I'm telling you a fact. And you know what?" said Tom, uttering words he immediately regretted. "I think I might enjoy carrying out Brewster's orders."

While Tom and Tony were getting things off their chests, strength coach Brad Ballings was getting-it-on with Jimbo Jenks, a teenage hustler Brad and his roommate Rob had met several weeks before at the Silo.

"Did you hear sumpin'?" drawled Jimbo, who was reclining on the bed in the guest room of Brad's condo.

Brad turned around and—"Oh my God!"—saw Rob.

"JIMBO! BRAD! YOU BITCH!" Rob burst into tears and ran down the hall. "How could you?"

"Rob! Rob!" Brad took off after him.

"Get away from me, you bitch!" screamed Rob, grabbing a lamp in his hands.

"Don't, honey!" *CRASH!*

"And here!" Rob picked up an imitation Steuben Glass vase Brad had given him on Valentine's day. "Here's your present back!" *CRASH!*

"Don't, Rob, no!"

"And this china you bought us," sobbed the distraught teacher, raking the cups, saucers and finger bowls off the shelves of the antique hutch cupboard in the dining room *CRASH! CRACK! SHATTER!* "Oh I hate you!"

"Wait a minute, Rob, please!" Brad chased his roommate into the kitchen where Rob grabbed Brad's car keys off the table and scooted out the front door.

"Stop! Rob!!" Brad threw on a raincoat as Rob jumped into his Lexus and started the engine.

"Get away! Or I'll run you over!" screamed Rob, wildly backing down the driveway with Brad running beside him trying to yank open the door. "Rob, get out of that car. WATCH OUT! WATCH OUT!—"

As Rob pulled into the street, a United Parcel truck slammed into Brad's Lexus with such force that the car spun around ninety degrees. Fortunately for the truck driver, who was knocked unconscious when his head hit the windshield, there was a police car cruising down the street.

"We need an ambulance down here at River Road (*crackle*)."

Unfortunately for Brad, who stood there barefoot in his trench-coat, the presence of the police was to prove his undoing. For in the collision, the trunk of the Lexus had popped open and two boxes of illegal steroids had spilled into plain view.

"And what's this here?" asked Sergeant Grizzard, lifting up one of the vials from Brad's trunk.

"It's ah, some medicine," stammered Brad.

"Uh huh. And just what kind of medicine is it?" asked the sergeant, smiling maliciously as he handed the vial to his partner.

• • •

Attorney Buddy Phillips had warned Tom that the news of Brad Ballings' arrest for "possession of controlled substances" might appear in the paper the next day. But when Tom breathlessly rifled through *The Tribune* Friday morning, he found no mention of it. "Thank God!" The story had temporarily been squelched by Clarence Drumbacher until Red Carlisle could dig up some further information.

"You know a good story, Red, is kinda like a piece a' meat. You leave it hangin' there for awhile and it gets more savory. Yuk yuk."

• • •

"So you're tired of him, already, huh?"

"No, that's not it, Val," said Jan Hanagan pensively munching on her enchilada at lunch later that same afternoon.

"I know it would take me a while to get tired of a hunk like him." Jan's fellow buyer, Valerie Carter, flagged down one of the illegal aliens who waited tables at El Coyote. "Some more iced tea, please, Juan. A real long time. Can I ask you a serious question, Jan?"

"Sure."

"Is he really as good as he looks?"

"Val!"

"Really," said the lonely and lascivious thirty-five year old, who hadn't dated a heterosexual male since she and her "boring husband" had divorced two years earlier. "Betcha that stallion can run all night, huh?"

"If you're asking me does Stefan have a lot of energy." Jan smiled. "The answer is yes."

"Some girls have all the luck." Valerie bit into her chili relleno. "But—"

"But what? You say he's five times more romantic, four times more exciting, and three times as energetic as you know who, and you wanna give him up?"

"I don't know, Val. I guess I feel—"

"Guilty? That's somethin' your husband's never felt playin' around with that little assistant of his."

"I know."

"And after all, honey, this is the twenty-first century. What's good for the goose is good for the gander."

"Ohh, and Stefan can be so cute sometimes, especially when he starts talking to me in Russian."

"Is that before, after, or while he's, ah—"

"Wicked, wicked girl," said Jan, suddenly turning serious as she reached for the guacamole. "Maybe it's being a Mother."

"I wouldn't know," said Valerie, with genuine jealousy.

"But that's not all of it either. In a way, I guess, I still feel something for Tom."

"Huh," huffed Valerie, who still kept a photo of her ex taped inside her bedroom closet at home.

"Even if it's only pity. The truth is the way things are going at the school, he needs me. Just between us," whispered Jan, "I wouldn't be at all surprised if he lost his job when this season is over."

"Are you serious?"

"I'm really afraid for him. The rumor is that Chancellor Brewster and the Board are very disappointed, especially after the way the season began."

"Oh, aren't they doing well anymore?"

"No, they aren't. And though Tom would never admit it, I know he's scared."

"Humm."

"And that's really why I've got to break this thing off with Stefan—that, and the kids."

"I guess so."

"Tom doesn't need any more anxiety at this point than he's already got."

"And is he still off the deep end about seeing the two of you at Ruby Tuesday'?"

"No, the past couple days he hasn't had enough energy to be suspicious, but I know he still doesn't trust me."

"That's not good."

"No, it's not. People have to trust each other for a relationship to work. And that's why I've decided to tell him the truth—the whole truth."

"I don't know if I'd—"

"No, Val, it's the only way this marriage of ours is going to work. Like it or not, I owe it to Tom to let him know the whole story. If he can't love me, the real me, with all my weaknesses included, then there's no sense in even pretending we can make it."

RING RING

"Abe, this is Milt calling at 10:00. . . . Hey, sorry to call so late. . . . Busy, huh? . . . I remember how it used to be for my Uncle Saul before the holidays. You remember Saul, don'tcha? . . . Right, with the toupée . . . Yeah, he sold out his toy business to Mattel and got into home computers. . . . That's exactly what he used to call them, too, toys for grown-ups. You play with 'em for a coupl'a weeks and then they sit around collectin' dust until they're obsolete. Anyway, what I'm calling about—Yeah, I'll hold."

Milt looked down from the second story of the Lee and Jackson office building at a bunch of former farmhands who were loading up a van with junk food advertising inserts for the morning issue of *The Tribune*. . . . "Ah, there you are. Anyway, what I called to tell you is, I think I got enough shirts. . . . Yeah, I'm over-stocked right now. . . . I know I should'a listened to you. After last Saturday they stopped moving completely. But now that you've heard the bad news, here's the good. As I'm gettin' ready to leave the office the otha' day, who should happen to call me but Dudley Dunning. . . . That's right. 'We need to talk,' he says to me. 'About what?' . . . 'About business,' he says. 'Meet me at the Metro Club for lunch one o'clock tomorrow.' . . . Right, Dunning's the one who's been callin' the shots at the University since Brewster got there, him and his buddy, Boomer Cox, the contractor. Anyway, to make a long story short, we're sittin' there havin' lunch the next day when all the sudden Dunning says, 'How much have you made off those Kick Butt souvenirs?' ... 'Off what,' I say? ... 'You don't need to play dumb with me, Milt,' he says. Then he leans over the table and says in a low voice, 'I like the way you do business, Milt. I think maybe our Alma Mater could use somebody like you.' 'Oh really? Like how?' 'Like maybe as Executive Director of the National Camelot Club. It's just an idea, but I thought you might be interested.' 'Well, that would all depend'— 'On the money?' he says. 'I don't think that will be any problem....' You're right, Abe. It could be a great opportunity."

• • •

The Morgan faithful looked forward to Saturday's match-up with the Tigers in nearby Sparta with all the enthusiasm that one has for a prostate exam. At 8 and 1, the Roarin' Tigers were tied for first place in the Mid-South and ranked number eight in the nation. They were mean, deep, and motivated by a monomaniacal martinet named Knox Newcomb, who took pride in his squad having decimated the roster of every school they played that season. "Yeah, these guys can put the hurt on you," bragged Newcomb when questioned about accusations of unnecessary roughness in a pre-game interview. "But whad'da ya expect, this isn't touch football we're playin'."

Against such a professionally trained and obsessively motivated football squad—exactly the type that the fathers of Morgan University had hoped Tom Hanagan and Tony Star would build for them— Chancellor Brewster knew his Knights had little or no chance.

"You just never know, Bill," said Winnie, trying to console her husband after they'd taken their seat behind the Morgan bench in Tiger Stadium.

"We'll find out in a minute," said Brewster as the squads lined up for the kick-off.

Actually it took three minutes—for Tiger quarterback Trent Reeves to hit Hollis Henry with a sixty-five yard touchdown pass.

And five more for Tiger linebacker Majik Mays to pick up a Gentry fumble and run it in for another.

GROWWLLLLL TIGERS!!!!!

"I can't watch this," said Brewster to his wife as the Tigers made the point after and the crowd went roaring wild in anticipation of the Bowl-impressing slaughter Coach Newcomb had promised the press all week.

Two hours and fifty-three agonizing minutes later, it was over. U.K. Tigers 63, Morgan Knights 3. It was the worst drubbing the team had suffered in eight years, "the most humiliating day" Chancellor Brewster could remember, and the end of the line for Coach Star.

"So we're all agreed then," said Dudley, talking to Brewster and Boomer over the speakerphone from Kansas City later that evening.

"I sure as hell am," said Brewster."

"Me too," said Boomer.

"Well then, I'll tell Beerbauer that we got a deal. We'll find that extra 85,000 he wants somewhere."

"And tomorrow I'll tell Hanagan to fire Star," added Brewster.

"You sure you don't want me to tell him?" asked Dudley.

"No, that's something I'll enjoy doing myself."

CHAPTER 26

Sunday, November 20

When Tom arrived home from picking the children up at Sunday school, there was a message from Chancellor Brewster on his answering machine.

"Call me as soon as you get in. 943-0017."

Tom had been dreading this call since he'd looked up in the stands Saturday afternoon at half-time and seen Brewster looking darts at him from the third row. Heads were definitely going to roll. What he didn't know was how many.

RING RING

"Brewster here!" came the annoyed sound of the Chancellor's voice over his car phone.

"Hel-lo, Bill, this is Tom returning your call."

"Hanagan," said Brewster in a cool and level voice beneath which blazed a bonfire of frustration and anger. "I want you to fire Star."

"Today?"

"Immediately, damn it!"

"And is there anything else?"

"No, that's it—*for now.*"

"I've seen enough," sighed the Coach, shutting off the tape player and turning on the lights in the War Room with his remote control. "Does anybody have anything they'd like to say?" *Silence.* "Awright then, we'll meet back here at 1:30. And by the way, Gene, make sure Turk runs us the offensive series from the second half of last year's State game."

"Okay, Coach."

"And, Jet, I need a full report on Badders and Bobinski. If we're gonna have a chance against State, we gotta find some way to stop them."

Once the War Room door was closed, Coach Star, like a balloon that someone has let the air out of, collapsed into his chair. Unable to reach either Mike Tubo or Hamilton Pigg for three days, he was emotionally played out. And as visions of acne-faced teenage football players and dingy high school locker rooms smelling of mildew and dirty socks loomed up before him, he cursed Hamilton Pigg and all the rest of the *fat, rich motherfuckers who don't give a damn about anything or anybody but winning football games. Win win win, that's all they care about*!

RING RING

"Coach Star here . . . Yes, yes," he said, straightening up in his chair. "Yes, Mr. Pigg, I was just thinkin' of you. I've been tryin' to reach—busy, huh?"

"That's right," said Hamilton Pigg, leaning back and throwing his feet on top of his desk in Cosmopolis. "And I'm not gonna bullshit you, Star. There's a lot of folks down here who are tellin' me to call it off. . . . Yeah, I know how the contract reads, but right about now I don't think I could convince the committee to give you the job even if I wanted to. Personally, I know you're a good coach. If you wadn't, you would'a never won any games with the players you got. But that's beside the point. Unless you can knock off State this weekend, I'm afraid we're just gonna hafta hold to the letter of intent and call the whole thing off. . . . Well that may be. But that trouble you had with those colored boys didn't make matters any. . . . I know it wadn't your fault. . . . Hol' on a minute, would'ja? . . . Yeah, come on in," said the financier, smiling at the curvaceous masseuse who had come to knead his muscles, "Una momento, honey. . . . But, like I was sayin', you beat State this Saturday and then we'll talk. "

As the Coach sat there tottering over the abyss from which there again arose a vision of pimply-faced teenagers and their booster parents, he buzzed the tape room.

"Listen, Turk. I almost forgot. I need a tape with all Muggins' third and longs on it."

Tom Hanagan's stomach was churning as he pulled his Mercedes into the Calhoun parking lot later that evening. Thankful that he had been spared, but dreading the task that lay ahead, he decided that regardless of their estrangement, he owed his old friend Tony the decency of breaking the news in person. Tom appeared in the doorway of Tony's office at 8:15.

"Hey Tony, can I come in?"

"Tom!" said the Coach, startled though not surprised at his friend's unexpected visit. "Yeah, come on in! I was just watchin' the Cottonpickers game. You know State didn't look very good yesterday, or the week before either."

"Really." Tom sat down in front of Tony's desk.

"So anyways"—Star turned off the video player and whirled around in his chair to face his friend—"what's up?"

"I got a call from Brewster this afternoon."

"Yeah."

"And he told me that we, ah, that there need to be some changes around here."

"Yeah ... And?"

"Well, I don't know how to say this, but he thinks that—"

"You need a new head football coach?"

"Yeah, Tony, that's right, but I want you to know—"

"Hey, save it."

"Really, Tony, I want'cha to know—"

"Listen, Buddy, you don't need to do the old song and dance with me. This is a business. And—"

"I know it is, Tony, but all the same—"

"I know exactly where you're at," said Star matter of factly.

"And you're not—"

"Angry? Hell no."

"Oh," said Tom, suddenly aware that the man sitting across the desk from him, whom he had looked up to all his life and considered

334 · KICK BUTT

his best friend, regarded him as little more than a meal ticket—and a used-up stub at that.

"This is a dog eat dog business we're in, Tom. You gotta do what you gotta do. And I gotta do what I gotta do."

"Sure, but—"

"No buts about it, that's the name of the game. And I guess when you get right down to it, it ain't much different than any other business. We're all expendable. I don't blame you for nothin', Tommy. You got a family to feed just like me. That's the bottom line. And anybody who tells you it ain't is either lyin' or too fucking stupid to know what's goin' on, right?"

"I guess so, Tony."

"It's survival, plain and simple. But anyways, Tommy, I don't got time to sit around and bullshit right now. I gotta get with Jet a minute before I go do my show."

"Yeah, okay, Tony."

"Hey, we gotta look at the positive side of this," joked Star, "at least I'll never have to talk to that asshole Carlisle again, right?"

CHAPTER 27

The Week of November 20

The "poop" that Red Carlisle had uncovered on Brad Ballings over the weekend was smeared on the front page of *The Tribune* Monday morning and tossed on everyone's doorstep.

MORGAN WEIGHT COACH ARRESTED
ON DRUG CHARGES

As Tom Hanagan stood in his living room foyer and read the *The Tribune's* headline story, he knew he was reading his own obituary.

"No, and nobody else is gonna care about the fine points of the law either, Dudley, you're right," agreed Brewster, who was on the phone long distance with the industrialist. "Yes, I did talk with Hanagan after I saw the headlines.... What could he say?... That's right, but the way I figure it, it'll just give us a chance to clean house. ... Star?... Yeah, Hanagan gave him the news last night.... Hanagan?... I'm writing the letter right now. Boomer talked with Clifton this morning and he agreed. In fact, Clifton told Boomer it would probably be the best thing that ever happened to him.... I know, Clifton just hasn't been right since that attack. All right, Dudley, take care. And now, Anita," said Brewster as he hung up the phone, "where were we?"

"From the beginning, sir?"

"Please."

Mr. Thomas P. Hanagan
Director of Athletics
Calhoun Hall
Morgan University

Dear Tom,
I have enjoyed working with you over the past six
years. It has been a pleasure and a privilege for me
to have associated with a man of your intellectual
capability, moral character—

"That part's fine, go down to the last paragraph."

Again, let me wish you the best in all—

"That's as far as we got."

"Hmm, let's see," said the Chancellor, "the best in all of your
future endeavors, period. And if there is anything I can do for you,
please don't hesitate to call. Signed, Sincerely—no, make that Your
friend, William R. Brewster, and let me have a look at it before it
goes out."

"Yes sir." Anita ran into her office to answer the phone. "Chancellor, it's General Ridley, do you want to take it?"

"Yes, yes." Brewster cleared his voice and reached for the phone.
"Yes, General Ridley, how are you on this beautiful Monday
mornin'? . . . Well good. . . . Yes, it's been nippy down here too, just
in time for Thanksgiving. And to what do I owe the pleasure of this
call?" Brewster had heard from a friend in Washington that the
research lab project was all but a done deal. "Oh really? Between us
and Rice, great! . . . And after further consideration they decided on
Rice? . . . Ohh . . . I know you do, General. . . . Yes, I'm sure. . . . Of
course, I understand . . . Yes. . . . I'll be in Washington in March for
the NAIUCA meetings. . . . I'll be sure to call you. . . . All right, sir,
good day. GODDAM IT!" roared Brewster, so loud that Anita
rushed back in the room.

"Are you all right, sir?"

"Yes—I mean no! DAMN IT! Do you know what that sono-fabitch just told me?"

"No," lied Anita, who had listened to the call.

"He said, oh never mind what he said. Get Thackston in here. I need to go over that DeeDee Grimes case with him before he leaves for Thanksgiving."

• • •

Tom had been unable to reach the Chancellor since they had spoken Monday morning. On Tuesday afternoon, he found out why.

"This letter just came for you," said Savannah when he walked into his office after lunch.

Tom stood in the reception room and read the Chancellor's letter, and went numb. *I can't believe it,* he said to himself, finally confronting what he knew had been inevitable for the last two weeks.

"Are you all right, Tom?" asked Savannah.

"Yes, I'm all right," he muttered and walked into his office. *Sacked. Fired. Canned.* As many times as he read through the letter desperately pretending that he had misconstrued its meaning, the fact remained that he had been cut from the Chancellor's team. Crushed at first, Tom, after a tumbler of Grey Goose, began to grasp at straws of pride. *The hell with numbnuts. If he hadn't fired me, I would'a quit anyway. This is probably the best thing that's ever happened to me. Now I can get myself a job someplace where they'll appreciate my talents.* But his righteous indignation soon cooled under the hard cold fact that jobs like his were hard to find, especially when you'd been dismissed in the midst of a drug scandal, from a program with a mediocre record. Tom meekly reached for the phone to call "his friend" the Chancellor.

"No, Tom, he's not in right now," said Anita, after buzzing the Chancellor to see if he wanted to take Tom's call. "Would you like to leave a message?"

Suddenly finding his spacious office unbearably confining, Tom walked into his waiting room to tell Savannah that he was feeling ill and was going home.

"Is there anything I can do?" she said, hanging up the phone on which she had been talking with Bill Conner about what she was going to wear to Dudley Dunnings' house on Thursday for Thanksgiving dinner.

"No, I'm all right," he said, walking past her desk in a daze.

Tom made his way home slowly, taking several lengthy detours to give himself time to sort out his thoughts and summon up courage. He knew the worst was yet to come. Reconciling oneself to being fired is painful, but having to tell your loved ones and friends about it is excruciating. Everyone will, of course, give you their sympathy and encouragement. But for Tom, returning home to his subdivision unemployed was tantamount to a Confederate officer returning to the plantation with a minie ball in his behind.

But before his housekeeper Aretha he felt no shame.

"Oh, you surprised me, Mista' Tom. Ain't you feelin' good?"

"No, Aretha, I'm not. I lost my job today."

"Ohh honey," said the maid mournfully, taking his raincoat and shaking her head, "dat's terrible. But you knows dey's a lot of otha' jobs in this world, specially fo' a smart and goodlookin' young man like yourself."

"Thanks, Aretha." He smiled.

"It's the truf."

"I know." He patted her on the shoulder and hugged her. "Are the girls home yet?"

"No, not yet."

"Good, I think I'm gonna go upstairs and lie down for a while. Did Mrs. Hanagan call in yet this afternoon?"

"Not yet, Mista' Tom. Should I tell her you at home?"

"No, I'll just wait till she gets in. In fact, Aretha, why don't you take the afternoon off. I'll drive you to the bus stop in an hour or so."

"Oh no, Mista' Tom, I wouldn't think of it."

"Go ahead, Aretha." He smiled magnanimously. "You can get

your Thanksgiving shopping done early this year for a change. I insist. Come get me in forty-five minutes, I'll be in the guest room."

"Well, Mista' Tom, if dat's what you wants."

Jan also left work early that afternoon. Though everyone at the store was in a frenzy preparing for Friday's onslaught, she had made up her mind to have it out with Tom. It was time to clear the air and make a full confession. She knew that he needed her. Even Uncle Clifton, who never meddled, had told her as much on Sunday. It was time to bridge the troubled waters between them, time to stand by the man to whom she had pledged herself. But before she could do that, she had to tell him the truth.

"Tom! Tom! Are you here?" she called as she walked in through the front door shortly after 5:30.

But her husband could not hear her. He was slumped over the kitchen table. An empty Johnny Walker bottle stood amid dirty dishes and the coagulated remains of his daughters' pork and beans.

"He's in there, Mommy!"

Shaking her head in disgust, and then pity as she pulled off her pigskin driving gloves, Jan could wait no longer.

"Tom," she said as her befuddled husband looked up at her through bloodshot eyes. "We need to talk!"

"Whaa...."

"I said we need to talk," she repeated, removing her coat and abruptly sitting down at the table across from him.

"Hallo, Jan." He blinked and smiled drunkenly at his stone-faced wife.

"Tom...."

"Yesss, dear."

"There's something I need to tell you." She drew in a deep breath and looked at the ceiling.

"Something you need to wha...." he said, blinking at her again.

"Something I need to confess, damn it!" she said, flashing an annoyed look. Jan had wanted this moment to erupt with passion, but his drunkenness was spoiling the whole effect.

"Tom," she said, sniffing significantly once or twice and biting her lip, "I have been . . . unfaithful to you."

She sat there trembling, awaiting the rage, the fury, even the violence that she had anticipated. Her husband said nothing. "Tom, did you hear me? I have been having an affair with Stefan."

"Oh really. Well, I lost my job today."

"What?!!!"

"I said I lost my job, Jan. I got fired, axed, shit-canned."

"Oh my God!" She burst into tears. "I can't believe it!"

• • •

With afternoon classes canceled Wednesday afternoon for the Thanksgiving holiday, the football team was on the practice fields at 1:00.

"Awright, Reggie! Good move! Good move!" shouted Coach Star from the sideline, clapping his hands together in encouragement.

As a cold rain fell on the shivering players and staff, he ran the offense through the fundamentals of the T-bone.

"Awright guys. Now let's run it down again! Well Jet, whad'da you think?" Star wiped the freezing rain off his face.

"I don't know what the hell Muggins is on, but I'd sure like to get me some."

"Yeah, me too," said Star, who alone of the coaches knew it was desire and pride, the two most powerful stimulants known to man, that were driving Reggie.

"I just hope he don't bang himself up too much before Saturday."

But as Reggie pulled himself off the muddy turf and limped back to the huddle, he felt no pain. Indeed it was only when he was crashing headlong into the opposing line that he was free from the sickening sense of shame that had dogged him like a blitzing linebacker since he had cut and run at Bow Wow's.

"That sonofabitch is gonna kill himself," said Pete Cossacky with admiration.

For ten agonizing days after the shoot-out Reggie Muggins had suffered the torments of the damned. The product of an asphalt jungle—in which there was no worse sin than running from a fight—he had committed the ultimate transgression. And as he lay there jonesing for coke in his apartment, and then in his darkened dormitory room the following week, he was unable to forgive himself. Over and over he saw himself fleeing Bow Wow's in a panic ... again and again he heard gunshots and Tootie's cries.... So low, in fact, had Reggie fallen in his own estimation that the day before he returned to practice he had dropped to his knees, with Teeny McAdoo by his side, and begged forgiveness from the God he had prayed to as a boy at the Gospel Truth Baptist Church in Memphis.

"JESUS CHRIST, KUZNOWSKI!" roared Ed Tarmeenian as Reggie bowled over the third string nose guard for another first down. "What the fuck are you doin', playin' with yourself? Bring that man down!"

But Muggins was not to be stopped, at least not by Walt Kuznowski. And on the next play the born-again quarterback once more lowered his head and churned forward for six more yards of self-esteem.

"ATTABOY, REGGIE!" yelled Star, too desperate to think about the absurdity of pinning his hopes for Saturday—and his future at Cosmopolis—on a suicidal adolescent whom he had seen, a week and a half earlier, curled up on his bedroom floor crying like a baby. "AWRIGHT, REGGIE! THAT'S MY MAN!"

• • •

It was the custom in the Dudley Dunning family, since Manley had started to spend his Thanksgivings in Pebble Beach, to have dinner at home while they watched the traditional NFL Thanksgiving day games.

"I told you the Packers were gonna whip 'em, Pop," said Hartley, the industrialist's son, who was presently in his second year of law school at Duke. "You owe me five bucks."

"That I do, Hartley," said Dudley, annoyed, ushering his guests into the dining room.

"Now then, Bill, why don't you sit over there?"

"Thank you, Mr. Dunning," said Bill Conner, seating himself between Dudley's daughter, Josephine, a pudgy thirty somethingish set designer from New York, and Dudley's mother-in-law, Nelly, a frail, blue-haired septuagenarian, whom Dudley and his wife brought to the house on holidays from the Methodist retirement home.

"Clarissa, you're over there. And Ridley, you sit next to her." Dudley motioned to his older brother, a prematurely aged sixty-four year old, who had never been quite right after spending six months in a North Korean prison camp. And last but not least, Savannah," said the industrialist, his hand lingering on the small of her shapely back, "you're right here next to me."

"Oh thank you, Mr. Dunning," she gushed as he helped her wriggle into her seat.

"Good. I think we're ready now." Dudley nodded to the butler to begin serving dinner.

"Yes," said Dudley, buttering a piece of cornbread twenty minutes later, "I feel certain that you'll be able to handle the job, Bill."

"I hope so, Mr. Dunning," said Bill Conner modestly.

"I'm sure you will. I have every confidence in you."

"I appreciate that, sir."

"And, besides, if for some reason that I can't imagine,"—Dudley winked at Dawn, "you don't like bein' Director of Athletics here at Morgan, well then, you can just resign at the end of your interim appointment, and we'll all go away feelin' like winners. Now here you go, have another piece of this ham."

"Thank you, Mr. Dunning, it's delicious."

"I have 'em flown in special from Jonesboro every year. When it comes to hogs, there's no place like Arkansas."

"Umm."

"Yeah, Bill, I like the idea of bein' able to use somebody like you from the inside. It'll help us make the transition as smooth as possible. Last thing we need to do is waste time and energy showin' somebody new the ropes, 'specially with basketball season gearing up."

"I agree, Mr. Dunning."

"It's a great opportunity for you, son. And believe me you'll have all the help you need getting the ball rolling, from myself and Mr. Cox and"—Dudley hesitated—"from all of us at the school who want to see you succeed. 'Course it's gonna be a little unpleasant at first having to let so many people go. But I think you can handle it. You kinda remind me of myself when I was working my way up. What's that, Ridley? . . . Of course he will. . . . Leon! Get Ridley another beer, would'ja? Now, what was I sayin'? Oh yes, when I was workin' my way up. . . ."

Dudley Dunning, like thousands of dejected and disgruntled Morgan fans, had hoped to be giving thanks for considerably more than the bounty of the earth on Thursday, but he was not about to let disappointment ruin his holiday. Deprived of his elusive Bowl, Dudley was not blind to life's compensations. He had, after all, just closed a multi-billion-dollar deal to move his auto parts manufacturing operation to Mexico, received a letter of intent from the head coach he wanted and, last but not least, secured a verbal commitment from a very promising, young administrative assistant he'd had his eye on.

"And now I have an announcement to make." Dudley tapped his silver fork against his wine-glass after the pecan and chess pie had been served. "Well, actually two announcements." He grabbed Savannah's hand and gave it a squeeze as everyone turned to the head of the table. "As you all know by now, as of January 1, Bill Conner will be the Acting Director of Athletics at Morgan University."

CLAP CLAP.

"That's the first announcement. And the second is that Savannah McLane will be coming to work for me as my assistant starting January 1."

OOO! AHH! CONGRATULATIONS! (Only Mrs. Dunning seemed to be unimpressed by Savannah's good fortune.)

"And now," said Dudley, rising to his feet, Savannah's hand still tightly clasped in his talons, "a toast to the future happiness of all!"

• • •

"Whew, I'm exhausted!" said Bill Conner, loosening his tie and plopping himself on the couch in the living room of Savannah's apartment four hours later. "I thought Dudley was never gonna let us go, especially after he started showing us his tennis trophies."

"He's a very good tennis player," said Savannah, sitting down on the other end of the couch.

"A regular *Borin' Borg*," laughed the ex-football player.

"Personally I think Dudley is a very charmin' gentleman."

"Yeah, so is George Steinbrenner."

"Who?"

"George—Oh never mind."

"Really, Bill, I can't believe, after all he's done for you, for both of us."

"He needs me, baby. That's the only reason I've got the job. Well, that and the fact that I'm good."

"Billy...."

"C'mere, honey.... c'mere."

"Honestly though, Bill"—Savannah scooted over and laid her blond head on Bill's shoulder—"don't you think Dudley is distinguished?"

"What?" said Bill, who was day-dreaming about his new position.

"I said, don't you think Mr. Dunning is nice?"

"Dudley nice? I'll give you the answer to that question after he hires me for the directorship full-time." Bill reached for the remote control. "Is there anything you want to watch, baby?"

"No, I don't care, Bill," she said, dreamily snuggling up to him, thinking about what kind of tennis dress she should buy for the lesson that Dudley had promised to give her on Sunday.

CHAPTER 28

Saturday, November 26

An hour before game time the Stadium Club was abuzz with rumors of Tom Hanagan's and Tony Star's "resignations."

"And I hear they're dumpin' Hanagan too," said Harlan Gooch reaching for a biscuit with his gnarled fingers.

"It's about time," said Felton Potts, who six weeks earlier had been "honored" to have Tom autograph his copy of *Sports Illustrated.*

"Scandals like this are a disgrace to an academic institution of our caliber," grumbled high school-dropout Wendell Sinks.

"You're right, Wendell," agreed Dr. Lucius Thompson, helping himself to a fried catfish filet. "Things like this give intercollegiate sports a bad name."

"Naw," sneered Buster Hooper, "Hanagan wouldn't have the balls to show up here today."

But to everyone's surprise, Tom did show up shortly before 12:00, sporting a Morgan blazer and the ghost of a smile on his haggard face.

"So, is there any truth to what we've been hearin', Tom?" asked Roy Nash.

"Truth?" said Tom, looking out at Roy from the sockets of his sunken eyes. "I'm not sure what you mean."

In the press box, meanwhile, Red Carlisle was being his usual affable self.

"Anybody wanna make any bets on this game?" he jeered,

squeezing Butch Sanders and Rudy Marrow on the shoulders as they readied themselves to go on the air.

"I don't think so, Red," said Rudy.

"You're sure now?" asked the reporter.

"Yeah, I'm sure."

"Well all I can say is, I tol' you so! Har har har."

"Five seconds to go guys ... 4, 3 2, 1, you're on!"

Hello folks! This is Butch Sanders—

And Rudy Marrow—

Comin' to you today from the press box high atop Fulsom Field where in just a few minutes the Morgan University Fighting Knights will be doing battle with 'cross state rivals, the University of T. Coonhounds. Boy, we've got a whale of a crowd on hand for this one today.

We sure do, Butch. Not even the frigid weather has kept the fans away from Fulsom this afternoon.

You're right, Rudy, but that's how it always is for one of the oldest and greatest rivalries in college football.

Ten minutes to go until kick-off, the Morgan players were waiting for Coach Star. At 12:55, he burst through the locker room door.

"AWRIGHT!" he yelled, climbing up on a bench. "LISTEN UP! As you've prob'ly heard, there's a rumor goin' around I've been fired. Well ... this time the rumor's true. ... That's right, gentlemen, I've been sacked. This is gonna be my last game here at Morgan— and the last game for a lot of you too." He looked around at the seniors—or more correctly speaking, those players whose eligibility would be up at the end of the term. Now I'm not gonna tell you I'm happy about what's happened, 'cause I'm not. It's not gonna be easy to leave here. I believe in this program and I believe in you. In a lot of ways I feel closer to you guys than any bunch of players I've ever worked with. It's gonna hurt to go. But then again I keep tellin' myself that maybe it's for the best. *Grumbles of protest.* No, wait a minute," he said raising his hands, "hear me out. The reason I say that is, when you got a bunch of players on a team with as much talent, and heart, and guts as you guys, the only person you can blame when things go wrong is the Coach.... It's true. Maybe I ain't the guy who's meant to lead this football program to the greatness you've proved you're capable of. (*No way, Coach! We want Coach Star! We want Coach Star!*) But I tell you one thing ... HOLD ON just a minute.... And I mean this from the bottom of my heart. Even if I'm not the man for the job, they'll never find anybody else who loves you guys more than me. And that's the truth, gentlemen.... And now that I've said that, LET'S GO KICK SOME ASS!

"AWRIGHT, YOU GUYS! LET'S WIN THIS ONE FOR COACH STAR! KICK BUTT! KICK BUTT!"

Chancellor Brewster's heart was heavy as he waited for the toss of the coin. He had just spent a half hour in the gallery being barraged by the Morgan faithful with questions he couldn't answer and looks that said "*Don't even think about asking for money.*"

"I know how Nixon must have felt," he said, trying to be funny as the bartender mixed him a double at the skybox bar.

"Ahh, don't pay any attention to 'em," said Boomer, hunting for the Tigers-Wave game on the Cable. "This is gonna be one helluva ball game today."

"What's that, Boomer?" said Brewster, gazing abstractedly out the sky box window.

"I said this Tigers-Wave game's gonna be a doozy."

"I suppose so."

"You suppose?! Are you feelin' all right, Billy Bob?"

"Oh Boomer, leave Bill alone." Winnie stroked her husband's arm. "He's been feelin' grumpy ever since Sweetie Pie told him she wasn't comin' home for Thanksgiving. Isn't that right, honey?"

"That's not it at all," huffed the Chancellor—who was in fact disappointed with his daughter—though not nearly as much as he was with his football team.

As the Chancellor watched the referee signal that the Knights would receive on the south end of the field—a sight that would normally have quickened his pulse—he felt very tired and very very old. Here he was at the end of another season, New Year's coming up, and still his heart's desire eluded him. Not even the distant sight of a new purple and gold Medi-Vac helicopter landing on the roof of the University Hospital was any consolation. All he could think about as the teams lined up was what *Sports Illustrated* had said two months ago about this being Morgan's year.

"They're just about ready to start, Billy Bob!" Boomer dipped a shrimp in cocktail sauce and watched the Tigers and the Wave take to the field in Apaloochee.

On Fulsom Field the Coonhounds had just kicked off.
CUBBINS ON THE RETURN FOR THE KNIGHTS
A GAIN OF 23
And despite the finger-numbing cold, the Morgan offense seemed fired up.
A GAIN OF SIX ON THE PLAY
SECOND AND FOUR
Especially Reggie Muggins, who, as he had done all week in practice, threw himself into the teeth of the defense.
MUGGINS ON THE CARRY
A GAIN OF TWO
Over and over again, with no apparent thought for his own physical well-being, he ran right at State's front four.
MUGGINS WITH THE BALL
A PICK-UP OF THREE.... FIRST DOWN!
"Atta boy!" Star pumped his fists as Muggins once more butted his way forward for another four yards. "Whadda you think, Jet?"
"I hope Doc's got plenty of pain killers."

"Well, Obie?" said Coonhound head coach Hoss Humphreys to his defensive coordinator after the Knights crossed the 50 four minutes later.

"Terrence is gettin' off kinda slow, but he'll warm up." Obie Gamble fingered a baggie full of amphetamines he had in his pocket. "Don't worry about that. And if Star keeps runnin' Muggins at us, he won't be able to walk by half-time."

"I hope you're right, Obie."

"Look out! Look out, Reggie! . . . UMPH!"

"Man, I could hear that one all the way up here," said Pete Cossacky in the spotter's booth.

"Yeah, that was a mean lick," said Star into his headphones, giving the sign for P.U. Pointer to go on the field and punt. "But I think you're right, Pete, we can run on Black today. C'mere, Reggie. You okay?"

"Yeah I'm okay," said the quarterback, disgustedly shaking his head, his breath visible on the freezing air.

"We'll get it back."

Tom Hanagan was having trouble staying focused as he sat at the end of the Morgan bench. Traumatized by the events at work and at home, for the first time in his life he felt like one of the ninety-nine percent of humankind he had always regarded as "losers."

"Pshew, it's freezin' out here," said Doc Willis, blowing on his fingers. "Aren't you cold?"

"Did you say something, Doc?" said Tom, who was thinking about his wife and Stefan Bazitski.

"I said you oughta button up your coat, it's freezin' out here."

"Oh sure," said Tom, his addled mind wandering again to Jan and Bazitski . . . then to the Chancellor's letter of termination . . . and to the 60,000 fans in the stadium he was sure were talking about him behind his back.

PASS COMPLETE! FIRST DOWN STATE!

"That's exactly what I mean!" said Dudley Dunning after State quarterback Spenser Thurmond hit his wide receiver with a 30-yard pass. "But I promise we're gonna get this football program in shape." Dunning was standing in front of his sky box window lecturing Milt Lee, Lamar Tubbs, Bill Conners and Savannah McLane about the future of Morgan athletics. "Building a great athletics program is no diff'rent than puttin' together a successful business operation. It takes guts, determination, and a whole lotta hard work. But take it from someone who's had to fight for everything he's ever got in this world, if you want it bad enough, there's nothin' you can't do."

I tell ya, Rudy, I'm beginning to get that feeling that this one's gonna go down to the wire this afternoon.

No doubt about it, Butch. Here we are, three minutes left to go in the first quarter and neither team has come near their opponent's goal line. And what a beating Reggie Muggins has taken so far this quarter.

"You sure that hand is okay, Reggie?"

"I'll be all right, Coach," said Muggins, holding an ice pack on his left hand, the pinky finger of which had been broken on the last play.

"It's good that's not your throwin' hand." Star looked worriedly downfield where Coonhound halfback Ozzie Baldwin had just broken loose for 14 yards.

"Yeah."

"You're doin' good, Reg. Just keep the pressure on. We're gonna win this one. . . . We got to," he said under his breath, repeating the words that Rose had uttered when he left for campus earlier that morning.

HOOOOORAY STATE! GO! GO! GO!

"I don't know if I can take this," groaned Brewster, walking away from the window after Coonhound quarterback Spenser Thurmond hit his wide receiver with another first down strike at the Morgan 41.

"We got it! We got it!" yelled Boomer at the TV over the bar. "Yahoo! The Tigers just scored one!"

"I don't think we're ever gonna get ourselves a team like that here," said Brewster, wistfully watching the Tiger fans going crazy on the TV.

"It'll happen, Bill. It'll happen."

"In our lifetime?"

"This Beerbauer boy we're hiring is as good as they come. And like he told Dudley, if he doesn't have us a Bowl contender in four years—"

"Four years?!"

"Well, nothin' happens overnight," said Boomer as the stadium shook beneath their feet, after All-American Rayon Taylor broke loose for fourteen yards up the middle.

GO STATE! GO HOUNDS! ARF ARF ARF!

"'Course I know how you feel, Bill. Four years is a long time, considerin' everything."

"A very long time," sighed the Chancellor. "Who knows where any of us will be in four years."

"You aren't thinkin' of retirin', are you, Bill?"

"Retiring?" said Brewster, suspiciously recalling how Dudley had asked him the same question earlier in the week. "What gives you that idea?"

"Oh nothin' … I was just wonderin'.… Kinda been thinkin' about it myself lately," said the contractor. "Sure would be nice to kick back, not hafta worry about anything anymore, play golf all the time, fish whenever you want to, maybe even go on a safari."

"Well that might sound nice for you, but I've still got some things I want to accomplish here at Morgan."

"Of course you do, Bill. I just thought maybe you were planning on sneakin' off on your ole buddy."

"Not soon," said the Chancellor, as he and Boomer watched Coonhound place kicker Clem DeWitt break the ice with a thirty-five yard field goal. State 3 Morgan 0.

HOORAY HOUNDS!

Four minutes later, the ball was again back in the hands of the Hounds. And seven minutes after that—with Rayon Taylor in again at halfback—the Coonhounds were threatening at the Morgan 23.

DEFENSE! DEFENSE! DEFENSE!

"No, Cliff wasn't int'rested in comin' today," sniffed Inez, clapping her frozen hands together.

"To the State game?!" said Peaches Perdue in disbelief as she shook her pompom at the Coonhound offense.

"That's right. And I gotta tell ya, honey, I really am worried he may have suffered some kinda brain damage. I mean sometimes I hardly know him anymore. C'mon! Defense! Defense!"

"Really?"

"Like the other night for instance, I was talkin' to him about this new coach we've got comin' in. And he just sat there pretending like he didn't hear a word I said. And when I started askin' him what he thought about the basketball team, I'll be darned if he didn't just get up and walk out of the room. OH NO! First and goal! And if that's not enough, just this mornin' Jan called me— OH LAWD! TOUCHDOWN! I can't believe it!"

COOOOOOOON HOUNDS! ARF! ARF! ARF!

"How is Jan doin'?" asked Peaches after the Hounds extra point kicker made it 10–0 and the crowd quieted enough for her to be heard.

"She said Tom's taking things pretty hard."

"He doesn't look very good, does he?" Peaches peered down at the bench where Tom sat catatonically gazing at the scoreboard.

"No he doesn't. Jan's afraid he might be having, what did she call it, some kinda identity crisis."

A nervous breakdown was more like it. And Tom wasn't the only one on the Morgan bench who looked as if he could have used some professional help. Since the start of the second quarter, Reggie Muggins had been showing signs of what Psychology Professor Lou Sazlow and his colleagues call acute anxiety reaction. Fidgeting, mumbling to himself, rippling from head to toe with uncontrollable surges of nervous energy, each time the crowd let out a roar the quarterback spun around thinking he heard gun shots and someone calling his name. *HOOORAY!*

Then suddenly the stadium was on its feet as Ricky Ritter ran a quick-out all the way down to the Coonhound 36.

"AWRIGHT!! C'mon now, you can do it," hollered Coach Star.

"Yeah, we can do it," said Reggie Mugins to himself, stepping up to the line.

That was a nice move by Ritter, Rudy!

You got that right, Butch. And now we'll see if the Knights can put some points on the board.

Second and 8 from the Coonhound 31, under a minute left to go in the first half. Muggins takes the snap . . . heads for the near side . . . looking for dayligh. . . . wrestled to the ground by Simmons just short of a first down. And Coach Star takes his last time out.

DON'T LET AN INJURY KEEP YOU ON THE SIDELINES
COME TO THE PROFESSIONALS AT THE
MORGAN SPORTS MEDICINE CENTER
OPEN WEEKDAYS 7 TO 9
AND WEEKENDS TILL 6

Back to the action at Fulsom. third and 1 at the Coonhound 32. Muggins with the ball . . . breaks to the far side . . . in trouble . . . dropped behind the line by Terrence Black for a loss of two!

BOOOOOO HISSSSSSS!

"Tarnation!" exclaimed Jacky Joe Wallace, rocking forward in his easy chair as Fernando DeGama trotted in to attempt a field goal with 22 seconds left to go in the first half. "If they'd 'a had you in there, Jimmy Joe, we wouldn't be goin' for no field goal. Idn't that right, Momma?"

"Absolutely." Tammie looked at the TV screen as DeGama's kick sailed up . . . up . . . and through the uprights, 10 to 3! "At least we got somethin'. Y'all want some snacks now?"

"Sure, honey," said Jacky Joe as his wife headed for the kitchen of their suburban ranch house to get her menfolk some half-time treats. "No, we wouldn't be trailin' by no seven points now if you were playin'."

"I guess so, Paw," said Jimmy, who, at his neurologist's suggestion, had stayed in Shreveport over Thanksgiving rather than returning to Metro for the game.

"Hell, boy! You were the hottest quarterback in America at the beginnin' of last month."

"I guess," said Jimmy Joe, staring blankly at the coffee table on top of which lay an October 12th edition of *Sports Illustrated*.

"But don't worry." Jacky Joe patted his sedated son on the shoulder. "You'll be back out there, good as new, 'fore you know it. Those doctors don't know what they're talkin' about. If you want it bad enough, there's nothin' you can't do. Idn't that right, Momma."

"Amen," said Tammie, walking back into the den with a bowl of Nachos and bean dip, two bottles of Budweiser and a protein supplement shake for Jimmy Joe.

"This is not going to be fun." Chancellor Brewster drained his highball glass in preparation for his descent into the gallery at half-time.

"Oh it won't be that bad," said Winnie, opening up the door of the sky box. "What are they gonna do, fire you?"

Before the Chancellor had time to answer, Dudley Dunning appeared in the hallway with his party of guests.

"Hullo, Dudley."

"'Lo, Bill." Dunning barely acknowledged Brewster's presence as he breezed past, intently discussing something with Milt Lee.

"There you are, Lamar, you ole horse thief!" hooted Boomer Cox when he saw the attorney with Savannah and Bill Conner. "Helluva game today!"

"What's the score?" whispered Lamar. "Dudley's been talkin' so much I haven't had a chance to follow it."

"Tigers 21, Blue Wave 14 at halftime."

"Well awright!"

"And how's our new Athletics Director doin'?" Boomer slapped Bill Conner on his broad back. "Glad to have you aboard, son."

Buoyed up by DeGama's last second field goal, the Morgan players were confidently apprehensive as Doc Willis and the coaches went around the locker room dispensing medication and encouragement.

"You feel okay, Reggie?" asked Star.

"Yeah, I'm okay." Muggins sat on a bench having his left pinky worked on while Pat Pitouchi taped his ribs.

"You sure that's not too tight?" asked Pat.

"No, it's okay," he winced.

"You're doin' good. I mean it. We got these bastards runnin' scared. I doubt if Black will be back. And Bonds was limping when he left the field."

"How's Mongol?" asked Muggins.

"He's okay. We got the swelling down on his knee. He'll be fine. And like I was sayin', just keep up the pressure and remember the next time we cross their 35, go to the no huddle and hit 'em with the bomb before they can line back up."

"I got it."

"Good man." Star rubbed Muggins on the head. *"AWRIGHT YOU GUYS! LISTEN UP!"*

As the Morgan band marched off the field to an up-tempo version of the theme from *Man From LaMancha*, the fans nestled down with the $150,000 worth of rain gear, mittens, scarves, and hats they had purchased during intermission. Then the teams reappeared on the sidelines for the start of the second half.

HOWLLLL! ARF ARF! GO HOUNDS!

KICK BUTT! KICK BUTT! GO KNIGHTS!

And the Knights and Coonhounds went at it again.

TAYLOR ON THE CARRY

A GAIN OF 8. SECOND AND TWO

Temporarily numb to the pain in his left shoulder and swollen right knee, Coonhound Rayon Taylor looked like his old self as State began to drive the ball upfield.

TAYLOR OUT OF BOUNDS AT THE 33

FIRST DOWN!

And like all great running backs, the more he got the ball,

TAYLOR FOR A GAIN OF SEVEN

the stronger he got.

TAYLOR ON THE CARRY AGAIN. A GAIN OF 12

"We're gonna bust this wide open in a minute, Hoss," said offensive coordinator Obie Moss, spitting a gob of tobacco on the ground.

"Could be, Obie." The Coonhound coach shook himself and stamped his cold feet. "How 'bout tryin' a reverse?"

"Yeah, good idea." Moss signaled in a reverse with a yank of his belt-buckle and tug of his ear lobe.

"I smell a bomb," said Rod Carver to Ed Tarmeenian over the phones. "They did the same thing against the Pickers three weeks ago."

"Awright, Rod," said Ed, scratching the end of his nose and grabbing his crotch, giving the sign for a safety blitz.

Hut one, hut two.

As the Morgan defense blitzed through the line, Thurman dropped back as if to pass and handed off to Taylor, who handed off to Adams going the other way at the 40, the 35, 30, he's gonna go all the way! TOUCHDOWN! State 17, Morgan 3.

"I tol' you so!" crowed Red Carlisle, getting up to go relieve himself just as Tom Hanagan stepped through the press box door.

"Well if it ain't the Di-rector himself," laughed Red. "What's goin' on, BIG MAN?"

"Not much," replied Tom, who had spent half-time in his office finishing up a bottle of Grey Goose while he wondered what he was going to do for the rest of his life.

"You're sure you don't wanna put some money on the game?" taunted Red, winking at the crowd.

"You know that's against regulations, Red."

"Oh sorry—I musta forgot," mocked the pock-marked reporter, pushing his way out the door.

Down on the field, Morgan kick-off return man Asswad King had just run the ball back to his own 37. Then Tutomo Tongo—trying to impress a sports agent who had come from Dallas to see him—shed a tackler at the 40, two more at the 45, and ran it down to the Coonhound 34 before he was pushed out of bounds.

HOOORAY MORGAN! GO! GO! GO!

As the officials trotted downfield with the first-down markers, Coach Star ran behind them whirling his fist in the air, shouting encouragement to his troops. This was the first break they'd had all afternoon. If his boys could capitalize on this one—then suddenly Muggins brought the team to the line without a huddle. *"Oh no, he's gonna throw it like I told him at half-time. TIME OUT! TIME OUT!"* he yelled, but it was too late. Muggins took the snap, dropped back in the pocket, and let one go over the middle for Holmes. . . . COMPLETE! at the 2. . . . TOUCHDOWN MORGAN!!

HOOOOOOORAAAYYYYYY!

Man oh man, that was a sweet combination by Muggins and Holmes.

Unbelievable, Rudy! And it's like they just turned on the heat here at Fulsom.

The thaw, however, did not last long. A frigid and scoreless thirty minutes later, the crowd was again in hibernation.

I tell ya, Rudy, after those fireworks at the beginning of the half, it's been defense all the way.

Yes it has, Butch. And here come the Coonhounds back on the field, a little under seven minutes left to go, State 17, Morgan 10. Hound's ball on their own 37, second and three.

"Awright now . . . You got it. . . . You got it. YAHOO!" Boomer rose unsteadily from his barstool in front of the skybox television.

"Tigers score again?" asked the Chancellor.

"You betcha. That makes it 34 to 21. Whaddagame!" he said, tottering over and hugging his friend. "I tell ya what, Billy."

"What?" said Brewster, unable to hide his annoyance with his drunken friend.

"No matter what happens, I want'cha to know I'll always be your pal."

What the hell is he talking about? thought Brewster, irritably straightening his sport coat, beginning to wonder if Boomer and Dudley were hiding something from him.

"Here Buddy, shake," said Boomer, thrusting out a hairy paw. "C'mon! Shake my hand, Billy."

"You're loaded, Boomer."

"Yeah, I guess I am, Bill, but no matter what, I'm still your bes' frien' and don'tchoo forget it."

Back on the field, meanwhile, Coach Humphreys had just signaled in a power sweep to quarterback Spenser Thurmond who, as ordered, handed off to Adams, who pitched out to Baldwin, who slipped through two frostbitten Morgan tacklers at the 50, and churned down to the Morgan 21.

HOORAY HOUNDS! ARF ARF ARF! HOWLLLL!

But the Knights' defense—after getting roasted with a ten-yard long string of profanity by Ed Tarmeenian—froze the Coonhounds in their tracks.

Fourth and 5 at the Morgan 16, the Purple Knights Band began to beat out the opening bars of *Thus Spake Zarathustra.*

Then Thurmond set them down, took the snap, and rifled it—into the arms of ATILLA WILSON!

INTERCEPTION! WILSON AT THE 22
FIRST DOWN!

The Morgan fans let out a roar and Reggie Muggins once again thought he heard someone call his name. He spun around and saw that he was right. Across the track stood Teeny McAdoo, calling to him in a voice inaudible above the din of the crowd. He read her lips. *I love you, Reggie! I love you!*

Reggie charged back onto the field, more determined to win than he had ever been before in his life. He got the ball and fought his way forward for five. And on the next play he went around end for four more.

"You know, Mel, I like this little sonofabitch Muggins," said sports agent/attorney Lou Gross who had come from Atlanta to watch his clients Rayon Taylor and R. T. Simmons.

"Yeah, the kid's got balls," said the attorney's junior partner, Melvin Shabazz, watching Muggins get pounded to the turf at the 39.

"You got any stats on him?"

"Back at the hotel."

"Make a note on him. Monty said that Turner is looking for a headbanger with good hands in Detroit."

Back to the action here at Fulsom Field, third and 4, Muggins with the ball, breaks left, sees Holmes open at the Coonhound 42. . . . HOLY TOLEDO! What a catch by Holmes.

And what a shot Muggins took as he got rid of that ball!

"You sure that arm's all right, Reg?"

"I think so, Coach." Muggins grimaced as he bent over on the sideline kneading his elbow.

"It'll be okay," said Star, sending Reggie back into the fray, "be cool. You can do it."

Back at the line, Muggins again took the snap and started over tackle— when he got yanked by his face-mask under a stampede of stomping cleats. *TWEEEEEEET!* Fifteen seconds later, he came back to his senses on the Coonhound 42 yard line.

"You okay, Reg?" asked center Ron Cluck, bending over him as Pat Pitouchi and Doc Willis arrived on the scene.

"I think so," he said, making sure that all his body parts were still working.

"You sure?" Doc Willis knelt by his side.

"Yeah, I'm awright." Muggins pulled himself into a sitting position to the nervous applause of the hometown fans.

"Positive?"

"Yeah I can make it," he said, rising slowly to his knees and looking across the field to where linebacker K. T. Simmons stood with his hands on his hips and a "fuck you" grin on his face.

As the teams huddled on the sidelines preparing to resume play, Red Carlisle stood up, took a drink of the Wild Turkey in his Coke can, and declared in a voice loud enough for everyone in the press box to hear that he had a hundred dollars that said State was gonna win.

"Ain't nobody gonna take me up on my bet?" he shouted in Tom Hanagan's direction.

Unable to tolerate Red's needling any longer, Tom rose unsteadily from his seat and said he'd take him up on his bet.

"I mean, whaddaya got to lose, right? Har har har."

"Come to think of it"—Tom pushed his way from behind his chair—"nothing."

"You're right about that." Carlisle pulled a hundred out of his wallet and thumped it down on the table in front of him. "There's mine."

"And here"—Tom reached back as if to grab his wallet and smashed his fist into Carlisle's face—"is mine."

As Red dropped to his knees, blood spurting from his broken nose, the press box fell silent.... Then someone yelled, "AWRIGHT HANAGAN!" and everyone exploded in a round of applause.

On the field, meanwhile, Muggins, set them down, took the snap, and started for the same hole he'd tried to run through before. But this time when Simmons tries to grab him Reggie buries his head in the lineman's belly and bulls forward to the Coonhound 35.

HOOOOORAYYYYY!!!!

No huddle, Reggie again gets the ball and slashes his way over tackle for seven more. FIRST DOWN, MORGAN!

KICK BUTT! KICK BUTT! KICK BUTT!

As Coach Star gathers with his team on the sideline and tries to make himself heard over the crowd, the stormy sky begins to dust the field with a flurry of white confetti.

Then the Knights come to the line—and Harris gets dropped at the 28 for a loss of two.

DEFENSE! DEFENSE! DEFENSE!

Coach Star calls his last time-out and the crowd lets out a sigh of relief—which they suck back in as the play clock begins to tick. Muggins with the ball ... drops back ... looks long ... looks short ... sees a seam, and jukes his way to the 17.

MUGGINS ON THE CARRY, A GAIN OF 8
THIRD AND 2

Twenty-nine seconds and ticking. Reggie takes the snap, breaks to the near side, finds a hole at the 10, 9, 8 ... Driven out of bounds on the 4. First and 10 MORGAN!

KICK BUTT! KICK BUTT! KICK BUTT!

As Reggie and the Coach confer on the sideline, the quarterback once more thinks he hears his name. He spins around. And—for one brief moment he and Teeny are the only ones inside the stadium.

Then the clock starts. . . . Reggie takes the snap . . . breaks to the near side. . . . He's got room! 4, 3, 2 . . . TOUCHDOWN, MORGAN! *HOORAY!*

As Fulsom Field explodes in a supernova of snowflakes, pompoms, confetti and streamers, Star and his coaches huddle at the 20. Down by one, twelve seconds left. Do they kick and send it into O.T., or go for two?

"I say let's go for it," yells Ed, trying to be heard over the crowd. "Too risky," shouts Jet.

Star thinks a moment—about the conditions of Pigg's contract. "I think you're right, Jet, we better kick."

And so the Morgan kicking team, amidst a fortissimo of 60,000 screaming voices, sets up for the point after.

KICK BUTT! KICK BUTT! KICK BUTT!

Then DeGama measures off five steps, Cluck takes a long breath snaps it to Gentry, who BOBBLES IT! And in a panic heaves it to DeGama, who as he's hit tosses it into the end zone, where it bounces out of the arms of R.T. Simmons . . . off the helmet of Arlo Plummer . . . into the hands of Dewey Dobbins

HOOORAAAYYYYY MORGAN!

for two points

KICK BUTT! KICK BUTT! KICK BUTT!

and a victory

YAHOOOOOO KNIGHTS!!!!

that will live forever in the gridiron annals of J. P. Morgan University.

HURRAAAAAAAAHHH!!!!

OVERTIME

Which is as a bridegroom coming out of his chamber,
and rejoiceth as a strong man to run a race.

Psalm 19:5

CHAPTER 29

Monday evening, December 21

om Hanagan sat in the cocktail lounge of the Regency, alternately watching the Chicago-Miami game and the holiday partyers coming and going in the hotel lobby. *They all look so fucking happy,* he thought. *No wonder so many people commit suicide over Christmas vacation.* Tom pictured himself hanging from the landing of his Fox Chapel home by a string of blinking lights and had to laugh.

It had been a horrible day: meeting with Jan and Dr. Redman in the morning, cleaning out his office in Calhoun after lunch, and then interviewing with a friend of Uncle Cliff's about an assistant manager's job at the SunTrust branch office that was opening at the River Bend Mall. While everyone he knew was running around town, doing last minute shopping and toasting each other on a successful year, he was printing resumes to send to the junior colleges and prep schools in the area. The only good thing that had happened all day was when Red Carlisle's attorney had called to tell him that Red was willing to drop the assault charges if Tom paid for his medical expenses.

Then the Dolphins took a time-out and Tom turned around on his bar stool and saw Bobby Brooks getting off the elevator across the lobby. He instinctively rose to go say hello, then he remembered that for the past month and half she hadn't returned any of his calls. So he sat back down and watched as Bobby, looking better than ever in the new cocktail dress she'd purchased for Coach Star's Cosmopolis send-off that evening, went over and gave a big hug to—*BILL CONNER! That son of a*—

"DADDY! DADDY!" Tom's youngest daughter was suddenly yanking him by the leg of his pants.

"Is the show over?" he asked, looking toward the entrance of the Dixie Ballroom where the crowd from the Gingerbread Fairy Puppet Show was now exiting.

"There's Momma, Daddy!"

Tom saw Jan and his other daughters coming toward him, along with Reggie Muggins, Teeny McAdoo, and a little African-American boy in a sailor suit.

"Tom dear, look who I ran into," said Jan, suspiciously eyeing Tom's empty cocktail glass.

"Hey, Reggie, Teeny. And this is? —"

"Malcolm, shake hands with Mr. Hanagan."

"So," said Tom, after reaching for his handkerchief to remove the candy-cane goo that Malcolm had left on his hand. "I hear they're interested in Detroit?"

"They were," said the quarterback.

"Were?"

"Actually, Mr. Hanagan," broke in Teeny, "Reggie's decided he's going to work part-time and try to finish up his degree next year."

Tom didn't know what to say.

"Reggie and I are going to be married."

"That's wonderful," gushed Jan.

"This June after he graduates." Teeny took Reggie's hand.

"We're so happy for you. Aren't we?" Jan looked at Tom.

"Ah—yes. Very happy."

"Thank you, Mr. and Mrs. Hanagan. We're happy too."—Malcolm saw one of Santa's helpers and tugged on Teeny's arm.—"Well, I guess we better get going. Y'all have a Merry Christmas!"

"And a happy New Year," said Jan, waving good-bye as the young lovers walked across the gaily decorated lobby and disappeared through the hotel's revolving door.

Printed in the United States
63561LVS00003B/40

9 780970 621498